DE QUINCEY'S DISCIPLINES

De Quincey's Disciplines

JOSEPHINE McDONAGH

CLARENDON PRESS · OXFORD
1994

Oxford University Press, Walton Street, Oxford OX2 6DP

Oxford New York Toronto
Delhi Bombay Calcutta Madras Karachi
Kuala Lumpur Singapore Hong Kong Tokyo
Nairobi Dar es Salaam Cape Town
Melbourne Auckland Madrid
and associated companies in
Berlin Ibadan

Oxford is a trade mark of Oxford University Press

Published in the United States
by Oxford University Press Inc., New York

British Library Cataloguing in Publication Data
Data available

Library of Congress Cataloging in Publication Data
McDonagh, Josephine.
De Quincey's disciplines / Josephine McDonagh.
Includes bibliographical references.
1. De Quincey, Thomas, 1785–1859—Knowledge and learning.
2. Great Britain—Intellectual life—19th century.   3. Knowledge,
Theory of—History—19th century. 4. Romanticism—Great Britain.
I. Title.
PR4537.M37   1994
828'.809—dc20   93-39460
ISBN 0-19-811285-8

1 3 5 7 9 10 8 6 4 2

Typeset by Best-set Typesetter Ltd., Hong Kong
Printed in Great Britain
on acid-free paper by
Biddles Ltd.
Guildford and King's Lynn

In memory of my parents

Acknowledgements

Like a De Quinceyan text, this book has undergone various revisions; it has also benefited from the influence of many people, whose help I should like to acknowledge. An earlier version of the book was submitted as a Ph.D. thesis at the University of Southampton. Particular thanks are due to Robert Young, for his scrupulous supervision, and to Isobel Armstrong, Maud Ellmann and Anne Swadling for their good advice and warm encouragement. Paul Hamilton, my examiner, suggested ways in which I could develop and expand the work. Many people have discussed ideas with me or kindly read parts of the manuscript at various stages of its production; in particular, I thank Joe Bristow, Derek Duncan, Liz Farr, Anne Janowitz, Sally Ledger, Jane Spencer, Peter Taylor and Andrew Thacker. The final stages of revision have benefited from the astute comments of my colleague, Michael Wood. My sister, Sarah Harvey, has been very supportive. Colin Jones has helped me inestimably in the process of refining and consolidating my ideas, for which I thank him warmly.

Material from Chapter 2 was previously published in 'Debt and Desire: Thomas De Quincey and the Psychology of Political Economy' in *Wordsworth Circle*: Volume XXV, no. 2 (Spring 1994).

Material in Chapter 3 was included in 'Writings on the Mind: Thomas De Quincey and the Importance of the Palimpsest in Nineteenth-Century Thought', *Prose Studies* 10 (1987), 207–224, © Frank Cass and Co.; an earlier version of Chapter 5 has appeared as 'Do or Die: Problems of Agency and Gender in the Aesthetics of Murder' in *Genders*, 5 (1989), 120–134, © University of Texas Press; and an earlier version of Chapter 6 appeared as 'Opium and the Imperial Imagination' in *Reviewing Romanticism*, edited by Philip W. Martin and Robin Jarvis (Macmillan, 1992), 116–133, © Macmillan Academic and Professional Ltd. I gratefully acknowledge permission to reprint this material. Thanks are also due to the Keeper of Manuscripts at the National Library of Scotland, for permission to quote from material held there. Grevel Lindop has kindly supplied information about De Quincey's editions. The revisions of the book were assisted by a grant from the University of Exeter Research Fund.

Contents

Bibliographical Note

References to *Confessions of an English Opium-Eater*, *Suspiria de Profundis*, and *The English Mail-Coach* are to *Confessions of an English Opium-Eater and Other Writings*, ed. Grevel Lindop (Oxford: Oxford University Press, 1985), and are given parenthetically in the text with page numbers, in the form, for example, C, 42.

Unless otherwise stated, references to other works by De Quincey are to *Collected Writings*, 14 vols., ed. David Masson, (Edinburgh: Adam and Charles Black, 1889–90). References are included in the text by volume and page number in the form, for example, X: 136.

Masson's text reprints De Quincey's revised editions of his works rather than original versions. In cases where the original deviates significantly from the revised version, and in the case of texts not included in *Collected Writings*, I refer to the original publication. References to *Blackwood's Edinburgh Magazine* and to *Tait's Edinburgh Magazine* are included in the text in the form *Blackwood's*, or *Tait's*, with volume, date and page numbers.

Introduction: The Bath of Knowledge

Called on De Quincey at Lothian Street. Found him in his room, with a small glass half filled with liquor of the colour of pale port, and a phial of undiluted laudanum beside it, on the table, which was covered as usual with books and papers.

J. R. Findlay, 1855 (cited XIV: 398)

I

Latterly, De Quincey tells us, he kept his papers in a bath. In it he tossed 'every paper written *by* me, *to* me, *for* me, *of* or *concerning* me, and finally, *against* me' (XIII: 252). When approached by the organizers of a Ladies' Bazaar to contribute an essay to a collection in aid of the Library of the Glasgow Athenaeum, having failed to meet the deadline, and in keeping with the spirit of charitable fund-raising, he called on the services of a young man who, dressed in a potato sack tightly laced at throat and legs, dipped into the bath and fished out papers at random.[1] Four dips produced only a dinner invitation, two bills, and a lecture addressed to him by a friend on the subject of moral improvement. The fifth yielded a blank piece of paper on which De Quincey, it turns out, would write a new essay, on 'Sortilege and Astrology', elaborating on the themes of fate and chance that were already dramatized by this tombola scenario.[2]

Whether or not the incident really happened in this or any form seems unimportant. What is interesting is that De Quincey wished to represent himself as the author of works lost in a bath. Bizarre as this episode is, it nevertheless captures something of the spirit of De Quincey's life and writing. In his biography, Grevel Lindop describes De Quincey's erratic methods of work-

---

[1] The extraordinary garb, De Quincey explains, was to prevent the young man from cheating, by 'secreting papers about his person' (XIII: 252-3).

[2] The account of the tombola is prefixed to the essay 'Sortilege and Astrology' in XIII: 251-269. It was first printed in *Glasgow Athenaeum Album* (1848).

ing: surrounded by piles of books and manuscripts with barely room to move, he constantly mislaid the crucial page as he was swamped by the glut of papers around him.[3] In his effort to keep all within his grasp, the significant pieces are lost, reduced to the status of litter within the bewildering mass that confronts him.

Lindop has recounted in particular De Quincey's efforts to revise his works for a collected edition, *Selections Grave and Gay*, to be published by his friend, the Edinburgh publisher, James Hogg. Up to this point, with a few significant exceptions, De Quincey's work had taken the form of contributions to periodicals and newspapers, notably *London Magazine*, *Blackwood's Edinburgh Magazine*, and *Tait's Edinburgh Magazine*.[4] *Selections Grave and Gay* was the second of three collected editions undertaken in the second half of the nineteenth century, the last of which, David Masson's, published in 1889–90, is still considered to be the standard edition of De Quincey's work.[5] Editors have faced massive problems in categorizing and organizing his works, for as a journalist and 'man of letters', he covered an astonishing range of topics: German philosophy, political economy, literary history, and biography, murder, the history and philosophy of ancient Greece and Rome, political commentary on current affairs, physiology, as well as gothic fictions, in addition to the autobiographical works for which he is renowned. That De Quincey was least of all immune to these organizational problems is made clear by the criticism of one contemporary reader, who remarked that *Selec-*

---

[3] Grevel Lindop, *The Opium Eater: A Life of Thomas De Quincey* (Oxford: OUP, 1985), 373–85.

[4] The only works to be published separately in their original form were *Walladmor: Freely translated into German from the English of Sir Walter Scott and now Freely Translated from the German into English* (London, 1825), and *Klosterheim; or, The Masque* (Edinburgh, 1832). After its success in the *London Magazine* in 1821, *Confessions of an English Opium-Eater* was reprinted in a single volume five times between 1822 and 1845. Blackwood published *The Logic of Political Economy* (Edinburgh, 1844) as a separate treatise. The other newspapers and periodicals to which De Quincey contributed included *Westmorland Gazette*, *Edinburgh Saturday Post*, *Edinburgh Evening Post*, and *Hogg's Instructor*.

[5] *Selections Grave and Gay*, 14 vols., (Edinburgh: James Hogg, 1853–60). The first edition was *De Quincey's Writings*, ed. J. T. Fields, 20 vols. (Boston: Ticknor, Reed, and Fields, 1850–1856), reissued in twelve volumes as the Riverside edition in 1877. David Masson's edition was published in 1889–90. A new edition, *The Works of Thomas De Quincey*, ed. Grevel Lindop (London: Pickering & Chatto, forthcoming) is currently in preparation.

tions Grave and Gay presented 'the most provoking jumble in the contents of the fourteen volumes: mixed kinds of matter in the same volume, and dispersion of the same kinds of matter over volumes wide apart, and yet all with a pretence of grouping, and with factitious subtitles invented for the separate volumes on the spur of the moment' (cited, XIV: 384).[6]

It is ironic, perhaps, that De Quincey should produce such an organizational disaster given that he intensely admired intellectual systems that proposed the organic incorporation of knowledge into an all-encompassing scheme. Thus his heroes included Kant, Leibnitz, and Ricardo, for the very reason that each proposed an encyclopaedic system that sought to unify knowledge.[7] In addition he esteemed Adelung's notion of the affinity of languages, the planetary system exposed by Rosse's telescope and written about by his friend John Nichol, and the new historiography of Niebuhr, all of them attempts to produce an organic, systematic, and totalizing approach to the study of language, astronomy, and classical history.[8] In De Quincey's own hands, however, such systems seemed to disintegrate, perhaps because he saw too many connections, too many relationships to arrange coherently. His impulse for coverage and incorporation militated against his pursuit of order.

De Quincey was searching for order at a moment, moreover, when systems of ordering were in a process of mutation. Michel Foucault has argued in *The Order of Things* that the end of the eighteenth and beginning of the nineteenth centuries saw an epistemological rupture, and the formation of a new form of knowl-

---

[6] In the face of these problems of categorization, Lindop's forthcoming edition of De Quincey's works, will present the works in chronological order.

[7] For an account of De Quincey's early enthusiasm for Kant, see Lindop, *Opium-Eater*, 116, and 131–2. For his interest in Leibnitz, 'the one sole potentate in the fields of intellect whom the Germany of [the 17th cent.] produced' (IV: 423), see David Groves, 'Thomas De Quincey, the *Edinburgh Literary Gazette*, and the *Affinity of Languages*', *English Language Notes*, 26/3 (1989), 55–69, esp. 58–9. In *Confessions*, De Quincey records his interest in Ricardo as a Kantian economist who had 'deduced, *a priori*, from the understanding itself, laws which first gave a ray of light into the unwieldy chaos of materials' (C, 65). For full discussion, see Ch. 2.

[8] For De Quincey's admiration of Adelung, see Groves, 'Thomas De Quincey'; on De Quincey and astronomy, see Lindop, *Opium-Eater*, 342–3, and 359–60. See also De Quincey's Essays 'System of the Heavens,' *Tait's*, NS, 13 (Sept. 1846), 566–579, and 'Niebuhr,' *Blackwood's*, 49 (May 1841), 565–583.

edge, a new episteme.[9] While the earlier period was concerned with taxonomy, that is the classification of the details of the empirical world in order to find identities and differences therein, the nineteenth-century episteme was characterized by a new introspection, as distinct disciplines erupted, each one inhabiting an organic structure of its own. Of the new disciplines which Foucault claims emerged in this period, he focuses in particular on economics, biology, and philology. We should also note that this is the point at which aesthetics developed as a field of philosophical enquiry, and the idea of literature as we know it was formulated.[10] The relations between fields of knowledge were now more complex, constituted through analogies between the relationships within the elements in each field. The nineteenth-century intellectual project, Foucault suggests, was an attempt to bridge the epistemological ravines that had opened up, as intellectual enquiry took on the burden of three different tasks: the empirical labour of the positive sciences; the metaphysical quest into the 'depth from which the objects raise up towards our superficial knowledge';[11] and finally the critical project, of which Kant's transcendental philosophy was the first instance, which sought a unifying principle in this incoherent and fractured arena.

Foucault thus provides a useful heuristic model for studying De Quincey, which, moreover, suggests something of the seriousness of his intellectual endeavours. As opportunistic and frivolous as De Quincey frequently was, his work was nevertheless in keeping with the aspirations of his age. By ranging across the new

[9] Michel Foucault, *The Order of Things: An Archaeology of the Human Sciences*, a translation of *Les Mots et les choses* (1966), (London: Tavistock, 1970). Foucault's account of history in terms of epistemic ruptures has been controversial. For a clear account of the theoretical debates raised by the episteme, see Robert Young, *White Mythologies: Writing History and the West* (London: Routledge, 1990), 73–77. Foucault's inaccuracies of historical detail have been well documented. See, for instance, J. Q. Merquior, *Foucault* (London: Fontana, 1985), 56–75. Cf. J. Christie, 'Human Sciences: Origins and Histories', *History of the Human Sciences*, 6 (1993), 1–12, esp. 6. As Christie remarks, empirical errors do not invalidate Foucault's larger theoretical project.

[10] On the development of aesthetics in the late 18th cent., see Terry Eagleton, *The Ideology of the Aesthetic* (Oxford: Blackwell, 1990), Chs. 1 and 2; on the emergence of literature, see Philippe Lacoue-Labarthe and Jean-Luc Nancy, *The Literary Absolute: the Theory of Literature in German Romanticism*, trans. Philip Barnard and Cheryl Lester, (Albany, NY: State University of New York Press, 1988).

[11] Foucault, *The Order of Things*, 245.

fields of knowledge on the pages of the periodicals, he not only attempted to popularize new disciplines; he also tried in vain to mimic Kant's critical project of epistemological unification. His writings thus highlight some of the strains of the intellectual programme of his time as it was carried out in one particular context. When we inspect De Quincey's contribution to the delineation of the disciplines, we will find areas of shared interest, collusions and contaminations, certain repressions, that compromise his epistemological scheme.[12]

It is the purpose of this book to trace De Quincey's formulation of disciplines—in particular political economy, literary criticism, linguistics, and aesthetics—and the relationships between them. The study differs from many earlier works which concentrate on what De Quincey himself considered his best works, and named, approvingly, the 'impassioned prose' or the 'literature of power':[13] these are principally his autobiographies, *Confessions of an English Opium-Eater* (1821), and its sequel, *Suspiria de Profundis* (1845). In this study, by contrast, the emphasis will be on works less frequently scrutinized, namely his political commentaries, his translations of German philosophy, his numerous essays, his treatise on economics, many of which would fall into De Quincey's category the 'literature of knowledge'. My objective is not to evaluate his contribution to these particular disciplinary fields in terms of significant developments in a gradual process of refinement and sophistication. Rather my interest lies in De Quincey's work as a popularizer and disseminator of other people's ideas,[14] and as a writer who, because of his range, suggests links between fields that might otherwise be considered discrete.

---

[12] On the always repressed interests between discrete fields of knowledge, see Jacques Derrida, 'La Loi du Genre/The Law of Genre', *Glyph*, 7 (1980), 176–232. See also Lacoue-Labarthe and Nancy, *Literary Absolute*.

[13] De Quincey invokes the term 'impassioned prose' in his preface to *Selections Grave and Gay*, reprinted in I: 14. He defines the terms 'literature of power and knowledge' in 'Letters to a Young Man whose Education has been Neglected' (X: 47) and 'The Poetry of Pope' (XI: 54–60). For discussion of these terms, see John W. Bilsland, 'On De Quincey's Theory of Literary Power', *University of Toronto Quarterly*, 26 (1957), 469–80; Sigmund K. Proctor, *Thomas De Quincey's Theory of Literature* (Ann Arbor, Mich.: University of Michigan Press, 1943); and Ch. 3.

[14] De Quincey's position as a popularizer of ideas attains iconoclastic status through his contributions to the *Encyclopaedia Britannica*. These include essays on the lives of Goethe, Pope, Schiller, and Shakespeare, published between 1837–38.

De Quincey's exposition of the new disciplines is always eccentric, frequently wrong-headed, compromised by his own
forthright political views, and sometimes scarred by misappre-
hensions. In view of this, it might be objected that I attribute
greater significance to De Quincey's non-literary works than they
warrant. Certainly, given De Quincey's various identities as an
addict, dreamer, debtor, sometime plagiarizer, and journalistic
hack, it is not possible to have total confidence in his intellectual
integrity as an impartial bearer of true knowledge. Moreover his
overriding motive for writing was a financial one.[15] All this, however, is precisely what makes his work interesting, for it lies on
the interface between pure knowledge and the social contexts in
which knowledge is generated, but which, as Foucault has force-
fully argued, are frequently overlooked within the insular concerns of the traditional disciplines. The economy of knowledge
that we will find in De Quincey's work is one formulated by a
commercial writer, with High Tory sympathies and a nostalgia
for Romanticism, working at a time of extreme social rupture as
political and class allegiances shifted in response to political
reform, industrialization, and the expansion of markets across
the world. Against René Wellek's vehement repudiation of De
Quincey's work in his 1944 essay, 'De Quincey's Status in the
History of Ideas', in which he asserted that De Quincey had
misunderstood the great intellectual movements of his time, I will
argue that the significance of his work within the history of ideas
is that it demonstrates the function of knowledge within particular social and institutional contexts, but not the anaesthetized
world of philosophical enquiry for its own sake.[16] Viewed this

---

Generally critics have viewed the work of popularizing as secondary to his 'original' work as a literary genius. See Albert Goldman in *The Mine and the Mint:
Sources for the Writings of Thomas De Quincey* (Carbondale, Ill.: Southern Illinois
University Press, 1965), who argues that although De Quincey's method of composition involved patching together scraps derived from the work of others, he
nevertheless dusted everything with his own eccentric wit and genius.

[15] De Quincey's economic motivation for writing is nicely illustrated by a letter
to his publisher, William Blackwood, in 1832: 'I wish to know whether you would
wish to have Klosterheim lengthened. . . . if you wish it, I can throw in a chapter of
8–10 or 12 pp. which would carry it so far beyond 300 pp. if you think that of
importance.' National Library of Scotland, MS 4032, fo. 191.

[16] René Wellek, 'De Quincey's Status in the History of Ideas', in *Confrontations:
Studies in the Intellectual and Literary Relations between Germany, England, and the
United States during the Nineteenth Century* (Princeton, NJ: Princeton University
Press, 1965), 114–152. See also *Immanuel Kant in England, 1793–1838* (Princeton, NJ:

way, the 'flaws' and eccentricities of his work take on a new significance because they illustrate the ways in which forms of knowledge might serve particular groups.

A study of the neglected non-literary works also helps to situate the literary writings, the impassioned prose, in a context that is more appropriate than the suspended moment of Romanticism that they are often held to inhabit.[17] Partly because of the connections which he forged with the Wordsworth circle in the Lake District as a young man, and exploited later in his literary reminiscences produced for *Tait's* in the 1830s, long after relations had been all but severed,[18] De Quincey is frequently considered as a latter-day Romantic. It must be remembered, however, that his prolific writing career spanned some forty years, from 1818 until his death in 1859, and thus straddled two literary periods. The view that De Quincey was an unproblematic Romantic writer is in keeping with critical approaches to Romanticism that endorse a strain in Romantic writing itself that celebrates literature as the site of transcendent values and monumental timelessness, a tendency that is the target of the current historicist revisions of the Romantic terrain.[19] It also necessitates a restriction of the De Quincey *œuvre* to the impassioned prose, and relegates the rest of his work to the status of mere curiosities.

Princeton University Press, 1931), 172–180; and 'Thomas De Quincey' in *The Age of Transition*, iii, *A History of Modern Criticism* (London: Jonathan Cape, 1966), 110–120. For a brief but pertinent defence of De Quincey against Wellek, see Robert Maniquis, 'Lonely Empires: Personal and Public Visions of Thomas De Quincey' in *Literary Monographs*, 8, ed. Eric Rothstein and Joseph Anthony Wittreich, jun. (Madison, Wis.: University of Wisconsin Press, 1976), 202–3, n. 44.

[17] Cf. John C. Whale, '"In a Stranger's Ear": De Quincey's Polite Magazine Context', in *Thomas De Quincey: Bicentenary Studies*, ed. Robert L. Snyder (Norman, Okla.: University of Oklahoma Press, 1985), 35–53. Whale argues that the bourgeois, Victorian periodical context of De Quincey's writing makes the 'extremes of his Romanticism . . . more provocative' (52). See also Whale's *Thomas De Quincey's Reluctant Autobiography* (London: Croom Helm, 1984), ch. 6, in which he discusses De Quincey's style as a product of his ambiguous position between Victorian and Romantic periods.

[18] On the relationship between Wordsworth and De Quincey see John E. Jordan, *De Quincey to Wordsworth: a Biography of a Relationship, with the Letters of Thomas De Quincey to the Wordsworth Family* (Berkeley, Calif.: University of California Press, 1963).

[19] See in particular Jerome McGann, *The Romantic Ideology: A Critical Investigation* (Chicago: University of Chicago Press, 1983); Marjorie Levinson (ed.), *Rethinking Historicism: Critical Readings in Romantic History* (Oxford: Blackwell, 1989); and Clifford Siskin, *The Historicity of Romantic Discourse* (Oxford: OUP, 1988).

The failure of past literary critics adequately to confront the historical context, and consequently the political content of De Quincey's work, has allowed the construction of his persona as one of a gentle dreamer, a benign eccentric, an amusing and harmless wit. In the light of this, I have shared with other readers surprise on finding expressed in his writings social and political views informed by intense class and racial prejudice, advocating practices of extreme violence on the part of the state that are in some ways more sinister than his essays, 'On Murder Considered as one of Fine Arts' (1826, 1839, 1854) which can at least be read in the spirit of the joke that was intended. Part of the aim of this book is to continue the work begun by Robert Maniquis in his monograph, *Lonely Empires*, and John Barrell in *The Infection of Thomas De Quincey*,[20] to understand as connected and integrated projects De Quincey's political works and his dream visions and impassioned prose, and not see the latter as conveniently inoculated against the former by their status as works of literature.

One of the reasons that this project is particularly difficult is that in various ways De Quincey himself divided his works into separate categories. For instance, in the preface to *Selections Grave and Gay* he separates them into works for amusement, instruction, and for the uplifting and spiritual transcendence of the reader. But, as we shall see, he also formulated other devices that obscured the reader's free passage from one kind of work to another. In order to piece together the various facets of his works, to reconcile the dreamer and the John Bull ranter, we must read against the grain of De Quincey's own orderings. When we delve into the murky logic that sustains his discursive economy we will find repressed material that informs his works in ways he hardly knows.

II

In the twentieth century, De Quincey's fortunes in literary criticism have fluctuated. Chameleon-like, he has provided different readers with versions of himself that indulged their literary interests and desires. In the 1960s, for instance, De Quincey was the

---

[20] Maniquis, 'Lonely Empires'; Barrell, *The Infection of Thomas De Quincey: A Psychopathology of Imperialism* (New Haven, Conn.: Yale University Press, 1991).

Opium Eater, psychedelic guru *par excellence*, whose vivid dream visions, and frank confessions of extravagant pleasures and tortuous pains fired the imagination of a generation in turns excited and terrified by drugs. In 1968 Alethea Hayter's influential work *Opium and the Romantic Imagination* was published, followed by a second edition of M. H. Abrams's *The Milk of Paradise* in 1970.[21] Between 1964 and 1974 four biographies were published, including a new edition of Edward Sackville-West's *A Flame in Sunlight*,[22] and a wide range of works by De Quincey were reprinted, some in new paperback editions.[23]

In the late 1970s and 1980s a new De Quincey was discovered: this was the proto-deconstructionist. Now critics influenced by the work of Jacques Derrida and Paul de Man found in De Quincey a writer whose ironic method matched their own critical position. Thus his digressive and frequently incoherent style, and his interest in psychology and idealist philosophy became the centre of attention, and critics typically focused on questions of subjectivity and desire, tracing the circuities of his subjectivity constructed in and riven by language and literary history. Among the best work of this kind was Stephen Spector's 'Thomas De Quincey: Self-Effacing Autobiographer' (1979), which found in

---

[21] Alethea Hayter, *Opium and the Romantic Imagination* (London: Faber and Faber, 1968); M. H. Abrams, *The Milk of Paradise: The Effect of Opium Visions on the Works of De Quincey, Crabbe, Francis Thompson, and Coleridge* (1934; New York: Harper & Row, 1970). The themes of dreaming and drug addiction preoccupied critics at this point. See for instance, John W. Bilsland, 'De Quincey's Opium Experiences,' *Dalhousie Review*, 55 (1975), 419–30; Fredrick Burwick, 'The Dream-Visions of Jean-Paul and Thomas De Quincey', *Comparative Literature*, 20/1 (1968), 1–26; and Michael Cooke, 'De Quincey, Coleridge, and the Formal Uses of Intoxication', *Yale French Studies*, 50 (1974), 26–40.

[22] Hugh Sykes Davies, *Thomas De Quincey* (London: Longman, 1964); Françoise Moreux, *Thomas De Quincey: La Vie—l'homme—l'oeuvre* (Paris: Presses Universitaires de France, 1964); Judson S. Lyons, *Thomas De Quincey* (New York: Twayne Publishers, 1969); Edward Sackville-West, *A Flame in Sunlight*, ed. John E. Jordan, (1936; London: Bodley Head, 1974).

[23] e.g. *Confessions and Other Writings*, ed. Aileen Ward (New York: New American Library, 1966); *Recollections of the Lakes and the Lake Poets*, ed. David Wright, (Harmondsworth: Penguin Books, 1970); *Confessions of an English Opium-Eater*, ed. Alethea Hayter (Harmondsworth: Penguin Books, 1971); *New Essays by De Quincey: His Contributions to the Edinburgh Saturday Post and the Edinburgh Evening Post, 1827–1828*, ed. Stuart M. Tave (Princeton, NJ: Princeton University Press, 1966); *Selected Essays on Rhetoric*, ed. Frederick Burwick (Carbondale, Ill.: Southern Illinois University Press, 1967); and *De Quincey as Critic*, ed. John E. Jordan (London: Routledge & Kegan Paul, 1973).

the autobiographies 'a self-portraiture that exists always as a simultaneous erasure', and Arden Reed's 'Abysmal Influence' (1978) which read the Piranesi dream in *Confessions* as a demonstration that De Quincey was a writer caught up in an abyss of literary relations, in which his own identity was formulated and lost.[24] This approach to De Quincey has certainly enlivened the study of his works by finding a serious philosophical project within it, and rescuing it from the dismissive criticisms of Wellek. The present study owes much to this work, in both its approach and its findings.

The current upsurge of historicist criticism has produced yet another layer in the critical crust that overlays De Quincey's works. Another De Quincey has been fashioned, this one more sensitive to the social and political context of his life and work. Barrell's *The Infection of Thomas De Quincey* is among a number of recent works, including Edmund Baxter's *De Quincey's Art of Autobiography*,[25] that have paid particular attention to the political writings, in addition to literary and philosophical works, in order to find a way of understanding De Quincey's eccentricities in their historical contexts. Thus Barrell presents a case history of De Quincey in the manner of a psychoanalyst, finding somatic material in a wide range of texts, including De Quincey's own writings and contemporary accounts of public and personal events. In this way, Barrell constructs what he calls a 'psychopathology of imperialism'.

---

[24] S. J. Spector, 'Thomas De Quincey: Self-Effacing Autobiographer', *Studies in Romanticism*, 18 (1979), 501–20; Arden Reed, 'Abysmal Influence: Baudelaire, Coleridge, De Quincey, Piranesi, Wordsworth', *Glyph*, 4 (1978), 188–206. See also Mary Jacobus 'The Art of Managing Books: Romantic Prose and the Writing of the Past', in *Romanticism, Writing, and Sexual Difference: Essays on* The Prelude (Oxford: Clarendon Press, 1989), 126–58; Bryan Tyson, ' "The Frightful Co-Existence of the *To Be* and the *Not To Be*": Antinomy and Irony in De Quincey's "Sir William Hamilton" ', in *Philosophical Approaches to Literature: New Essays on Nineteenth- and Twentieth-Century Texts*, ed. William E. Cain, (London: Associated University Presses, 1984), 73–90.

[25] Edmund Baxter, *De Quincey's Art of Autobiography* (Edinburgh: Edinburgh University Press, 1990). See also Nigel Leask, *British Romantic Writing and the East: Anxieties of Empire* (Cambridge: CUP, 1992), ch. 3, and Charles J. Rzepka, 'The Literature of Power and the Imperial Will: De Quincey's Opium War Essays', *South Central Review*, 8/1 (1991), 37–45.

Barrell reads De Quincey's accounts of childhood events as primal scenes that will resonate throughout his life and works, and inform his political opinions. A compelling and suggestive analysis results which productively links the literary work with the political material. Nevertheless this reading allows one to view De Quincey's politics as a public working through of a private symptom, and history as a context in which to understand the activities of an individual whose autonomy is undermined by an unconscious that is fundamentally private, and not social. The present study is an exploration of the idea that the De Quincey we reconstruct through reading his works was a symptom of a public malaise, his writings the eruptions of a social group whose position was fraught with contradictions. As deviant as De Quincey undoubtedly was, the temptation to explain De Quincey as a special case, an extraordinary individual, should be resisted. The aim will be to draw him in from the margins and to suggest that he was indeed in many ways a representative Victorian. A High Tory, a Romantic dreamer, yet an impoverished journalist, displaced from his social and literary milieu, his home, and his time, his works elaborate on that sense of unbelonging that is one mark of a class attempting to adapt to the changing circumstances of its time.

III

The particular historical focus of this study is the period from 1830 to the mid-1840s, which is flanked by two important landmarks in British parliamentary and economic history: the Reform Act of 1832 and the Repeal of the Corn Laws in 1846. Both of these events may be viewed as part of the gradual accommodation of the interests of industry and commerce against the traditional concerns of land and agriculture: a restructuring of the political nation and a shift in the economic base of the country.[26] Sir Robert Peel, the Tory prime minister between 1834 and 1835, and again

---

[26] See David Cresap Moore, *The Politics of Deference: A Study of the Mid-Nineteenth-Century English Political System* (Hassocks: Harvester, 1976); Norman Gash, 'The Repeal of the Corn Laws', in *Sir Robert Peel: The Life of Sir Robert Peel after 1830* (London: Longman, 1972), 562–615.

from 1841 to 1846, aimed to make Britain the foremost industrial power in the world, reliant on world markets, and the importation of food supplies to supplement home production.[27] Despite this, it is important to bear in mind that by the 1850s the greater part of the population was still employed in the traditional occupations related to agriculture and small-scale manufacturing, and, as David Cannandine has pointed out, 'while Britain may have been the "workshop of the world", the workshops were both small in size and relatively few in number'.[28] Nevertheless, for De Quincey and other conservative writers—such as Carlyle, for instance—the development of industry and the appearance of big factories was a metaphor for a catastrophic shift in the location of political power in the nation.[29] Thus De Quincey writes disparagingly of the 'iron tubes and boilers' of the railway engine (C, 194), and monotonously of the iniquities of the press, its increased circulation, and the dangerous spread of literacy among the proletariat; he worries recurrently about the pernicious and devastating effects of the extended franchise; and, in line with the rhetoric of High Tory anti-abolitionists, he idealizes the social relations of slavery as the stuff of a pastoral idyll, for him not dissimilar to the nostalgic representation of English rural life that he had found in the poetry of Wordsworth. Although it is not presented with the thoroughness of a writer such as Tennyson, we can catch in De Quincey's writings snatches of fantasy of a feudal past as a political vision and a literary dream. In the face of modern decay, he invents a past in which an individual possessed freedoms that have since been lost—such as the freedom to act, command, and be obeyed, to dream, and to feel deeply.[30] For De Quincey, as we

---

[27] Bernard Semmel, *The Rise of Free Trade Imperialism: Classical Political Economy, the Empire of Free Trade and Imperialism, 1750–1850* (Cambridge: CUP, 1970), 146–150.

[28] 'The Context, Performance, and Meaning of Ritual: the British Monarchy and the "Invention of Tradition", c.1820–1977', in *The Invention of Tradition*, eds. Eric Hobsbawm and Terence Ranger, (Cambridge: CUP, 1983), 101–64, esp. 110; on this also see F. M. L. Thompson, *English Landed Society in the Nineteenth Century* (London: Routledge & Kegan Paul, 1963).

[29] On Tory debates about machinery, see Maxine Berg, *The Machinery Question and the Making of Political Economy, 1815–1848* (Cambridge: CUP, 1980), 253–68; on Carlyle and machinery, see Raymond Williams, *Culture and Society, 1780–1950* (1958; repr. Harmondsworth: Penguin Books, 1982), 85–98.

[30] On 19th cent. revisions of the past, see Hobsbawm and Ranger (eds.), *Invention of Tradition*.

shall see, Romantic poetry, opium, and the family will be the agents of the restoration of this imagined past.

Perhaps predictably, his feudal fantasy becomes attached to a nationalist rhetoric, instanced most clearly in the essay on 'The English Language' (1839), discussed in Chapter 4, in which the English language, itself a patriotic monument, is seen to endorse and reproduce the social relations of a kind of feudal society. The same year, however, De Quincey joined with free-traders in supporting the British in the Opium War (1839–42) against the Chinese. His motivation, however, was not a commercial but a nationalist one: British honour and British property were at stake. As his own party interests became outmoded and ceased to dominate the political scene, he recuperated them within a discourse of nationalism. Thus his writings chart a flagging but intransigent High Tory response to contemporary events bolstered by a nationalism that aimed to strengthen his beleaguered position.[31]

If the political writings disavow the force of commercial society, elsewhere in De Quincey's work we will find its needs countenanced and interrogated. Between the 1830s and 1840s, throughout his writings there is an increased emphasis on the powers of the consumer. For instance his unorthodox version of Ricardian economics in 1842,[32] discussed in Chapter 2, is an eccentric psychology of consumption, which assesses value according to the desires of the consumer. Similarly his later works on literary criticism outline its role as a readers' guide, selecting works and assisting the general reader in the processes of literary digestion (see Chapter 4). This comes in the context of his famous explication of the Wordsworthian 'literature of power', a version of the affective theories that are characteristic of Victorian poet-

[31] De Quincey's conservative nationalist voice should be considered as one strand in a complex array of different nationalist voices in the first half of the 19th cent. On the development of nationalism in Britain, see Linda Colley, 'Whose Nation? Class and National Consciousness in Britain, 1750–1830', *Past and Present*, 113 (Nov. 1986), 97–117, and *Britons: Forging the Nation 1707–1837* (New Haven, Conn.: Yale University Press, 1992). See also Benedict Anderson, *Imagined Communities: Reflections on the Origin and Spread of Nationalism*, 2nd edn., (London: Verso, 1991).

[32] 'Ricardo Made Easy', *Blackwood's*, 52 (Sept., Oct., Dec., 1842), 338–53, 457–69, and 718–39. De Quincey's treatise, *The Logic of Political Economy*, was based on these essays.

ics.[33] De Quincey's later works concentrate attention on the responses of the reader, and find in the literary text a strangely disembodied emotion, as though the emotional activity of the producer surrenders to the greater needs of the consumer. The result is an expunging of the writer's personality, a trend in literary thought that will develop throughout the century into the theories of impersonality of the early twentieth century.

De Quincey is a consumer who cannot stop consuming, who loses his identity and will to opium. In this respect he is an ideal writer of the literature of power, for his personality has already been in a sense divested, as he soars the sublime heights of his opium-induced Elysium. But just as his opium pleasures give way to its pains, and bodily transcendence is followed by bodily obsession, addiction for De Quincey is always double-edged. Thus in his political thought, addiction represents to him the problems implicit in policies that serve the interests of trade, for not only do they incur a change in the constitution of the political nation, witnessed in 1832, but they also enforce a dangerous dependency on foreign markets that challenges national sovereignty. In Chapter 6 I will explore this double response to addiction between his late autobiographical work, *Suspiria De Profundis*, in which addiction is celebrated as the dynamic of his literary production, and his essay, 'The Opium Question with China' (1840) in which Britain's addiction to the Chinese opium market causes a vulnerability that must be protected by drastic military action.

IV

The broad argument of this book is that, as a popularizer of knowledge, De Quincey participates in the formulation and consolidation of the new discourses or disciplines that have currency in the first half of the nineteenth century; and that, as such, his work proposes a possible investment, on the part of this epistemology, in a particular political order. Underlying this work is

---

[33] See *The Victorian Poet: Poetics and Persona*, ed. Joseph Bristow, (London: Croom Helm, 1987), 27–116; W. David Shaw, *The Lucid Veil: Poetic Truth in the Victorian Age* (London: Athlone Press, 1987); Alba H. Warren, jun., *English Poetic Theory, 1825–1865* (Princeton, NJ: Princeton University Press, 1950).

Michel Foucault's compelling analysis of power. In the first volume of *The History of Sexuality*, Foucault suggests that individual events and practices should be seen within a larger network of power relations that form 'a dense web that passes through apparatuses and institutions, without being exactly localized in them'.[34] This critique is helpful because it sees power as operating in and informing local contexts as well as national or global ones, between not only governments and their subjects, but also in interactions between (using De Quincey as an example) a mother and her wayward son, an opium addict and his children, a landlady and her middle-class tenant, a hack writer and his poet-heroes,[35] or even an impoverished Tory and the classes he despised. De Quincey's various texts can be analysed as strands spun out of, but also woven into, a complex social fabric, each one informed by, and constituting, layers within its texture. Foucault's denial that the individual subject acts as a sovereign agent within the practices of power and resistance has been a point of contention,[36] but it is helpful in a study of De Quincey, because it allows us to view him as a conduit for a range of contemporary opinions and beliefs, and to recognize in his work bids both to take power and to resist power when it is inflicted on him by others.

We must therefore inspect every level of utterance in his works in order to see the relationships of power that are implicit in them: the relations they presuppose between the writer and audience, between the representation and the material world in which it is produced. I will argue that De Quincey formulated two distinct forms of representation—distinguished precisely by the different versions of these relations they imply. The first is a form of representation in which the will of the writer constantly recedes; it is a testimony to his inability to take control over his life or his writ-

---

[34] *The History of Sexuality, i, An Introduction*, trans. Robert Hurley (London: Penguin, 1981), 96.

[35] De Quincey's relationship with Wordsworth is discussed in Ch. 1. Also relevant is his ambivalent relationship with Coleridge which unfortunately I do not have room to discuss in this study. On this see John Beer, 'De Quincey and the Dark Sublime: The Wordsworth–Coleridge Ethos', in *Thomas De Quincey: Bicentenary Studies*, 164–198, and Leask, *British Romantic Writing*.

[36] On Foucault's notion of power see Mark Cousins and Athar Hussain, *Michel Foucault* (London: Macmillan, 1984), 243–7, and Young, *White Mythologies*, 85–7.

ing, the proper style of an addict. This abnegation of his selfhood lies at the heart of his 'impassioned prose', for it generates the style for which he is famed. Thus he describes his writing in *Suspiria* as

those parasitical thoughts, feelings, digressions, which climb up with bells and blossoms round about the arid stock; ramble away from it at times with perhaps too rank a luxuriance; but at the same time, by the eternal interest attached to the *subjects* of these digressions, no matter what were the execution, spread a glory over incidents that for themselves would be—less than nothing. (C, 94)

Digressive, rambling, parasitical, writing that always effaces the writer, that in a sense inscribes his death;[37] this style operates on the principle of contagion, spreading limitlessly, exceeding its subject, transforming, and annihilating. I will call this mode of writing *representation as contagion*.

The second form of representation functions on the principle of compulsion. In this a representation is figured as a spectacle designed to compel the audience or reader to repeat the represented action. This is the aesthetic of force, or *representation as compulsion*. Unlike contagion, it represents and enforces the subject's will with coercive force. A good example is presented to De Quincey by the English language, which, I shall argue, he sees as impelling people to repeat the social relations that it endorses. Constructed at a time of parliamentary reform and popular agitation for universal male suffrage, the aesthetic of force enters this debate as a form of representation that counters reform by endorsing a political ideology of subservience.[38] Thus De Quincey will tell us that the family is a spectacle that imparts to servants the importance of hierarchies and the value of submission; and that the British army is a spectacle representing its superior strength to a Chinese people who should respect it. The examples are all different, but they present the same scenario: a crude version of ideology, in which people succumb to the incontrovertible message revealed before them by the text.

[37] For the best account of this see Spector, 'Self-Effacing Autobiographer'.

[38] Cf. Catherine Gallagher's discussion of Coleridge's notion of symbolic representation in poetry as the basis for his views on political representation. See *The Industrial Reformation of English Fiction: Social Discourse and Narrative Form, 1832–1867* (Chicago: University of Chicago Press, 1985), 187–200.

The representations of contagion and compulsion are clearly related, but in no straightforward way. Both tell a story of loss of will and submission, but one from the point of view of the writer, and the other from that of the reader. The trajectories of these stories, their convergences and departures, form the subject of the later chapters of this book.

1

De Quincey in History: Terror and Amnesia

[T]hough you may find many more minds more congenial with your own—and therefore proportionately more worthy of your regard, you will never find any one more zealously attached to you—more full of admiration for your mental excellence and of reverential love for your moral character—more ready (I speak from my heart!) to sacrifice even his life—whenever it could have a chance of promoting your interest and happiness—than he who now bends the knee before you. And I will add that, to no man on earth except yourself and *one* other (a friend of your's), would I thus lowly and suppliantly prostrate myself.
Dear Sir!
Yours for ever,
Thomas De Quincey.

Letter to Wordsworth, 1803[1]

In 1803, the seventeen-year-old Thomas De Quincey sent a fan letter to Wordsworth that belied the worldliness acquired through his adolescent wanderings and low-life adventures he would later recount in *Confessions*. The letter marked the beginning of an 'attachment' that grounded De Quincey's literary career. The passage of the peculiar relationship between the two writers has been well documented by John Jordan in *Wordsworth to De Quincey: A Biography of a Relationship*:[2] a short correspondence led to their eventual meeting in 1807 in the Lake District; in 1809 De Quincey moved into Dove Cottage, the Wordsworths' former

---

[1] John E. Jordan, *De Quincey to Wordsworth: A Biography of a Relationship with Letters of Thomas De Quincey to the Wordsworth Family* (Berkeley, Calif.: University of California Press, 1962), 31.

[2] See also Margaret Russett, 'Wordsworth's Gothic Interpreter: De Quincey Personifies "We Are Seven"', *Studies in Romanticism*, 30 (1991), 345–65, for a good account of De Quincey as a reader of Wordsworth.

home, and was based there for about eleven years. Thus his life as an early adult was spent in the company of the literary coterie that gathered around Wordsworth. He also developed intense relationships with Wordsworth's family, in particular the women and children.[3] But the friendship between De Quincey and the Wordsworths soured, partly on account of the former's opium addiction that intruded more and more into his daily life, and partly because of his marriage in 1817 to Margaret Simpson, a farmer's daughter of whom the Wordsworths disapproved, who had already given birth to De Quincey's first son.[4] In 1830, with his wife and now seven children, he moved to Edinburgh, where for the past five years he had worked intermittently as a writer for *Blackwood's*, *The New Times*, and *Edinburgh Saturday Post*, drawing to a close this significant episode of his life.

In 1803, Wordsworth was known to De Quincey as the brilliant author of the *Lyrical Ballads*, poems which De Quincey admired for their evocation of 'the lovely scenes of nature'.[5] Although, as has been amply documented, these poems bear the marks of Wordsworth's serious political engagement, developed during his experience of the French Revolution,[6] De Quincey praised

---

[3] Jordan notes that De Quincey's grief on the death of Wordsworth's son was more excessive than Wordsworth's. See Jordan, *De Quincey to Wordsworth*, 229. De Quincey was particularly attached to Catherine Wordsworth. His account of her death, aged three (II: 440–45), has been isolated as an elaboration of one of the central motifs of his work: the dying woman. See Stephen J. Spector, 'Thomas De Quincey: Self-Effacing Autobiographer', *Studies in Romanticism*, 18 (1979), 501–20; John Barrell, *The Infection of Thomas De Quincey: A Psychopathology of Imperialism* (New Haven, Conn.: Yale University Press, 1991), 39–40; and Angela Leighton, 'De Quincey and Women', in *Beyond Romanticism: New Approaches to Texts and Contexts 1780–1832*, ed. Stephen Copley and John Whale (London: Routledge, 1992), 160–78.

[4] Dorothy Wordsworth wrote to a friend, 'Mr. de Quincey is married; and I fear I may add he is ruined. . . . This is in truth a melancholy story! He utter'd in raptures of the beauty, the good sense, the "angelic sweetness" of Miss Sympson [*sic*], who to all other judgments appeared to be a stupid heavy girl, and was reckoned a Dunce at Grasmere School . . .'. Cited in Grevel Lindop, *The Opium-Eater: A Life of Thomas De Quincey* (Oxford: Oxford University Press, 1985), 220.

[5] Jordan, *De Quincey to Wordsworth*, 31.

[6] On Wordsworth's politics in the 1790s see Nicholas Roe, *Wordsworth and Coleridge: the Radical Years* (Oxford: Clarendon Press, 1988); on the political project of the *Lyrical Ballads*, see Olivia Smith, *The Politics of Language, 1791–1819* (Oxford: Clarendon Press, 1984), 202–26; on the legacy of his revolutionary politics in the *Prelude*, see Ronald Paulson, *Representations of Revolutions (1789–1820)* (New Haven, Conn.: Yale University Press, 1983), 248–75.

them as poems of landscape and feeling, and made no reference to their political content. By the 1830s Wordsworth, the one-time radical, whose poetic style had been forged as part of his complex responses to political events of a revolutionary period, had shifted dramatically to the Right, and was beginning to become a secure, establishment figure: in 1842 he was awarded a state pension, and in 1843, the laureateship. In 1844, in an ironic repetition of De Quincey's teenage supplication to the author of the *Lyrical Ballads*, Margaret De Quincey, his eldest daughter, wrote another letter to Wordsworth—this time to obtain Wordsworth's influence in gaining an army commission for her brother Frederick.[7]

The relationship with Wordsworth shrouded De Quincey's entire writing life, and the spirit of Wordsworth's poetry remained a lasting influence. In 1818, Wordsworth in effect launched De Quincey's journalistic career by procuring for him the post of editor to the *Westmorland Gazette*. Although this appointment was short-lived—he was asked to resign the following year—nevertheless it was at this point that his considerable talents as a writer began to emerge. Three years later, the *London Magazine* published *Confessions of an English Opium-Eater*, the work on which his reputation was established and still rests. *Confessions* calls on the major tropes of Romanticism that Wordsworth and Coleridge had long established: a youthful spirit is oppressed by social institutions—not unlike Wordsworth in the *Prelude*, which De Quincey had read in 1810; he wanders alone in the countryside and the city; he befriends the poor and dispossessed (such as the prostitute, Ann)—whose noble spirits resemble those of the rural peasants in the *Lyrical Ballads*; he recounts his opium dreams, yet more graphically than Coleridge; and so on. In the second part, as an emphatic reminder of his connections with the Lakeland poets, De Quincey represents himself 'in a cottage among the mountains, on a stormy winter evening' (C, 61)—the cottage being Dove Cottage, and the mountains, those of Cumbria.

Even after he had left Grasmere and cut ties with the Wordsworths, his eleven-year residence in their company continued to figure at the centre of his work. In 1833 he began a series of

---

[7] The letter is reprinted in the catalogue to the exhibition, *Thomas De Quincey: An English Opium-Eater, 1785–1859*, Introduction and notes by Robert Woof (Cumbria: Trustees of Dove Cottage, 1985), 100–1.

anecdotal essays for *Tait's*, which included his essays on Coleridge and his 'Lake Reminiscences'.[8] The years from 1834 to 1838 saw the temporary abatement of the publication of his work in *Blackwood's*, as his relations with the editor had suffered under the strain of De Quincey's failure to meet deadlines.[9] The *Tait's* essays therefore provided his main and only consistent source of income at a time when his predicament had been exacerbated by an unfavourable financial arrangement that he had entered into in order to remortgage some property belonging to Margaret Simpson's family.[10] His former intimacy with the Wordsworths presented his best saleable commodity, since his frank discussion of the private lives of these public figures contributed to the popularity of the *Tait's* essays. Needless to say, they also incurred the irritation of Wordsworth, who disavowed De Quincey as 'a pest to society and one of the most worthless of mankind' (*c.*1836).[11]

It is significant that the essays on the Wordsworth circle should have been published in *Tait's*, and not the High Tory *Blackwood's*, for whom De Quincey had been a regular contributor since 1826. William Tait, the founder and publisher of *Tait's Edinburgh Magazine*, was a Benthamite who had established it as an organ for the dissemination of Utilitarian thought, and its writers included John Stuart Mill, John Bright, and the radical Ebenezer Elliott.[12] In 1834 it merged with *Johnstone's Magazine*, which billed itself as 'cheap reading of the most amusing kind'.[13] Now under the

[8] The series of essays entitled 'Sketches of Life and Manners: from the Autobiography of an English Opium-Eater' began in *Tait's* in Feb. 1834, and was made up of twenty-five parts, the last published in Feb. 1841. During this period he also contributed other pieces to *Tait's*, including 'Samuel Taylor Coleridge' (in three parts in 1834), and 'Lake Reminiscences' (in five parts between Jan. and Aug. 1839). Little or no distinction is maintained between 'Sketches', which are nominally autobiographical pieces, and the biographical essays.

[9] William Blackwood died in 1834, and his sons, who took over his affairs, were less indulgent regarding De Quincey's erratic methods of producing his work. See Grevel Lindop, *Opium-Eater*, 324.

[10] See Lindop, *Opium-Eater*, 290–1, and 308–9.

[11] Jordan, *De Quincey to Wordsworth*, 347.

[12] See Mark A. Weinstein, '*Tait's Edinburgh Magazine*', in *British Literary Magazines: The Romantic Age, 1789–1836*, ed. Alvin Sullivan (Westport, Conn.: Greenwood Press, 1983), 401–5.

[13] The expression is used in an advertisement for a compendium of writing from *Johnstone's Magazine* in *Tait's*, NS, 1 (June 1834), 363.

editorship of Christian Isobel Johnstone, the new *Tait's* dropped its price to one shilling and went on to become one of the most widely read magazines in Britain, with a large middle- and working-class, and in particular female, readership. Although at this point the main emphasis shifted from political to literary matters, it nevertheless remained true to its liberal and radical convictions, and included essays on, for instance, the Corn Laws (a 'misnomer for what is generally signified by them—namely, *the Taxes on Food*'), and advertisements for reading material for 'every reformer, nay, every Englishman'.[14] It was not extraordinary for a writer to contribute to *Blackwood's* and *Tait's*: the literary men John Galt and William Edmondstoune Ayton, for instance, also wrote for both. But for De Quincey, whose deep-seated political views were expressed on the pages of *Blackwood's*—his contempt for all radical thought, his distrust of the press as an organ for the dissemination of ideas, his hatred of working-class, and especially female readers—the financial expediency that forced him to write for *Tait's* indicated the extent to which he was caught up in a system he could not resist.[15]

De Quincey's work is marked throughout by such ideological compromises. The clearest example of all is provided by his work on Ricardo's political economy. As I shall suggest in the next chapter, his admiration for the arch-Whig, Ricardo, was in itself peculiar for a High Tory, but this is complicated further by his strange misreading of Ricardo's work: for instance, in *The Logic of Political Economy* (1844) he regarded the idea of rent as the 'golden tessellae' (IX: 237) of the economic system, when for Ricardo, rent was a leech on the system threatening its downfall. Moreover De Quincey's failure to pay his own rent in Edinburgh in the 1830s had forced his retreat into Holyrood, a debtors' sanctuary, where

[14] 'How Do Poor Men Live?' *Tait's*, NS, 6 (Jan. 1839), 13 n.; advertisement for *The Constitutions of Great Britain, France, and the United States of America*, in *Tait's*, NS, 1 (Mar. 1834), 219.

[15] Indeed De Quincey made some attempt to match the political opinions of the magazine. For instance, in the first essay of 'Sketches' he is careful to point out that his father, although a merchant, was antipathetic to the 'kidnapping, murdering Slave-trade' (I: 18–19). Nevertheless, he also presented a controversial essay, true to his political sympathies, 'A Tory's Account of Toryism, Whiggism, and Radicalism in a letter to a friend in Bengal', published in two parts in Dec. 1835 and Jan. 1836.

ironically he fell further into debt on account of his inability to pay his rent there. Rent, the 'golden tessellae', in the end, was the cause of his total impoverishment. Under these circumstances, it is hardly surprising that De Quincey was and has since been considered eccentric.

This chapter will attempt to make sense of the ideological entanglements that mark the writings of the 1830s, when De Quincey, the Tory, continued to fashion himself as a Romantic fellow-traveller in a magazine addressing a popular and radical audience. The situation was complicated by the fact that at the beginning of the decade, between 1829 and 1832, he published his first cluster of political essays in *Blackwood's*. In these essays he was responding to a series of important constitutional changes, the repeal of the Test and Corporation Acts (1828), the emancipation of Catholics (1829), and the Great Reform Act (1832), which, combined with outbreaks of popular violence across Britain,[16] and the 1830 Revolution in France, made the period seem as though it were a dangerous re-enactment of the 1790s. As De Quincey consciously adopted the rhetorical flourishes of Edmund Burke, in *Reflections of the Revolution in France* (1790), he returned his readers to the initiating moment of Romantic poetry, albeit in a way that was quite different to the nostalgic Romantic scenarios evoked in his essays in *Tait's*.

De Quincey's works of the 1830s produce two different versions of Romanticism. In the political essays, he claims that the 1830s saw a repetition of the revolutionary conditions of the 1790s, which were also the source and subject of Romantic writing. As a consequence the essays bear many traces of Romanticism, which serve to remind the reader of the imminent crisis that continued to face civilization forty years later, as, in De Quincey's analysis, the social infrastructure fractured under the pressures of industry and trade. In the context of the political essays, therefore, the spirit of Romanticism figures as something dangerous, to be avoided at all costs. A very different story is told in the literary reminiscences in *Tait's*. Here Romanticism is presented in the form of a particular group of writers, a landscape, and a capacity to feel deeply. It has been divested of its historical roots and

---

[16] Eg. the Swing Riots. See E. J. Hobsbawm and George Rudé, *Captain Swing* (London: Lawrence & Wishart, 1969).

political content, to become instead a means of articulating a nostalgia for a lost rural past. Moreover, for De Quincey, to speak about Romanticism is to invoke a set of personal associations, which assure his commercial viability as a contributor to the literary magazines. In *Tait's*, Romanticism becomes a kind of commodity, reconstructed in the absence of its authentic past.[17] Romanticism's revolutionary history is charted only in the political commentaries, as evidence of the tyranny of revolution that continues to haunt the nation.

This distribution of historical and literary knowledge has a number of effects, one of which is a strangeness and sense of dislocation that we will find throughout De Quincey's work. Moreover it provides a key to understanding the violence that is characteristic of De Quincey's rhetoric, but which rests uneasily beside his persona as the gentle and unworldly dreamer. Violence is a product of the process of commodification, as aspects of Romanticism are wrenched from their historical context; it is also evident in De Quincey's political programme, which must go to any length to cling on to the social conditions that are fast slipping away.

Romanticism and Reform

In an essay entitled, 'On Wordsworth's Poetry', De Quincey will observe in 1845 that '[T]he French Revolution has not even yet . . . come into full action. It was the explosion of a prodigious volcano, which scattered its lava over every kingdom of every continent, everywhere silently manuring them for social struggles; this lava is gradually fertilizing all' (XI: 310). The sense that a shadow had been cast over future generations by the events sparked off in 1789 was experienced widely throughout the nineteenth century. For De Quincey, the events of 1792–4 had already been rehearsed in July 1830, when the Bourbon monarchy had been overthrown after the so-called Three Glorious Days. Although the Revolution soon fell into a more moderate, bourgeois mould, this spell of violence, when the people rioted in the streets,

---

[17] On the commodity form, see Karl Marx, 'The Fetishism of the Commodity and Its Secret', in *Capital: A Critique of Political Economy*, i. Trans. Ben Fowkes (Harmondsworth: Penguin Books, 1982), 163–77.

brought back painful memories of the Terror. 'Far more danger-ous, every way more full of change and fear,' wrote De Quincey in 1830, 'because more insidiously smiling upon all around her, is the Revolutionary France of August and September, 1830, than that of January, 1793' ('France and England', *Blackwood's*, 28 (Oc-tober 1830), 702).[18] Whereas for Marx the tragic events of the Terror in 1793–94 would only ever be repeated as farce, for De Quincey, the revolution accumulated power through its repeti-tion, for the fact that it had happened twice suggested that it could happen again and again, and not only in Paris.[19] Revolution is figured as a French contagion that in De Quincey's eyes had spread across Europe once before under the Jacobins, and subse-quently under the leadership of the imperialist warmonger, Napoleon. If this had happened in the 1790s, how much worse might it be in 1830?

Retrospectively, his estimation that the events of August 1830 were more terrifying than those of 1793 and 1794 proved errone-ous. However, De Quincey perceived a similarity between the situations in France and Britain that inflamed his fear of conta-gion. The so-called ultra-royalist Bourbon regime in France had attempted to re-establish in France the conditions that had existed before the Revolution. The king, Charles X, was ousted by a bourgeoisie wishing to reclaim the political powers it had won during the revolutionary years; in his place was instated Louis-Philippe, who introduced a more liberal form of government, an extended franchise, and ended Catholicism's privileged status. For De Quincey and other High Tories, the clamourings of the Reform agitators in Britain echoed too closely the cries of the French bourgeoisie, for they also sought enfranchisement for a previously under-represented, but ever-growing, and increas-ingly monied middle class. Moreover De Quincey considered that the bill for the emancipation of Catholics, that had been passed by Wellington in 1829, and which had severed the ties between Church and State in a similar way as French events of 1830,

---

[18] Louis XVI was executed in Jan. 1793.
[19] Karl Marx, 'The Eighteenth Brumaire of Louis Bonaparte' (2nd edn., 1869), in *Surveys from Exile*, ii. *Political Writings*, trans. David Fernbach (Harmondsworth: Penguin, 1973), 143–249. See Jeffrey Mehlman, *Revolution and Repetition: Marx/ Hugo/Balzac* (Berkeley, Calif.: University of California Press, 1977).

merely opened the floodgates to insurrection, creating a state of instability in the nation that would be inflamed by revolutionary infection from abroad.[20]

High Tories, such as De Quincey, experienced the period that culminated in the Reform Act of 1832 as the end of the *ancien régime*, when ties between Church and State and the identification of the traditional aristocracy with government were lost once and for all.[21] The Bourbon Charles X's failed attempt to revive such a state in France sent ambiguous messages to British Tories. For some, it suggested that the government should listen and yield to the demands of reformers in order to prevent the insurrection evidenced in France.[22] For others, the Ultra Tories (a name which emphasized support of the French Right), of whose views, in this case, De Quincey was representative, reform was a Frenchification, a pustulating sore that needed to be eliminated for the health of the nation.

According to De Quincey, the effects of Reform would be felt in all departments of government and in all aspects of social life, both in Britain and in the colonies. In an unpublished essay from 1831, entitled, 'On Reform as Affecting the Habits of Private Life in a Second Letter to a Friend', he painted a vision of a reformed Britain that was loosely based on his knowledge of revolutionary France: church property would be taken over, metropolitan control of the colonies would be lost, revolutionary ideas would be instilled in marauding native populations, divorce would be legalized.[23] In the essay, divorce in particular becomes a sign of the decaying body politic in Britain, soiled in its most private places by the activities of unruly mobsters who mimic the behaviour of past revolutionaries—Jacobins and Americans.[24] In De Quincey's

[20] On the French Revolution in 1830, see David H. Pinkney, *The French Revolution of 1830* (Princeton, NJ: Princeton University Press, 1972), and *1830 in France*, ed. John M. Merriman (New York: New Viewpoints, 1975).

[21] The view that 1832 marked the end of the *ancien régime* is explored sympathetically by J. C. D. Clark in *English Society 1688–1832: Ideology, Social Structures, and Political Practice During the Ancien Régime* (Cambridge: CUP, 1985).

[22] In *Blackwood's* this opinion was expressed by Archibald Alison in a series of thirteen essays, 'On the Late French Revolution', published between January 1831 and January 1832.

[23] National Library of Scotland, MS 4789 fo. 37–55.

[24] On divorce laws in this period, see Roderick Phillips, *Putting Asunder: A History of Divorce in Western Society* (Cambridge: CUP, 1988), 227–78.

rhetoric, all revolutions merge into one, and the activities of their protagonists are divested of all content and historical specificity to become merely the agents of an indiscriminate will to revolt.

'Revolutions', De Quincey noted, 'do not stop at the point marked out by their projectors;'[25] their effects are boundless and unpredictable. Revolutions cause an epistemological crisis in which one can never be sure of the consequences of a particular act. As the certainties of cause and effect are interrupted, so are the sequences of chronology. Commenting on parliament as it debated the Reform Bill throughout 1831, De Quincey compared it with a woman 'who deliberates on a proposal of dishonour [and] is already dishonoured' as a consequence. He continued:

Except the first French Revolution, nowhere do we read of one so extensive in the spirit of its changes, as this which is now agitated. Yet it is undeniable, and the gravity of regular history must descend to record, that, for its origin, it is built on a mere reverberation of one petulant word, dropped in a moment of irritation by the Duke of Wellington. ('On the Approaching Revolution in Great Britain, and its Proximate Consequences in a Letter to a Friend', *Blackwood's*, 30 (August 1831), 316)[26]

In these extracts a sense of sequence is lost, and replaced by the repetition of events that have already taken place—the 'dishonour[ing]' of an already dishonoured woman, or the 'reverberation' of Wellington's 'petulance', displayed when he resigned from parliament the previous year. In the face of this loss of chronology, De Quincey summons the memory of Edmund Burke as he calls on the 'gravity of regular history . . . to record' the pernicious spread of disorder and chaos threatened by Reform.[27] In an attempt to re-establish order, De Quincey invokes 'regular history', a record of sequential events, to counter the feminized orderlessness of petulance that reverberates in the shadow of the

---

[25] National Library of Scotland, MS 4789 fo. 43.

[26] Wellington resigned in Nov. 1830 over his defeat on a vote on the Civil List Accounts, two weeks after he had declared against parliamentary reform.

[27] Here De Quincey mimics Burke, who writes: 'History will record, that on the morning of the 6th of October 1789, the king and queen of France, after a day of confusion, alarm, dismay, and slaughter, lay down . . . to indulge nature in a few hours sleep.' Edmund Burke, *Reflections on the Revolution in France and on the Proceedings in Certain Societies in London Relative to that Event*, ed. C. C. O'Brien (Harmondsworth: Penguin, 1969), 164.

French Revolution.[28] His return to Burke, as a rhetorical device that marks his resistance to any kind of political change, indicates that his politics are based on a nostalgic vision of the past, registering a sense of suspended time, which ironically bears in structure a resemblance to the timelessness he considers to be the pernicious effect of revolution.

The representation of revolution as a destroyer of chronology and of sequences of causation, the agent of an epistemological crisis, was a familiar one from the 1790s onwards, for it corresponded with the dominant category in aesthetic theories of the time—the sublime. The eighteenth century had seen a revival of interest in the sublime, and Edmund Burke's *Philosophical Enquiry into the Origin of our Ideas of the Sublime and Beautiful* (1757) provided one of its most influential accounts. For Burke, the term sublime should be applied to objects that provoked terror in the spectator—for example, a tiger, a storm, or a tyrant; this terror, which 'robs the mind of all its powers of acting and reasoning', was experienced as a kind of negative pleasure, such as the feeling which one would experience on the brink of death.[29] Such a description suggested that revolution could be represented as a sublime object, but as Burke demonstrated in his later work, for him the negative pleasures of fear are best enjoyed in the realm of the aesthetic. As political realities, 'danger or pain press too nearly . . . and are simply terrible.'[30]

For Romantic poets, however, the sublimity of the French Revolution provided both the occasion of and a model for poetry. In their case, however, the sublime was perhaps less close to Burke's than Kant's version of the sublime, outlined in *Critique of Judge-*

---

[28] De Quincey was not alone in designating the revolution as a feminizing influence. On the Republic as a woman, see Maurice Agulhon, *Marianne into Battle: Republican Imagery and Symbolism in France, 1789–1830*, trans. Janet Lloyd (Cambridge: CUP, 1981). See also Neil Hertz, 'Medusa's Head: Male Hysteria Under Political Pressure' in *The End of the Line: Essays on Psychoanalysis and the Sublime* (New York: Columbia University Press, 1985), 161–91.

[29] Edmund Burke, *A Philosophical Enquiry into the Origin of our Ideas of the Sublime and Beautiful*, ed. James T. Boulton (Oxford: Blackwell, 1987), 57.

[30] Burke, *Philosophical Enquiry*, 57; on the relationship between Burke's political and aesthetic thought, see Ronald Paulson, 'Burke's Sublime and the Representation of Revolution', in *Culture and Politics from Puritanism to the Enlightenment*, ed. Perez Zagorin (Berkeley, Calif.: University of California Press, 1980), 241–69.

ment (1790).[31] Kant shifted the referent of the term from the terrifying object to the perceiving subject's experience of that object.
In this way, the sublime became a potentially empowering model
in which the subject, at first overwhelmed by terror or incompre-
hension, as in Burke's account, then had recourse to the faculty of
Reason, and became assured of its own independent powers of
consciousness.[32] Although as I shall indicate in Chapter 5, the
empowerment that is available in Kant's sublime is always pro-
visional and compromised, nevertheless this model provided the
basis for developing a revolutionary poetics.[33] Thus the social and
ontological chaos incurred by revolution would inspire not terror,
but a sense of individual freedom and a vision of egalitarian
societies that were the subject of Romantic poetry.

De Quincey's accounts of Revolution and Reform share a great
deal with his fictional and autobiographical works, which suggests that for him too revolution was a source of imaginative
inspiration. For instance, the systematic devastation of both private and public spheres brought about by revolutionary situations is not unlike that described in his gothic fictions, *Klosterheim*
and *The Household Wreck*, that will be discussed in Chapter 5.
Moreover the sense of repetition—the fact that 1793 is repeated in
1830, and will be repeated again and again throughout the century—in form presents a familiar scenario for De Quincey. His
opium dreams recounted in *Confessions* and its sequel, *Suspiria de*

---

[31] On the sublime see Samuel Monk, *The Sublime: A Study of Critical Theories in
Eighteenth-Century England* (1935; repr. Ann Arbor, Mich.: University of Michigan
Press, 1960); Thomas Weiskel, *The Romantic Sublime: Studies in the Structure and
Psychology of Transcendence* (1976; Baltimore, Md. and London: Johns Hopkins
University Press, 1986); and Frances Ferguson, 'Legislating the Sublime', in *Studies
in Eighteenth-Century British Art and Aesthetics*, ed. Ralph Cohen (Berkeley, Calif.:
University of California Press, 1985), 128–47.

[32] The best account of this process, which Neil Hertz names as the 'blockage' of
reason, is given by Hertz in 'The Notion of Blockage in the Literature of the
Sublime' in his *End of the Line*, 40–60.

[33] As Theresa Kelley has pointed out, the reading of Kant's sublime as the basis
for a revolutionary poetics has been taken up by post-structuralist critics. Kelley
argues that, in Wordsworth at least, the tempering influence of the politically
conservative *beautiful* should also be recognized. See Theresa Kelley, *Wordsworth's
Revisionary Aesthetics* (Cambridge: CUP, 1988). Other critics, notably Terry
Eagleton, in *The Ideology of the Aesthetic* (Oxford: Blackwell, 1990) 70–101, have
argued that Kant's sublime conforms to the needs of bourgeois culture.

Profundis, are full of coincidences and repeated events, and De Quincey's most characteristic anxiety is that of a man caught up in events that are not only beyond his control, but beyond control itself. A useful example is the nightmare vision described in *Suspiria*. In this, the boy De Quincey, greedy for books, makes an order from a bookseller that unexpectedly exceeds his boyish desires: as the books are piled up outside his house, De Quincey is swamped by the sheer mass of them, and by the seemingly endless debt they will incur. The nightmare is compounded when De Quincey realizes that his story has already been told in the *Arabian Nights*—that he has been 'contemplated in type a thousand years before on the banks of the Tigris' (C, 135). Fact and fiction merge, and history and cultural difference are effaced. As terrifying as this may be, it is nevertheless the sublime source of literary pleasure. At the heart of his literary project are situations such as this, in which De Quincey is trapped in circumstances beyond his domain. The repetition of the Revolution throughout the century would seem to present the ideal context for the production of literary fantasies.

As with Burke, however, De Quincey's political essays acknowledge no pleasure, no matter how negative, in the political realization of sublime fantasies. De Quincey draws a clear distinction between his aesthetic works—works of 'impassioned prose'—and the political essays. This is emphasized by the categories he established in the preface to *Selections Grave and Gay*. The political essays, had they been included in this collected edition, would have fallen into the second category, as works of instruction whose relevance is restricted to the particular events they describe, and their moment of production and publication. The works of 'impassioned prose', on the other hand, are transcendent works of universal significance, which surpass the strictures of time and place.[34] As I shall explain in Chapter 3, 'impassioned prose' is a category based on the idea of the suspension of time and place; such literature is characterized by its ability to transport the reader to a timeless zone beyond the concerns of the material world. The figure of the palimpsest, outlined in *Suspiria*, neatly encapsulates the desired effects of

[34] See De Quincey's 'Preface' to *Selections Grave and Gay*, repr. in I:10–15.

literature. This was a piece of vellum on which the inscriptions had been erased by successive generations in order that it might be reused. When new chemical discoveries enabled nineteenth-century archaeologists to reconstitute its lost writings, the palimpsest served as a storehouse in which the inscriptions of different generations were gathered together in a single surface that acknowledged no chronological difference between them. For De Quincey, 'impassioned prose' functioned like the palimpsest in its capacity to dissolve temporal difference, whereas the political writings were different precisely because they were bound to the transitory concerns of contemporary life.[35]

Ironically, the revolutionary state that the political essays described was one which provoked a similar suspension of time. But the dominant thrust of De Quincey's rhetoric dispelled this paradox, for the 'impassioned prose' is supported by a very different political vision: the retrieval of an imagined idyll of an *ancien régime* England, that will be, or has been lost as a result of parliamentary reform. So in *Suspiria*, De Quincey argues that literature along with opium are modes of retrieving the values that have been lost in the industrialized and democratized world. In particular, he says, people have lost their capacity to dream; it is as though the creative spirit has been crushed by the pressure of steam and the expansion of the franchise. The idea that literature might revive a lost, idealized past is of course reminiscent of a dominant strain in Wordsworth's poetry, and indeed, in De Quincey's works, the landscape and personae of Romantic past weave into his own nostalgic visions. The 'Lake Reminiscences' in *Tait's* begin with his incantation of the places in the Lake District, the 'scenery in which this most original poetry had chiefly grown up and moved', 'the very names of the ancient hills—Fairfield, Seat Sandal, Helvellyn, Blencathara, Glaramara; of the sequestered glens—such as Borrowdale, Martindale, Mardale, Wasdale, and Ennerdale' (*Tait's* (January 1839), 1–2), and so on. The names evoke not only the landscape of the region, but also a pastoral history and a poetic tradition with which De Quincey feels himself to be so strongly connected that he claims that his own life was in fact prefigured by the landscape before he even laid eyes on it.[36]

---

[35] On the palimpsest, see Ch. 3, pp. 85–8.   [36] *Tait's*, NS, 6 (Jan. 1839), 1–2.

The idea of Romantic poetry thus functions as a reminder of the past that he considers to have been lost since 1830: a natural landscape before industrialization, and the social relations that supposedly existed before the democratic advance spurred on by reform. The political radicalism of the initiating moment of Romanticism is erased; the individual freedoms that were once considered to be the fruits of revolution, are now considered to be aspects of an imagined feudal past in an *ancien régime* rural England. This is a political vision that dominates De Quincey's work, and it is important to acknowledge its investment in a particular reading of Romantic poetry.

In De Quincey's literary reminiscences, Romanticism forgets its own past and instead evokes an imagined feudal past, a glorious fantasy erected at the moment at which traditional order is at threat. Curiously we will find a similar kind of amnesia in evidence in the political essays. In these, images that have particular political histories are used in ways that seem oblivious of those alliances. The result is a set of texts that, in their use of rhetorical devices, seem opportunistic, taking whatever means possible to display the dangers of the forces of revolution.

The Organic, the Mechanic, and the Lex Equilibrii

When De Quincey described the revolution as 'silent manur[e]' in his 1845 essay, he recalled an image that he had used many times in the political essays of the 1830 period: that of revolutionary fervour as an organic growth, a weed, whose rampant growth might destroy the husbandry of tradition. For example, in November 1830 he warned, '[T]he plants, therefore, were ready; but the soil was not then prepared to receive them. Now, in 1830, all this is changed; Europe is overshadowed, as by some great Hercynian forest, with a rank growth of anti-social desires and disorganizing principles' ('Political Anticipations', *Blackwood's*, 28 (November 1830), 720). If he were not describing the forces of revolution, the emphasis on organic imagery would call to mind Burke's use of organicism, in particular in the *Reflections*, when he used it to evoke the naturalness of social hierarchies and traditions. Burke's rhetoric fuelled a powerful strain in conservative discourse that continued throughout the nineteenth century and beyond, which figured the nation as an organism and its institutions as natural as the growth of plants. In the context of the late eighteenth and early nineteenth centuries, the emphasis on organic growth enforced a sense that political authority rested in the land, or more particularly, in the ownership of land. The political implications of this were clearly articulated by J. S. Mill in 1840 when he praised Coleridge as the philosopher who

reviv[ed] the idea of a *trust* inherent in landed property. The land, the gift of nature, the source of subsistence to all, and the foundation of everything that influences our physical well-being, cannot be considered a subject of *property*, in the same absolute sense in which men are deemed proprietors of that in which no one has any interest but themselves.[37]

In view of De Quincey's political opinions, his association of the imagery of organicism with the revolutionaries is striking, for, despite the scatological implications of manure, it seems to have more in common with Thomas Paine's subversion of Burke's imagery. In *The Rights of Man* (1791–2), Paine described the revolutionary spirit of the 1790s as a burst of new buds on a tree in spring time.[38] For De Quincey, however, the growth of revolutionary forces was too rampant, and his images bear a Malthusian message of the destruction implicit in nature's overabundance; in this, the descriptions recall his accounts of oriental landscapes in the *Confessions*, which, 'swarming with human life' (C, 73), threaten his sanity. The overabundance of organic growth, such as that represented by a forest, was a familiar theme in gothic imagery, as the immense and unknowable power that produced it became an object of sublime terror. Indeed the ruling principle of gothic architecture was that its structures should resemble those of an organic being.[39] In which ever way we look at it, De Quincey's use of organic imagery to figure the revolutionaries

---

[37] J. S. Mill, 'Coleridge' (1840), reprinted in *Mill on Bentham and Coleridge*, introd. by F. R. Leavis (London: Chatto & Windus, 1950), 158. For a discussion of this essay, see Raymond Williams, *Culture and Society, 1780–1950* (1958; repr. Harmondsworth: Penguin, 1982), 65–84.

[38] See Ronald Paulson, 'Burke's Sublime', 244–69.

[39] See John Ruskin, 'The Nature of the Gothic', in *Stones of Venice* (1853), ii, *The Sea-Stories*, in *The Works of John Ruskin*, 39 vols., ed. E. T. Cook and Alexander Wedderburn (London: George Allen, 1904), 180–269.

imbues them with an inspirational power that obscures the political contempt he feels for them.

However, if the revolutionaries were organic, in De Quincey's rhetoric they were also mechanical. In 'Political Anticipations' he wrote, 'the political revolutionists of our time have a fulcrum in the very name of Paris, for supporting the machinery of those enormous levers, by which they operate the rest of the world' (723). In the same way that organic imagery was steeped in the political messages of conservatism, images of machines bespoke the politics of liberals and radicals whose philosophy had developed from a Utilitarian belief in the value of education and the development of science and industry as the basis for economic growth and social progress. While conservatives embalmed traditional hierarchies in the mysteries of organic life, Utilitarians subscribed to an enlightenment belief in rationalism and empiricism, and this lay at the heart of their support of the democratizing movements of the time, such as movements for parliamentary reform, the expansion of education, the abolition of slavery, and emancipation of Catholics. In his rhetoric, De Quincey moved the industrial centre of the world to Paris, and thus made a clear alignment between these groups and the Revolutionaries of France.

One of De Quincey's recurrent targets was the growing movement for education, for it was this that in his eyes politicized an otherwise subservient working class. 'In 1793,' he wrote in 'Political Anticipations', 'Jacobinism relied upon man with his natural infirmities; in 1830 it relies upon man trained and disciplined to discern an interest in pursuing their suggestions' (720–1). He described a class mechanized by education, its natural instincts subsumed by the robotic responses impelled by its leaders.[40] The imagery of mechanization stumbles between material and symbolic motivations, referring at once to industrial machines, the machine-like character of the working class, and the metaphorical

---

[40] The most powerful icon of a monstrously mechanized industrial working class is to be found in Frankenstein's monster, another organic machine. See Franco Moretti, 'Dialectic of Fear' in *Signs Taken for Wonders* (London: Verso, 1983), 83–109. The image of the monster reverberates throughout the century. For an account of its various meanings and applications, see Chris Baldick, *In Frankenstein's Shadow: Myth, Monstrosity, and Nineteenth-Century Writing* (Oxford: Clarendon Press, 1987).

machinery of educational institutions that produced it. As in other conservative writings of the time, these merge as the printing industry is isolated as the most dangerous manifestation of the new mechanization.[41] Later in the same essay he decried the influence of the press, disseminating its material to the 'humblest poor', a process that needed to be halted by the 'very wise' practice of taxation on newspapers which will apply a *'sufflamen*, or drag, to the ruinous diffusion of political irritation, in carrying speculations so intelligible, and so easily abused, to the firesides of the poor' (724).[42] This attack on the popular press and a working-class reading public recurs throughout his work.

De Quincey's representations of revolutionaries as both organic and mechanical present a confusing mixture of ideologically invested metaphors. However, it is not unusual to see the two sets of terms mixed together. Indeed many intellectuals throughout the century declared an aim to achieve unity or 'balance' between the opposing intellectual traditions of organicism and mechanism, and the political interests that each represented.

Kant's attempt to integrate idealist and empiricist philosophical modes, which I will discuss in Chapter 5, should be seen as an initiating work in the development of the nineteenth-century endeavour to achieve epistemological unity. Coleridge's *On the Constitution of Church and State*, first published in 1829 as a response to Catholic emancipation, formulated a version of this project in its attempt to balance the competing interests of opposing social groups of the time, for each was embedded in the development of different intellectual traditions. The prime function of government, Coleridge claimed, was to maintain equilibrium between the forces of *permanence* (the interests of the aristocracy for whom power rested in ownership of the land), and *progression* (the inter-

---

[41] Cf. Thomas Carlyle, 'Signs of the Times' (1829) in *Selected Writings*, ed. Alan Shelston, (Harmondsworth: Penguin, 1971), 59–85.

[42] The tax on newspapers, Stamp Duty, was increased in 1797. The Newspaper Stamp Act of 1819 redefined 'newspaper' in such a way as to make the tax a method of political censorship. De Quincey calls it the 'one solitary barrier' which 'stands between the jacobins and [their] darling purpose' ('Political Anticipations', *Blackwood's*, 28 [November 1830], 724). The tax was reduced in 1836 and abolished in 1855. See Richard D. Altick, *The English Common Reader: A Social History of the Mass Reading Public 1800–1900* (Chicago: University of Chicago Press, 1957), 318–47, and Patricia Hollis, *The Pauper Press: A Study in Working-Class Radicalism of the 1830s* (Oxford: OUP, 1970).

ests of the new commercial middle class); between the needs of moral cultivation and those of personal freedom; and between the competing interests of various religious sects, since the new legislation had brought increased political rights to formerly suppressed groups. The duty of maintaining this balance, of implementing what he names the *Lex Equilibrii*, was bestowed on the National Church, which, in the form of the *clerisy* would inculcate national values through a process of education and surveillance.[43]

Despite this avowed commitment to the middle way, *On the Constitution of Church and State* is clearly a work of conservatism: Coleridge named his enemies as 'Utilitarians and Liberalists' who had brought about the breakdown of social cohesion through their programmes for mass education that taught science instead of literature and morality. As these educational programmes were based on the methods of empiricism, Coleridge blamed in part an engagement with tawdry matter for the loss of social and moral values he lamented. The National Church and the system of education governed by the clerisy was designed to correct the impairments of such an educational philosophy: he wrote, 'You begin, therefore, with the attempt to *popularize* science: but you will only effect its *plebification*. It is folly to think of making all, or the many, philosophers, or even men of science and systematic knowledge.'[44] Instead he recommended a process of quasi-religious education to restore to society a sense of proper order.

De Quincey shared Coleridge's conservative beliefs, and also included a version of this language of balance. But it was perpetrated in panic and heavy-handed by comparison, raising more problems than it resolves. For instance, writing in September 1830, the idea of balance provided him with the basis for what appears to be a rather bland defence of the existing constitution:

Philosophically speaking, neither Whigs nor Tories, taken separately, express the truth of our constitution—but both in combination. They are

[43] For *lex equilibrii*, see Samuel Taylor Coleridge, *On the Constitution of Church and State*, ed. John Colmer (1829; London: Routledge & Kegan Paul, 1976) in *Collected Writings*, x, 23. The idea of balance is emphasized by Henry Nelson Coleridge in his 1839 preface to the work, and also by J. S. Mill in 'Coleridge' (1840). On the clerisy, see Ben Knights, *The Idea of the Clerisy in the Nineteenth Century* (Cambridge: CUP, 1978).

[44] Coleridge, *Constitution of Church and State*, 69.

the antagonist forces of the English constitution, as necessary to each other as the centrifugal and centripetal forces in another system, which by mutual hostility produce an equilibrium, and a uniform motion, that could not otherwise have resulted. . . . To one party is confided the conservative charge of the popular powers—to the other of the powers of the crown. Either party, insulated, would represent an abortion; both together, make up the total constitution. ('French Revolution', *Blackwood's*, 28 (September 1830), 556)

It should be remembered that De Quincey was writing at the time at which his own party fractured from conflicting responses to the pressure for Reform,[45] and the language he uses belies the sense of panic this engendered. The cool judiciousness of his pseudo-scientific language of 'centrifugal and centripetal forces' jars beside the outrage expressed by the term 'abortion', which is used to represent either party in its isolation, and bespeaks De Quincey's agitation, his awareness of the precariousness of the present state. The two-party system sustains the status quo through the sheer opposition of two intractable positions. For De Quincey this is an effective measure because it drastically limits the boundaries of political debate: the 'truth of [the] constitution' lies in the irresolvable conflict between Whig and Tory; the interests of groups outside this partnership are unrepresented and lie beyond the scope of the constitution.

The sense of balance that Coleridge described has been replaced by a head-on collision, the force of which would maintain an unreformed parliament, and continue the exclusion of the interests of other groups. De Quincey's rhetoric is characteristically violent. In this case, the violence is indicative of the political panic he experienced as he attempted to maintain a vision of a social order, the conditions of which were gradually slipping from beneath him. His odd conflation of organic and mechanic imagery is part of this process, for as he introduced every available rhetorical device for representing the force of revolution as dangerous, the particular histories and allegiances of each image are forgotten; as before, the texts perform as surfaces that erase

---

[45] On divisions in the Tory party see Bruce Coleman, *Conservatism and the Conservative Party in Nineteenth-Century Britain* (London: Edward Arnold, 1988), 46–54, and Eric Evans, *Britain Before the Reform Act: Politics and Society, 1815–1832* (London: Longman, 1989), 68–75.

pasts and violate memories, and use images for the moment and no longer. Coleridge's image of delicate balance is transformed into a whirling juggernaut, that angrily devours all signs of dissidence within the nation.

The use of terms such as 'centrifugal and centripetal forces' suggests a mechanical basis for the constitution that De Quincey clearly sees as an organic entity. This is an example of a recurrent image in his work, that of a natural machine. The idea of a natural machine encapsulates something of the contradictions that his work embodies: if his visions of an *ancien régime* in England cannot be sustained in the political world, he constructs a version of it in his literary reminiscences that he presents to a reading public in *Tait's* that is unsympathetic to his political aims. De Quincey's whole life was bestrewn with similar kinds of contradictions: a High Tory who admired Ricardo; who deplored the press yet who made his living writing for it; who wrote about political economy while his life was spent avoiding debt collectors; and so on. De Quincey's writings constantly display symptoms which can perhaps best be understood as those of a writer forced by financial expediency to engage with the institutions of a society of which he disapproved. It is in this context that we should read his writings on Immanuel Kant.

Kant for Businessmen

At the beginning of his writing career, one of De Quincey's most frequent themes was the presentation of German literature and philosophy to a British reading public. As editor of the *Westmorland Gazette*, he incorporated essays on topics derived from the works of German philosophers,[46] and later, after the success of *Confessions*, he produced translations of philosophical essays by Kant and Lessing alongside fictions by Jean-Paul Richter and other German writers for the *London Magazine* and *Blackwood's*. Indeed, with the exception of 'On Murder Considered as One of the Fine Arts' (1827), his early contributions to *Blackwood's* were all translations from German texts, and his engagement with topics arising from German philosophy and literature was only interrupted by his first political essay published in March 1829, 'The Duke of

---

[46] See Lindop, *Opium-Eater*, 229.

Wellington and Mr Peel'. De Quincey was one of the few British intellectuals engaged with German topics at the time, and his attempt to disseminate this work to the British public was one area in which his function as a popularizer of knowledge was carried out most self-consciously and systematically.[47]

However, from the beginning, the philosophical works were heavily criticized. In 1824 William Maginn set the tone for subsequent responses to De Quincey's work as a Kantian when, writing in the *John Bull Magazine and Literary Recorder*, he dismissed De Quincey's claim to understand Kant as 'another humbug'.[48] The works on Kant have since been the occasion of René Wellek's most stinging critique of De Quincey, which claimed that not only did De Quincey not understand Kant, but the works are on the whole insubstantial and contentless.[49]

'Kant in his Miscellaneous Essays' was published in *Blackwood's* in August 1830, in the midst of his political journalism.[50] Presented as a review of Kant's *Vermischte Schriften* (1799–1807), it took the form of a letter to the editor, Sir Christopher North. In it, De Quincey addressed the particular demands of the *Blackwood's* audience, whom he characterized as busy and practical men, occupied in commerce, but none the less possessing intellectual appetites eager to be gratified.[51] 'It is not for its abstruseness that we shrink from the Transcendental Philosophy,' he wrote, 'but for *that* taken in connection with its visionariness, and its disjunction from all the practical uses in life' (VIII: 85). If only transcendentalism were a touch more practical, he claims, the British man would

[47] On De Quincey's contribution to the circulation of German ideas in Britain, see Rosemary Ashton, *The German Idea: Four English Writers and the Reception of German Thought* (Cambridge: CUP, 1980), 16–17 and 41–2. See also René Wellek, *Immanuel Kant in England, 1793–1838* (Princeton: Princeton University Press, 1931), 172–80, and 'De Quincey's Status in the History of Ideas' in *Confrontations: Studies in the Intellectual and Literary Relations Between Germany, England, and the United States during the Nineteenth Century* (Princeton, NJ: Princeton University Press, 1965), 114–52.

[48] *John Bull Magazine and Literary Recorder*, 1 (July 1824), 21–4.

[49] René Wellek, 'Thomas De Quincey', in *A History of Modern Criticism*, iii, *The Age of Transition* (London: Jonathan Cape, 1966), 110–20.

[50] 'Kant in his Miscellaneous Essays', *Blackwood's*, 28 (Aug. 1830, pt. 1), 224–68.

[51] Cf. Jon P. Klancher's suggestive discussion of the preoccupation with the development of self-consciousness, or *Mind*, on the pages of *Blackwood's*, in *The Making of English Reading Audiences, 1790–1832* (Madison, Wis.: University of Wisconsin Press, 1987), 52–60.

find it very useful. A peculiar mixture of transcendentalism and empiricism emerges: he will agree with Kant, that metaphysical questions are central to all intellectual endeavour, but maintains that a practical man can only consider them after the more immediate business has been attended to. He writes, 'when vassalage to the eye is most matured, and the empire of sense absolutely systematized by education, still, under every obstacle,—oppression, thwarting, stifling,—such is the imperishable dignity of the human mind, that all the great problems concerning its own nature and destination, which, without one exception, happen to be metaphysical, must and will victoriously return upon us' (VIII: 85). Metaphysical questions, therefore, are always self-reflexive, and exist almost as a luxuriant supplement to the weighty problems of material life.

In the light of this, De Quincey's task is a difficult one, for as weighty as metaphysical questions are, they are nevertheless of secondary concern to the practical businessman that he addresses. 'Metaphysics are pretty generally out of the reach of a nation made up of practical men of business,' he writes. 'To judge a metaphysician directly is therefore out of our province; but, indirectly, we may fairly enough compute his amount of power by observing how he acquits himself on that neutral ground which is common to all intellectual nations' (VIII: 90). The compromise he reaches, then, is to focus on the common ground between Kant's metaphysics and the interests of the business class: the three issues he names are civil polity, natural theology, and political economy. Attention is diverted from Kant's philosophical idealism, for Kant will be judged as a businessman among businessmen, a man directly engaging in the material details of 'real life'. As Wellek has noticed, De Quincey fails to engage with the central points of Kant's philosophical works, for in his effort to tailor the philosopher for the audience he addressed, the metaphysical aspect of the work was omitted. The omission makes for a bizarre rendering of Kant's philosophy.

There are two points that emerge from this. First, De Quincey blames the context for which he was writing for the compromises enforced on his work on Kant. It is the modern lives of his audience, he claims, that allow no time for contemplation of metaphysical questions; even a *Blackwood's* audience, whose class position and political aspirations most closely match De

Quincey's ideal, have been compromised by the spread of commerce and all that it entails. Thus in 1830, De Quincey indicates that he acknowledges that the past for which he is nostalgic is already irretrievably lost, displaced by the onward march of commerce, and he will always write in an awareness of that knowledge.

The second point is that De Quincey indicates that the transcendental questions—self-reflexive questions concerning the mind and so on—belong to that lost order. Thus his 'impassioned prose' which explores the interiors of his own mind in his elaborate accounts of his dream world, provides a new location for the discussion of philosophical questions. Under the social pressures of his time, the dematerializing space of literature becomes the new arena for metaphysical issues.

In his account of Kant for businessmen, De Quincey nevertheless traces the issues that he considers to go beyond the concerns of the periodical audience. In so doing, he gives expression to his longing for this idealized past. The text stands strangely dislocated between the agenda he desires to address, and that which he is permitted.

This sense of dislocation is characteristic of De Quincey's work, which expresses nostalgic longings that cannot be accommodated within the context of the periodical. It is this that lies behind the discursive economy that we have begun to trace. In the literary reminiscences, a version of Romanticism as an idealized pastoral past is produced that is incompatible with the history from which it emerged. Moreover the agenda of transcendental philosophy is also transferred, in spirit, to the space of literature. Politics remains isolated, identified now as the time-bound responses to contemporary events. The establishment of these discursive boundaries cause a strong sense of fragmentation that marks De Quincey's work.

Our sense of confusion is nowhere stronger than when facing De Quincey's works on political economy. For if his attempt to produce Kant for businessmen is bizarre, his production of 'Ricardo Made Easy' for the same High Tory audience is even more so. The following chapter will trace the contradictions and compromises of De Quincey's political economy.

2

Debt and Desire: The Psychology of Political Economy

My dear Sir,
  Would you favour me with £1?

De Quincey, letter to Robert Blackwood, 20 February 1841[1]

For De Quincey, the pleasures of opium include those of a *flâneur*:[2] 'I used often, on Saturday nights, after I had taken opium, to wander forth, without much regarding the direction or the distance, to all the markets, and other parts of London, to which the poor resort on a Saturday night, for laying out their wages' (C, 47). The Saturday night pleasures of the poor consist of the frivolous expenditure of the wages of bodily toil; and De Quincey, the aimless wanderer, happily imbibes the spectacle of their consuming pleasures. When possible to maintain his anonymity, he swaps from observer to participant, joins their parties, and empathizes with their economic lot: he shares their gladness at higher wages and sadness at lost wages. The poor, he glibly maintains, are 'more philosophic than the rich', showing 'cheerful submission to . . . irremediable evils, or irreparable losses' (C, 47).[3] For him, compensation is available through the agency of opium: saddened by the low wages of his acquaintances, he draws from 'opium some means of consoling [him]self'. Addicts and the poor share forms of consumption as the mode of reconciliation to their feelings of displeasure.

---

[1] National Library of Scotland, MS 4055 fo. 145.

[2] See Walter Benjamin, *Charles Baudelaire: A Lyric Poet in the Era of High Capitalism*, trans. Harry Zohn (London: Verso, 1983), 35–66.

[3] De Quincey recalls Wordsworth's condescension to the philosophic rustics in the *Preface* to the *Lyrical Ballads*; the language of rustics, Wordsworth claims, is 'more permanent and far more philosophic than that which is frequently substituted for it by Poets'. See William Wordsworth, *The Prose Works*, ed. W. J. B. Owen and J. W. Smyser (Oxford: Clarendon Press, 1974), i. 124.

Having wandered further than he should, De Quincey must find his way home. The city is now no longer familiar, and confounds him like an Eastern terrain:

instead of circumnavigating all the capes and head-lands I had doubled in my outward voyage, I came suddenly upon such knotty problems of alleys, such enigmatical entries, and such sphynx's riddles of streets without thoroughfares . . . I could almost have believed, at times, that I must be the first discoverer of some of these *terrae incognitae*. For all this, however, I paid a heavy price in distant years. (C, 47–8)

Lost in the inscrutable interiors of the city, De Quincey is a parodic explorer, colonizer of virgin territory, charting his uncertain knowledge of the mysterious city, as Mayhew will later do.[4] These, however, are guilty pleasures, for which he will pay the 'heavy price' of psychological terror that invades his dreams, spinning narratives of confusion and a bad conscience that constitute the 'Pains of Opium' in *Confessions*. This psychological expenditure incurred through wandering nevertheless yields a rich narrative production. It is the source of his best dreams, on which his literary reputation was built.

A complex economy begins to emerge in which the *flâneur's* wandering-to-consume renders an expenditure that is not reimbursed, but which is the source of a narrative that provides reconciliation of a kind, like opium or poverty. Frequently in *Confessions* we find moments at which unlike terms are exchanged in irregular and faulty transactions. For instance, a memorable section of the text is occupied by his attempt to repay, in money, Ann the prostitute for an emotional debt incurred when she saved his life. An attempt to attain surety for a loan produces a series of adventures: an eventful journey to Oxford on a coach, a brush with an escaped murderer, and so on. The loan is never obtained, and besides, when he returns to London, Ann has disappeared, to return only in his dreams. But if the debt remains unpaid, emotionally and materially, the text nevertheless offers reconciliation of another kind, in the form of the narrative of his search for the loan, and again in his dream in the 'Pains of Opium' when Ann returns, seventeen years later, 'more beautiful . . . but in all other

---

⁴ Henry Mayhew's documentations of the urban poor were published as *London Labour and the London Poor*, 4 vols. (1861–1862; repr. London: Frank Cass, 1967).

points the same' (C, 76). In this text, debts are not repaid but are articulated in another currency; the narrative and the dream transform the indebtedness of the writer into the pleasures of the text.

In the autobiographical text, narrative offers recompense for the guilt of unpaid debts. There is a neat comparison with his life, in which writing, in its material form, forestalled but never satisfied the debt collectors. His correspondence with his publishers from the 1830s shows the extent to which he literally wrote to pay off debts. Moreover recognizing the commodity value of the writings, on a number of occasions, landlords in whose debt De Quincey was, held his papers 'hostage' as guarantee against the debt.[5] And if in *Confessions* the wanderings of the *flâneur* incur psychic expenditure, the perambulations of the real De Quincey created expenses of a different kind. To evade his debts De Quincey moved from lodging to lodging and in the 1830s, entered Holyrood Abbey, the debtors' sanctuary, where he fell into debt again. Forced by his debts into a domain of the city that was regulated by another economy, he resided in a space on the underside of the city's economy, at times confined to bed, as his poverty forced him to sell his clothes and mimic an invalid.[6] But De Quincey's own wanderings became commodities of a kind when private detectives were hired by his creditors to follow him. A bill from 1838 gives an account of the movements of one such detective, William Muir, as he attempted to apprehend De Quincey over a period of a number of months, following his shadowy traces across the city; each of his day's movements are costed so that De Quincey's wanderings do indeed incur expenditure, as the detective's expenses of £8. 4 shillings are added to his debt of £30. The bookseller, Adam Black, paid the debt, on the condition that De Quincey reimbursed him with copy for the

---

[5] See for example the McIndoe incident, recorded by Grevel Lindop in *The Opium-Eater: A Life of Thomas De Quincey* (Oxford: OUP, 1985), 335–8. De Quincey owed Mr McIndoe seventy pounds; when he accepted McIndoe's offer of a bed, and became his lodger, Mr McIndoe took advantage of the situation by holding De Quincey's books and papers to ransom.

[6] De Quincey's correspondence during this period makes poignant reading. See for instance his letter to Robert Blackwood, dated 6 June 1838: 'Meantime, would you be so good as to let me have one pound? I am utterly aground. Without even paper or pens. And keep out of prison I must. Doing that I shall in 6 weeks be afloat for ever. If I fail, and ever get into prison, I am booked for utter perplexity for a year and more.' National Library of Scotland, MS 4046 fo. 141.

Encyclopaedia Britannica:[7] the structure of this transaction mirrors only too neatly that which was found in the autobiographical text.

The economic obsessions of *Confessions* are largely of a psychic kind, yet he returns to his penury frequently enough to suggest a connection between his psychic and financial concerns, and one corroborated by his biography. Throughout, he is obsessed by complex exchanges, in which debts are compensated by other pleasures. The significance of economic metaphors in his writings is heightened by the fact that he wrote widely and fairly influentially on political economy, earning something of a reputation as a Ricardian. Ricardo's version of the market offered De Quincey the perfect metaphor for the organic, totalizing system which fascinated him. However, for De Quincey, the addict and debtor, who was unable either to stop consuming or to pay his bills, the economic implications of the market and its unstoppable mechanisms, in which his own transactions were but a small and insignificant part, were at once soothing and terrifying.

Given his political affiliations, De Quincey's admiration for Ricardo was unusual. Critics have begun to trace connections between De Quincey's economic theory and his psychic and literary transactions, but they have tended to underplay the eccentricity of a High Tory's enthusiasm for Ricardo, particularly in the 1840s, and the extremely idiosyncratic nature of De Quincey's economic writings.[8] Of all De Quincey's works, his economic

[7] Bill from William Muir, Esq., to Mr Wilkie. National Library of Scotland, MS 1670 fo. 35–6. The incident is recorded in John Jordan, *De Quincey to Wordsworth* (Berkeley, Calif.: University of California Press, 1963), 339, and Lindop, *Opium-Eater*, 324–5.

[8] The best account of De Quincey's economic writings is Robert Maniquis, 'Lonely Empires: Personal and Public Visions of Thomas De Quincey', in *Literary Monographs*, 8, ed. Eric Rothstein and Joseph Anthony Wittreich, jun. (Madison, Wis.: University of Wisconsin Press, 1976), 111–27. See also Kurt Heinzelman, *The Economics of the Imagination* (Amherst, Mass.: University of Massachusetts Press, 1980), 89–94, and Edmund Baxter, *De Quincey's Art of Autobiography* (Edinburgh: Edinburgh University Press, 1990), 153–85. Tave acknowledges the anomalous nature of De Quincey's interest in Ricardo. See Stuart M. Tave (ed.), *New Essays by De Quincey: His Contributions to the Edinburgh Saturday Post and the Edinburgh Evening Post 1827–1828* (Princeton, NJ: Princeton University Press, 1966), 21. Robert Maniquis argues, on the contrary, that an interest in Ricardo was usual for an intellectual in the first half of the 19th cent., and cites Walter Bagehot who claimed that political economy was 'the favourite subject in England from about 1810 to about 1840' (115). This is an important point to bear in mind, but the intensity of De Quincey's admiration for Ricardo remains incongruous beside his political affiliations.

writings are the most baffling for a twentieth-century reader, for
they are knotted with ideological inconsistencies and political
entanglements that cloud their meanings. In this chapter, I will
contextualize De Quincey's economic writings and suggest that
Ricardo's work, as it provided the organic intellectual system that
appealed to De Quincey, paradoxically allowed him to find
therein a conservative social model that suited his political ends.[9]
De Quincey admired Ricardo primarily as the gothic architect
of political economy, for his theory revealed secret and phant-
asmatic chambers. De Quincey perceived that Ricardo's economy
was built on a model of scarcity, and that circulation rested upon
the impossibility that a consumer's desire would ever be fulfilled.[10] The market was thus in a sense indebted, because it promised more than it could provide. If in De Quincey's literary
writings his debts were compensated for by the pleasures of writing, he perceives in Ricardo's work a system in which the elaborate and astounding network of exchange and circulation were
themselves compensation for the debts which the system generated. By the 1840s, De Quincey had forgotten the lessons of
Ricardo in all but name; but he always maintained his fascination
for a system based on debt.

De Quincey and the Political Economists

From its early stages in the mid-eighteenth century, the discipline
of political economy, with its commitment to the market as a self-
regulating and benign social force, carried a political programme
that represented the interests of commercial society. While it is
true that party political divisions were less clear cut in the early
decades of the nineteenth century than they later became, and
that Tory liberals under Lord Liverpool were responsible for
implementing the work of political economists in Parliament,
it is also the case that broadly speaking, during this period,
political economists tended to be identified with the Whig

---

[9] Boyd Hilton points out that the Ricardian model was attractive to some Tories
because it offered a static and non-interventionist economic programme. See
Hilton, *Corn, Cash, Commerce: The Economic Policies of the Tory Governments 1815–
1830* (Oxford: OUP, 1977), 312.
[10] Cf. Michel Foucault, *The Order of Things* (London: Tavistock, 1970), 256–7;
Heinzelman, *Economics of the Imagination*, 88–92.

party.[11] Indeed, in High Tory circles, the term political economy became synonymous with Whiggism.[12] Such polarization appeared particularly acutely in the periodicals published in Edinburgh, the home of the major economists from David Hume and Adam Smith onwards: while the Whig magazine, the *Edinburgh Review*, was the repository of advancements in political economy, publishing the works of writers such as J. R. McCulloch, *Blackwood's* saw itself as the bastion of opposition to the economists and all they stood for.[13]

In the context of nineteenth-century party politics, De Quincey's admiration for Ricardo's economic theory is certainly idiosyncratic. Nevertheless he wrote extensively on political economy, first for the *London Magazine*, and later, between 1832 and 1843 for *Blackwood's*. His most significant works were 'The Dialogues of the Three Templars', printed in the *London Magazine* in 1824, and the series of three essays for *Blackwood's* in 1842, 'Ricardo Made Easy', the latter forming the basis of the treatise, *The Logic of Political Economy* (1844).[14] While the later works were more detailed—*Logic* in particular adopting a less anecdotal style and a more technical vocabulary than the other works—the project that he sustained throughout was to popularize the works of Ricardo and to make them accessible to a wider reading public. He saw his practice as the dissemination of knowledge within an

[11] On the party affiliations of political economists, see F. W. Fetter, *The Economists in Parliament: 1780–1868* (Chapel Hill, NC: Duke University Press, 1980), and Barry Gordon, *Political Economy in Parliament, 1819–1823* (London: Macmillan, 1976); on Tory assimilations of political economy, see Barry Gordon, *Economic Doctrine and Tory Liberalism 1824–1830* (London: Macmillan, 1979), and Hilton, *Corn, Cash, Commerce*; for an account of party political divisions in the first half of the century, see Peter Mandler, *Aristocratic Government in the Age of Reform: Whigs and Liberals, 1830–1852* (Oxford: Clarendon Press, 1990).

[12] See Maxine Berg, *The Machinery Question and the Making of Political Economy, 1815–1848* (Cambridge: CUP, 1980), 253–68.

[13] On the *Edinburgh Review*, see Biancamaria Fontana, *Rethinking the Politics of Commercial Society: The Edinburgh Review, 1802–1832* (Cambridge: CUP, 1985); on the response to political economy in *Blackwood's*, see F. W. Fetter, 'The Economic Articles in *Blackwood's Edinburgh Magazine*, and their Authors, 1817–1853', *Scottish Journal of Political Economy*, 7 (June 1960), 85–107, 213–31, and Berg, *The Machinery Question*, 252–68. Fetter notes that the second issue of *Blackwood's* (in 1817) contained a favourable review of Ricardo's *Principles*, and that it was only from the 1820s that it expressed its opposition to the political economists.

[14] 'Dialogues of Three Templars on Political Economy: chiefly in relation to the Principles of Mr Ricardo' was first published in the *London Magazine* for Mar., Apr., and May 1824. For 'Ricardo Made Easy', see Introd. n. 32.

economy of divided labour. In the 'Dialogues' he invokes the
artisanal context of the production of coins, as Ricardo is compared with the 'labourers of the *Mine* . . . who dig up the metal of
truth', and himself with the '*labourers of the Mint* . . . [who] work
up the metal for current use' (IX: 50–1). Later, in 'Ricardo Made
Easy' this vocabulary is dropped in favour of the Coleridgean
terms, *clerus* and *populus*: 'it was the *clerus* not the *populus*, whom
Ricardo addressed: he did not call attention from the laity who
seek to learn, but from the professional body who seek to teach'
(*Blackwood's*, 52 (September 1842), 341). Thus, although by 1842 he
had upgraded his role from labourer to teacher, and swapped the
metaphor of the circulation of money to a literal expression for the
dissemination of knowledge, in both cases De Quincey represented himself as a bridge between an elite body of knowledge
and an ignorant public.

Whatever the response from his imagined audience, his efforts
were reasonably well received by the political economists.
J. R. McCulloch, the philosophic radical, who as Ricardo's loyal
disciple was considered as the prime target of the anti-political
economy lobby in *Blackwood's*, admired the 'brevity, pungency
and force' of the 'Dialogues' which 'annihilate[d]' Malthus's ob-
jections to Ricardo's theory of value, and he deemed *Logic*, a 'very
clever work . . . intended to unravel intricacies and to expose sun-
dry errors in the application of the Ricardian theory of value',
although he also noted that it was too 'scholastic' and 'tiresome
and repulsive'.[15] De Quincey's works were considered significant
by writers including J. S. Mill and Karl Marx for their explication
of Ricardo's theory of value.[16] Most notable, however, was Samuel
Bailey's anonymously published work, *Critical Dissertation on the
Nature, Measure and Causes of Value* (1825), which claimed to have
been prompted by the insights of 'Dialogues'—namely, that there
is no standard measure of value, and that profits and wages exist

---

[15] J. R. McCulloch, *The Literature of Political Economy. A Classified Catalogue of
Select Publications in the Different Departments of that Science with Historical, Critical,
and Biographical Notices* (London, 1845), 33 and 20.

[16] J. S. Mill, review of *The Logic of Economy* by De Quincey, *Westminster Review*,
43 (June 1845), 319–31, and *Principles of Political Economy, with some of their Applications to Social Philosophy*, 2 vols., 2nd edn. (London, 1849), 540–2; Karl Marx,
Grundrisse. Foundations of the Critique of Political Economy (Rough Draft), trans.
Martin Nicolaus (Harmondsworth: Penguin, 1973), 557–9.

in inverse relation to each other. Bailey's critique of Ricardo has been singled out by F. W. Fetter as the 'best organized and most effective attack on Ricardo's theory of value and distribution'[17] during a period in which Ricardo was falling from favour even with liberal Whigs. However, far from seeking alliance with Bailey, De Quincey claimed in 1844 that despite 'all his ability, [Bailey] failed to shake any of my opinions' (IX: 119), and he remained a stalwart supporter of Ricardo.[18] Such a response begins to indicate the extent of the contradictions implicit in De Quincey's desire to popularize a body of knowledge considered by many as the ideological basis of the opinions of his political opponents.

De Quincey first recorded his interest in political economy in 1821 in *Confessions*, when he claimed that he had found in it the advantages of an organic science, in which the parts could be disaggregated and considered separately. Nevertheless this had been an unsatisfactory interest. He recounts how he 'had been led in 1811 to look into loads of books and pamphlets on many branches of economy', but found in them only 'the very dregs and rinsings of the human intellect; . . . any man of sound head and practised in wielding logic with a scholastic adroitness, might take up the whole academy of modern economists, and throttle them between heaven and earth with his finger and thumb, or bray their fungus heads to powder with a lady's fan' (C, 65). All this changed, however, on his discovery of Ricardo's *Principles of Political Economy* (1817): 'Mr Ricardo', he wrote, 'had deduced, *a priori*, from the understanding itself, laws which first gave a ray of light into the unwieldy chaos of materials, and had constructed what had been but a collection of tentative discussions into a science of regular proportions, now first standing on an eternal basis' (C, 65). Ricardo rescued him temporarily from the torpor of drug addiction, rousing him to plan a work, which he never completed, to be called *Prolegomena to all future Systems of Political Economy* (C, 66). In 1842 he wrote that Ricardo's interest was in the 'great basis that supported the whole. . . . [I]t was in the grounds, the causes, the conditions, of these phenomena that Ricardo saw or imagined a series of errors' (*Blackwood's*, 52 (September 1842),

---

[17] Fetter, 'The Rise and Decline of Ricardian Economics', *History of Political Economy*, 1 (1969), 67–84, esp. 79.

[18] See also De Quincey's response to Bailey in *Blackwood's*, 52 (Dec. 1842), 719.

340–1). As Ricardo brought order to De Quincey's life and body, similarly he restored health to political economy itself. The connection is useful for De Quincey, because it endorses his claim that political economy is an *organic* science: Ricardo is a physician-architect, reconstructing a healthy constitution within the body economic.

The theoretical nature of Ricardo's work differentiated it from that of Adam Smith, who had held political economy to be an empirical science, derived from observing the industrial and commercial world.[19] De Quincey was attracted by Ricardo's abstract method, but more conventional political economists were suspicious of it. According to Biancamaria Fontana, writers and readers of the *Edinburgh Review* found that the theoretical style of Ricardo's *Principles* did not gratify their expectations of a treatise in political economy which, she claims, should have formed 'a complete handbook for the enlightened statesman and citizen'.[20] As McCulloch pointed out, Ricardo's was not a 'practical work. . . . It is not even a systematic treatise, but is principally an inquiry into and elucidation of certain fundamental principles'.[21]

The abstraction of Ricardo's work that De Quincey admired so much in fact contributed to the decline of its reputation. By 1830, apart from a residual prestige that continued to be associated with Ricardo's name, Ricardian economics had fallen out of favour with even the political economists.[22] In 1831, Colonel Torrens

[19] On this, see Elie Halévy, *The Growth of Philosophic Radicalism*, trans. Mary Morris (London: Faber & Faber, 1928), 226–7.

[20] Fontana, *Rethinking the Politics*, 77.

[21] McCulloch, *Political Economy*, 17.

[22] Marx claimed that 1830 marked the decline in bourgeois interest in Ricardo, as the 'more explicit and threatening' form of class struggle that emerged made Ricardo's theory, based on the antagonism between landowning, capitalist, and working classes, too dangerous to be countenanced. See Karl Marx, *Capital: A Critique of Political Economy*, trans. Ben Fowkes (Harmondsworth: Penguin, 1976), 'Postface to the Second Edition' (1873), i. 96–7. For accounts of Ricardo's decline, see Fetter, 'Ricardian Economics'; Ronald L. Meek, 'The Decline in Ricardian Economics in England', in *Economics and Ideology and Other Essays* (London: Chapman & Hall, 1967), 50–67; and Keith Tribe, 'The Dissolution of Classical Political Economy' in *Land, Labour, and Economic Discourse* (London: Routledge & Kegan Paul, 1978), 146–58. Some economic historians have stressed Ricardo's sustained influence. See M. Blaug, *Ricardian Economics: A Historical Study* (New Haven, Conn.: Yale University Press, 1958); and Samuel Hollander, *The Economics of David Ricardo* (London: Heineman, 1979). For a response to Hollander see Keith Tribe, 'Ricardian Histories', *Economy and Society*, 104 (Nov. 1981), 451–66.

initiated a series of debates at the Political Economy Club examining the impact of Ricardian economics, and concluded that 'all the great principles of Ricardo's work had been successively abandoned, and . . . his theories of Value, Rent, and Profits were now generally acknowledged to have been erroneous.'[23] As the basis of the economy changed from agriculture to industry, Ricardo's theories, and in particular the belief that wages and profits existed in inverse relation to each other and the importance he laid on the landlord, were considered to be anachronistic, and moreover, to have encouraged the growth of a socialist movement, giving scientific grounding to working-class dissatisfaction with its social and economic conditions. Ironically this wider use of Ricardo had brought about his fall from favour in the world of political economy. Through morally improving tales by Mrs Marcet and Harriet Martineau that set out to illustrate the principles of political economy, lectures from the Society for Useful Knowledge, and the writings of Ricardian Socialists such as William Thompson, Thomas Hodgskin and J. F. Bray, artisans were educated in the intricacies of Ricardian economics.[24] But for non-Ricardian political economists, such as Longfield, Scrope, and Torrens, it was politically expedient that such knowledge be discredited: industrial experience of the 1830s led them to believe that wages and profits were not held in inverse relation, as Ricardo had argued, but both might rise simultaneously; and in an attempt to remove labour from the centre of the production of wealth, they proposed a notion in which capital was the new agent of profits.[25] For them, labour became just one more commodity to be included in the calculation of production costs. Aside from radical circles, the commitment to Ricardian theory had fallen to the extent that McCulloch felt himself to be among the last remaining Ricardians. Another sign of the deterioration in interest in Ricardian economics among middle-class exponents, was the cessation in 1831 of the course of lectures on political economy, the Ricardo Memorial Lectures. These had been established by James Mill at the University of London in 1824; by 1831 the enrolments had decreased to

---

[23] Cited by Meek, *Economics and Ideology*, 67–8.

[24] On the Ricardian socialists, see Meek, *Economics and Ideology*, 69–71, and Tribe, *Land, Labour, and Economic Discourse*, 155–8.

[25] On this see Tribe, *Land, Labour, and Economic Discourse*, 151–4.

such an extent that they were no longer considered worth running.[26]

In the light of this, De Quincey's later writings on political economy, published in the 1840s in *Blackwood's*, are even more surprising than his earlier works. Ironically they share certain aspects of the political economists' critique of Ricardo, in particular the removal of labour as the principal cause of value. In this De Quincey was clearly motivated by a similar sense of the impending threat of a radicalized working class. However, he was far from sharing the political views of the political economists. Indeed on points of economic policy, his sympathies lay with other *Blackwood's* writers, such as David Robinson, Archibald Alison, and James McQueen, who denounced free trade, the restitution of the gold standard, and the reduction of British tariffs, and argued vociferously against the abolition of the slave trade and for the continuation of the Corn Laws. But while their arguments were made from the point of view that the workings of the market had a pernicious and devastating effect on civilized society, De Quincey, on the contrary, invoked the market as the site of the problem, but also of its resolution.[27] For instance, he used Ricardo's law of diminishing returns on land to argue that the reduction of taxes on corn would bring about inflation, unemployment, and widespread poverty.[28] He denounced cases in which former slaves purchased sugar plantations on the grounds that they were able to do so only on the withdrawal of capital investment from the plantation.[29]

In De Quincey's economic writings, the market was in itself neither entirely pernicious nor benign: it was an analytic tool that provided a framework through which a problem might be understood and possibly resolved. Nevertheless such a role accorded the market unmitigated powers, which made it for him at once

[26] On the Ricardo Memorial Lectures, see Gordon, *Economic Doctrine*, 10–11, 138.
[27] Cf. Fetter, 'The Economic Articles in *Blackwood's*': 'the contributor to *Blackwood's* who came closest to being an economist, in the technical sense of being interested in the mechanism of the market, was Thomas De Quincey' (92).
[28] See IX: 280.
[29] See IX: 216 n. De Quincey argues that the accumulated wages that allowed the slaves to purchase the plantations had been paid from funds that should have been spent on the upkeep of the property. The property was thus run down, so that when the landowners sold to the slaves, they recouped their own funds, cheated the slaves, and withdrew capital from the colony.

repulsive and compelling. This ambivalence is recorded in the autobiographical and fictional works rather than the economic writings. In the 'literary' works, the market is the source of his most sublime fantasies, such as in the dream of the expanding book order in *Suspiria*, or the harbinger of terror, as in the gothic fiction, *The Household Wreck*.

Politically, De Quincey's 1840s writings on economics were peculiar on two counts: first, because he persisted in his claim that his project was to popularize the work of Ricardo, when for political economists this had become the impetus to militancy in the working class; and second, because he used his work as a platform for voicing opinions in favour of trade restrictions, in particular the Corn Laws, and against the abolition of slavery, views that he had developed in opposition to both Ricardo and the next generation of political economists. The most striking element in them is the attempt to establish the consumer at the heart of political economy, and in this respect it is difficult to recognize them as Ricardian works, except in the sense that they promote the idea of an overarching system guided by the principles of value and distribution. This is made clear in 'Ricardo Made Easy', which is subtitled 'What are the Principal Differences between Ricardo and Adam Smith?', the answer being the attention to the founding principles of the system. But the effective decline in liberal interest in Ricardo meant that the publication of such a work in the pages of *Blackwood's* was not, at least, politically disruptive. Paradoxically, Ricardo served De Quincey as a frame on which to hang certain High Tory opinions and around which he might weave his gothic imaginings.

De Quincey's writings on political economy present the same bewildering mixture of ideologically invested forms that we encountered in his political essays. As before, this is epitomized by the intertwining of mechanic and organic metaphors. Thus in 'Ricardo Made Easy' he compares the land with a natural machine, one that cannot be reproduced (*Blackwood's*, 52 (December 1842), 724; IX: 177–8), and in *Logic* he claims that society is like a 'working body', whose elements, '(like so many organs of a complex machine) must eternally operate by aiding or by thwarting each other' (IX: 208). A machine with organs, a body with mechanical parts: the two sets of terms are confusingly entangled. As noted in the previous chapter, gothic architecture, which was constructed so as to resemble an organic being, provides probably the best example of this miscegenation of organic and mechanic terms, and it is not surprising, therefore, that the gothic architect is a figure that dominates De Quincey's economic writings. One of the defining characteristics of gothic architecture is its challenge to Reason, as Coleridge exemplified in his description of a cathedral in *Biographia Literaria* (1817). In this example, Coleridge exchanged intellectual certainty for imaginative excitement and aesthetic pleasure: ' "Now in glimmer, and now in gloom"; often in palpable darkness not without a chilly sensation of terror; then suddenly emerging into broad yet visionary lights with coloured shadows, of fantastic shape, yet all decked with holy insignia and mystic symbols.'[30] This typically gothic transaction, in which aesthetic pleasure compensates for intellectual ungrounding (an exchange that is closely related to the aesthetic of the sublime[31]) is the same as that enacted in De Quincey's literary works. The interesting point is that the very architecture that is the occasion of this transaction will also provide a model for De Quincey's economic theory. When we consider the economic plots that the architectural model implies, we will find an economy whose glorious mysteries are derived from the impossibility of supplying demands, in the same way that the aesthetic pleasures of the gothic are derived from the withholding of Reason.

The Architecture of Political Economy

The 'Dialogues of the Three Templars' provides a more orthodox explanation of Ricardo's theory than that to be found in *Logic*. In it, De Quincey explicates two central points from Ricardo's *Principles*: that the grounds of all value is labour; and that there can be no standard measure of value. The work is a fleshing out in Socratic form of an earlier and much shorter essay, 'Malthus on Value';[32] in it De Quincey's own persona, XYZ, attempts to

---

[30] *Biographia Literaria, or Biographical Sketches of my Literary Life and Opinions*, ed. James Engell and W. Jackson Bate (London: Routledge and Kegan Paul, 1983), i. 301.

[31] For the emergence of this relation, see Peter de Bolla, *The Discourse of the Sublime: Readings in History, Aesthetics and the Subject* (Oxford: Blackwell, 1989).

[32] 'Malthus on the Measure of Value' was first published in the *London Magazine* for Dec. 1823.

convert two sceptical templars, Philebus and Phaedrus, to the Ricardian principles of value. XYZ explains:

The ground of value of all things lies in the quantity . . . of labour which produces them. Here is that great principle which is the corner-stone of all tenable Political Economy; which granted or denied, all Political Economy stands or falls. Grant me this one principle, with a few square feet of the sea-shore to draw my diagrams upon, and I will undertake to deduce every other truth in the science. (IX: 55)

Ricardo, the master-builder, lays the 'corner-stone' of political economy, the theory of value, from which, XYZ claims, he can 'deduce', or build, the entire theory of political economy. To do so, however, he requires a piece of sand on which to 'draw [his] diagrams'. The sand will provide the space for the representation of the edifice of political economy, another *grounding* for the 'truth' of political economy. Of course, his figurative description of this role as demonstrator may well be flippant rhetoric, but as it doubles the imaginative topoi of political economy, it questions the force of his metaphorical scheme and its presumed authority. Ricardo is the architect of political economy, establishing its true foundations; but De Quincey, as the disseminator XYZ, builds its edifice in diagrams in the sand: the model of constant superscription and erasure suggested by the sand rests uneasily beside the figures of permanence and solidity.

De Quincey's account of Ricardo's theory is marked throughout by similar kinds of ambivalences. The architectural structures through which he describes Ricardo's economic ideas frequently have a peculiar material status—gothic structures, occupying irregular dimensional spaces and possessing secrets. He finds Ricardo's logic compelling not only for the order it suggests, but also for its abstractions, and for its mysteries. Ricardo is a mystic in possession of special powers of insight, and his theory grants access to hidden places.

De Quincey praises Ricardo for his meticulous use of language for it is this that enables Ricardo to see elements that are concealed to the normal gaze. Ironically, however, De Quincey points out, his fastidious language makes less observant men find Ricardo obscure. In his defence, De Quincey claims that Ricardo's is sanctioned 'obscurity', because it is, paradoxically, the *effect* of his clear-sightedness:

The obscurity, where any exists in Ricardo, is rather permitted than caused by his style of exposition: in part it adheres to the subject, and in part it grows out of the lax colloquial application which most men have allowed to the words *value, labour,* and *rent*; so that, when they find these words used with a stern fidelity to one sole definition, they are confounded. (IX: 115)

But if Ricardo's clarity is another man's obscurity, Adam Smith's obfuscation gives the false impression of clarity:

Adam Smith *appears* to be right in some occasional passages upon this great question [value], merely because his words, having two senses, dissemble that sense which is now found to be inconsistent with the truth. Yet even this dissembling was not consciously contemplated by Adam Smith: he could not dissemble what he did not perceive. (IX: 180)

Ricardo's too precise use of language gives him insight and privileged access to hidden knowledge; Smith's too lax language is a sign only of his own blindness and remains an obstacle to the truth of political economy. For De Quincey, everything rests on words: a special use of language shows a writer's intent and marks the authenticity of his knowledge; but it also maintains the mystery of political economy, for the true language of political economy is like a secret code that empowers the privileged readers to decipher its enigmas, and leaves others puzzled and excluded from the arcane chambers of knowledge.

In the *Dialogues* his Ricardian attention to verbal accuracy allows XYZ to unravel a series of errors in Malthus's wages theory of value.[33] According to XYZ, Malthus fails to distinguish between two different uses of the term *determine*, and consequently conflates labour as a cause of value with labour as an effect of value, mistaking the rewards of labour (wages) for the quantity of labour.[34] Ricardo does not make this oversight. For him, the quantity of labour is the grounds of value. Wages are no accurate

---

[33] This is the point for which McCulloch admires the 'Dialogues' and which Bailey expands on in his *Critical Dissertation on Value*. On this, see Fetter, 'The Rise and Decline of Ricardian Economics', 79.

[34] De Quincey argues that the term *determine* can be used 'objectively' and 'subjectively', a point made on three separate occasions. See IX: 35–6, 92–100, 151–4. In its objective use, 'to determine' means to ascertain the ground of value, and as such it is its *principium essendi*; to determine subjectively is to apply some existing criterion or test, and is the *principium cognoscendi*. According to De Quincey, Malthus conflates the two, and this allows him to propose a wages

measure of the quantity of labour, as Ricardian socialists bitterly noted. According to XYZ, there can be no standard measure of value, for 'nothing could possibly be stationary in value . . . unless it were always produced by the same quantity of labour' (IX: 94). The conditions for the production of goods are under such variable determining factors that they can never be constant. At the centre of Ricardo's account of value is a term that is arithmetically unrepresentable;[35] in this account, we can only know for certain that value exists, but we cannot quantify it, since such measurements can only ever be contingent. The 'corner-stone' of political economy, on which the whole theory rests, is thus an unrepresentable term—a blank. The metaphorical architecture is structurally unsound, but its imaginative scope is sublime: the building is precarious, supported by an unstable term that is always shifting in response to the material circumstances around it; but as a metaphor it is limitlessly fecund.

In the later work, the instability of the system becomes associated with an idea that increasingly preoccupies De Quincey, namely, that debt is the foundation of the economy. I shall say more about this later, but here it is helpful to note a striking image in *Logic* which he uses to illustrate the architectural structure that Ricardo suggests to him. In this example, Ricardo is no longer the foundation builder, but the creator of some vast spectral annex which engulfs and undermines former stable edifices:

We have all read of secret doors in great cities so exquisitely dissembled by art that in what seemed a barren surface of dead wall, where even the eye forewarned could trace no vestige of a separation or of a line, simply by a simultaneous pressure upon two remote points, suddenly and silently an opening was exposed which revealed a long perspective of

theory of value. When Malthus writes 'labour determines value' he means: first, that labour produces, or causes value; but second, that the amount labour can command (i.e. wages) is the measure of value. Thus 'the quantity of labour required to produce the wages of a given number of men, with the addition of the profits upon these advances estimated in labour must always be exactly the same as the quantity of labour which the wages will command.' (T. R. Malthus, *The Measure of Value, Stated and Illustrated, with an Application of it to the Alterations in the Value of the English Currency since 1790* [London, 1823], 39). De Quincey argues that this implies an unbalanced equation in which the quantity of labour required for wages and profits is equal to the quantity of labour required for wages alone.

[35] The very unrepresentability of value suggests that it performs in the manner of a sublime object in De Quincey's imaginative scheme.

retiring columns—architecture the most elaborate, where all had passed
for one blank continuity of dead wall. (IX: 134)

These columns have no foundations and find magical growth in
the twice noted 'dead wall', for this is organic architecture *par
excellence*: a secret, self-reproducing enclave both within and beyond the barren wall. Ricardo offers enlightenment, a way of
seeing beyond the blank walls of other economic theories, but it is
as well to bear in mind the kind of spaces to which he leads us.
Represented spatially, the knowledge that Ricardo imparts is like
the hidden places in Edinburgh that De Quincey inhabited: the
debtors' sanctuary, or the streets in which he wandered, evading
the scrutiny of the private detective—places in the economic un-
derworld of the city. In De Quincey's account, Ricardo's economics return us again and again to the idea of debt: in his imaginative
scheme, this spectral architecture is the architecture of debt. It is
thus interesting to note that while De Quincey occupied the geographical space of the indebted in Edinburgh, the city itself was
also in debt: in 1835 the corporation of Edinburgh was declared
insolvent. The very infrastructure of the city concealed the endlessly receding marks of debt that are, like Ricardo's 'long perspective of retiring columns', hidden behind the blank surfaces of
the economy.

In the 'Preface' to *Logic*, De Quincey describes political
economy as a fragmentary or ruined science, and compares it
with a landscape that is 'renewing itself by parts, but eternally
tottering in some parts, and in other parts mouldering eternally
into ruins' (IX: 119). Ricardo's achievement, he claims, was to find
order within these ruins. In the 'Dialogues', De Quincey asserts
that his purpose was 'to draw into much stronger relief . . . that
one radical doctrine as to value by which [Ricardo] had given a
new birth to Political Economy' (IX: 119), like a phoenix rising
from the ruins. De Quincey's attraction to Ricardo's political
economy bears the legacy of the Romantic fascination for organic
form and fragments: the fragment always invokes the totality to
which it aspires but, by definition, can never achieve.[36] Like a

---

[36] In the essay on 'Style' (1840–41), De Quincey wrote, 'the Doctrine of Value,
for example, could you understand that taken apart? could you value it apart?' (X:
185). On fragments and organic form, see Philippe Lacoue-Labarthe and Jean-Luc
Nancy, *The Literary Absolute: The Theory of Literature in German Romanticism*, trans.

Romantic poet, Ricardo finds order within the disordered, and life within the decaying.

We find the ruined architecture of political economy elsewhere, for it is also the architecture of his dreams which he illustrates in the 'Pains of Opium' in *Confessions*. Here he describes Piranesi's etchings,[37] recalled from memory of an account of them by Coleridge. These represent 'vast Gothic halls' containing the props of industry: 'engines and machinery, wheels, cables, pulleys, levers, catapults, &c. &c. expressive of enormous power put forth and resistance overcome' (C, 69). Dotted throughout the structures in the precarious positions of his labour is the body of the hapless Piranesi, reproduced many times within the context of his own work:

> Creeping along the sides of the walls, you perceived a staircase; and upon it, groping his way upwards, was Piranesi himself . . . But raise your eyes, and behold a second flight of stairs still higher: on which again Piranesi is perceived . . . Again elevate your eye . . . and again is poor Piranesi busy on his aspiring labours: and so on, until the unfinished stairs and Piranesi both are lost in the upper gloom of the hall. (C, 70)

The multiplication of Piranesi mimics the reproduction of industry with terrifying implications for Piranesi, the labourer. Arden Reed has noticed how De Quincey's vision borrows from Coleridge, whose recollections he recalls, and Wordsworth, whose poem, *The Excursion*, he uses to illustrate this scene, and indeed from Piranesi whose etchings are the occasion of the scene.[38] The gothic architecture, with its intricate organic structures, lacking ceilings and foundations, and in which the architect is endlessly figured, is like the literary past that prefigures De Quincey's dreams, for his imaginative life is indebted to the

Philip Barnard and Cheryl Lester (Albany, NY: State University of New York Press, 1988). See also Marjorie Levinson, *The Romantic Fragment Poem: A Critique of a Form* (Chapel Hill, NC: University of North Carolina Press, 1987); Anne Janowitz, *England's Ruins: Poetic Purpose and the National Landscape* (Oxford: Blackwell, 1990); and Thomas McFarland, *Romanticism and the Forms of Ruin: Wordsworth, Coleridge, and the Modalities of Fragmentation* (Princeton, NJ: Princeton University Press, 1981).

[37] De Quincey is referring to Piranesi's *Prisons*, although he misnames them the *Dreams*. See C, 70.

[38] Arden Reed, 'Abysmal Influence: Baudelaire, Coleridge, De Quincey, Piranesi, Wordsworth', *Glyph*, 4 (1978), 188–206.

writers that preceded him. When he notes that 'with the same power of endless growth and self-reproduction did my architecture proceed in dreams' (C, 70), he should also have pointed out that while self-generating, the structure also borrows from elsewhere, and these borrowings are not repaid, creating abysmal deficits into which De Quincey, like Piranesi, is likely to fall.

He might also have added that this is the architecture of Ricardian economics, an organic structure of secret cavities and organic powers of self-reproduction. It is only in the later economic works that De Quincey imbues the secrets of political economy with full gothic significance. In *Logic*, he abandons Ricardian teachings to a large extent, and writes his own idiosyncratic version in which the consumer occupies central stage. Political economy now charts the vicissitudes of desire as though it is a work of psychology. The secret of this consumer economy is that desire is its generating principle, the term that supports the whole system; but it is also the cause of its destruction. As such it is the apotheosis of organic form.[39] The desire to consume is for the economy as it is for the body of the opium addict: the cause of its pleasures and comforts, but also of its pains and torments.

The Economy of Addiction

De Quincey's later writings on political economy are wider in scope than 'Dialogues', attempting a comprehensive coverage of all aspects of Ricardo's *Principles*, rather than restricting their interest to the question of value as in the earlier work. Moreover while 'Dialogues' constructed an economic theory based on an unrepresentable term, value, the purpose of the later works is to represent that very term, to define it in intricate ways. Value is deemed to be caused not by labour, as in the labour theory of value espoused in 'Dialogues', but by the desires of a consumer. Like the political economists, De Quincey has removed labour as the cause of value. At the heart of economy now lie the longings and needs of the consumer—insatiable desires that incur irredeemable debts. The new economic player is the addict, and the market is impelled by a need it can never fulfil.

[39] On Ricardo as an organic economist, see Foucault, *The Order of Things*, (London: Tavistock, 1970), 221–6, 253–63.

The *Logic of Political Economy* begins by returning to the idea of utility, which, since Adam Smith, had been central to the idea of value.[40] De Quincey refines this as utility *for* someone: 'Not what is useful, but what is used' (IX: 120). For an object to possess value, it must be useful to someone.

Utility is the precondition for value, but an object may also possess exchange value.[41] This, he claims, is 'an idea constructed by superadding to the original element of serviceableness (or value in use) an accessory element of power (howsoever gained) to command an equivalent' (IX: 126–7). Value in exchange parasitically incorporates the term on which it depends, utility, as one of its two constitutive components,[42] these being the usefulness of the object, or the consumer's desire for it, and 'the difficulty of attainment' experienced by the consumer. Thus use value, now named 'affirmative' or 'U' value, is the more significant factor of two at work in establishing the exchange value of an object. The second factor, difficulty of attainment, or 'D' value, comprises all costs of production including the labour costs, and is thus a 'negative' force, derived from factors extrinsic to the object. Labour is now subsumed as just one of the negative factors operating on an object's value, another obstacle in the way of the gratification of the consumer's desire.

To explain his terms, De Quincey uses a mechanistic vocabulary of power and resistance: the affirmative value (U) represents the object's power to produce pleasure in the consumer; the negative (D), the object's resistance to its own reproduction. Although the latter will frequently be a factor at work in the establishment of the price of an object, De Quincey claims that this in itself can

---

[40] 'The word VALUE, it is to be observed, has two different meanings, and sometimes expresses the utility of some particular object, and sometimes the power of purchasing other goods which the possession of that object conveys.' Adam Smith, *An Inquiry into the Nature and Causes of the Wealth of Nations*, eds., R. H. Campbell and A. S. Skinner (Oxford: Clarendon Press, 1976), i. 44.

[41] See *Blackwood's*, 52 (Dec. 1842), 725.

[42] The parasitic status of exchange value is similar to that of the supplement, which, as Derrida writes, 'adds only to replace' (145). See Jacques Derrida, '... That Dangerous Supplement...', in *Of Grammatology*, trans. Gayatri Chakravorty Spivak (Baltimore: Johns Hopkins University Press, 1976), 141–64. The analogy is useful because it demonstrates how exchange value functions in a similar way to the sign in symbolic representation, an observation that underlies De Quincey's later work.

never attenuate a consumer's primary will to buy. Affirmative value (U) is the overriding factor in all economic transactions:

As regards the price, what acts is alternately U and D; sometimes one, sometimes the other. But not so with regard to the general purpose of buying. Here only one thing acts. No man ever conceived the intention of buying upon any consideration of the difficulty and expense which attend the production of an article. He wishes to possess, he resolves to buy, not on account of these obstacles—far from it—but in spite of them. (IX: 150)

Economic power is located in the desire of the consumer to possess an object. Thus the end of all economic exchanges is the production of pleasure in the consumer, for the site of production has been transferred to the body of the consumer. Although the model suggests that these desires can be fulfilled, De Quincey also asserts that desire is an accumulating force that can never be quelled, for the power in the desire of the consumer is an unstoppable force that will never be forestalled even by the strictures of mechanical reproduction. Within this model is a blueprint for a desire that can never be satiated, the desire of the addict perhaps, who will always want more.

It is hardly surprising then that the examples he presents to illustrate the theory all come from the luxury end of the market: rhinoceroses, Italian masterpieces, the provinces of Rome, croton oil, salmon, *Paradise Lost*. The value of each is ascertained by weighing affirmative against negative values. In order for exchange to take place, affirmative value must exist; but the price may be derived from either affirmative or negative values. Thus the price of rhinoceroses was based on their affirmative value, since the public curiosity to see such exotic beasts far outweighed the cost of capturing and importing them. Similarly the value of an Italian masterpiece rested on its authenticity; its negative value, the cost of production, was in this case 'a mere inoperative curiosity' (IX: 168). These are both cases of monopoly value, when affirmative value is taken to its extreme, and 'you press to the ultimate limit upon the desire of a bidder to possess the article' (IX: 166). It is more usual, De Quincey concedes, that an object be valued by its resistance price. Thus *Paradise Lost* will sell for its negative value, since printing technology enabled cheap and speedy reproduction.

Among the examples presented to illustrate his theory, two are particularly noteworthy, for they demonstrate the distance De Quincey has moved from Ricardo. The examples are the slave and the land. He seemingly forgets that in Ricardo's scheme, labour and land stand beside capital as the central terms around which value is to be ascertained, not commodities to be evaluated alongside exotic beasts and luxury foods. According to De Quincey, labour, in the form of the slave, may sometimes be valued affirmatively according to the work it can do, and sometimes negatively, according to the cost of its upkeep. Land, on the other hand, will always be valued affirmatively, that is, 'for what it can produce, not for what will produce it' (*Blackwood's*, 52 (December 1842), 724). It is like a natural machine, whose design is a secret known only to its maker; if the secret were disclosed, the value of the machine would change immediately to its negative value, the cost of its production. In the case of land, however, this of course is not possible.

De Quincey expresses concern that Ricardo could have 'overlooked a case so broad as this' (*Blackwood's*, 52 (December 1842), 724), but more surprising perhaps is the fact that De Quincey in this instance has overlooked Ricardo's long explanation of rent, which plays a key role in his theory. Elsewhere De Quincey goes to some length to explain Ricardo's theory of diminishing returns for ascertaining rents: Ricardo argues that the land of the finest quality will always be cultivated first, and it would command no rent; only when the next quality of land is used, will the owner of the first land demand rent, which will be calculated according to the difference in quality between the first and the second land; when the third quality of land is used, the rent on the first will increase, and the owner of the second will demand rent, and so on. The model of the natural machine that De Quincey invokes is clearly inadequate to express the complexity of Ricardo's thinking on the value of land; De Quincey's model implies that the land is always natural and never worked on, while for Ricardo, land is always husbanded. This is significant because it is on the subject of landlords that De Quincey differs most extremely from Ricardo. For Ricardo, the landlord is the parasite of the capitalist system, skimming off profits in ways that are detrimental to the economy. But as far as De Quincey is concerned, Ricardo's doctrine of rent merely fires the 'wild ferocious instinct' (IX: 250) of

Ricardian socialists who falsely 'accredit themselves upon his authority' (IX: 251). True to his Tory principles, De Quincey holds on the contrary that there will always be a counteragency moving against this force in the form of the noblest class of all, the 'country gentlemen' (IX: 252), whose moral stature will sustain the traditional social order against all onslaughts.

In the late economic works, land and labour are both reduced to the status of commodities. But De Quincey introduces another term into his consumer economy which is crucial to its maintenance: that is credit, or faith. The example that he draws upon is that of a popish relic. Like the land or the unique machine, the relic has value only as an affirmative power: its productive power is its potential to produce miracles, and this depends on its absolute authenticity. However, unlike the land, relics may be counterfeited, and, laments De Quincey, 'too often they were . . . But this was not a fact to be confessed' (IX: 178). The value of the relic in the market depends not on the authenticity of the relic, but rather on the belief in its authenticity: for 'the too great multiplication of these relics, as derived from one and the same individual saint or martyr, was one of the causes, . . . which gradually destroyed the market in relics' (IX: 178). Not only does the value and power of the relic depend on the consumer's belief in its authenticity, but, in a more cynical way, the example proves that the entire market depends on an act of faith. One must believe in the market for it to function, for without faith there can be no exchange, and without credit, there can be no circulation.

So long as credit exists, capital will spread its magnificent and silent web of commerce connecting all parts of the nation and the world. He describes 'the great monied capitalist, standing at the centre of this enormous web, [who] throws over his arch of capital or withdraws it, with the precision of a fireman directing columns of water from an engine upon the remotest quarter of a conflagration' (IX: 273). The incongruous image of the capitalist-fireman, extinguishing fires across the world, clearly conveys the sense that De Quincey considers the force of capital to be a conservative one, protecting the status quo, guarding against change of any kind. But at the centre of the web is a debt. This is made clear in another passage in which he describes the invisible and silent progress of capital, the inaudible vitalization of civil life. He writes,

Not a man has been shifted from his station; possibly not a man has been intruded; yet power and virtue have been thrown into vast laboratories of trade, like shells into a city. But all has been accomplished in one night by the inaudible agency of the post-office, co-operating with the equally inaudible agencies of capital moving through banks and through national debts, funded or unfunded. Such is the perfection of our civilization. By the simple pressure of a finger upon the centre of so vast an organization, a breath of life is hurried down the tubes. (IX: 273–4)

Within the miscellany of references from science, commerce, and battle, De Quincey insists on the calm necessity of capital, the 'breath of life' of the body politic, unseen and unheard but vital to the well-being of civilization. And near the heart of this organic network is debt, the 'national debts, funded and unfunded', the conduit of capital.

De Quincey's late economic works describe an economy founded on debts—the debts of the market that creates demands it cannot supply, and the debts of the consumer who wants more than he can afford—and in which value is derived from the powerful needs of the consumer. This is the economy of the addict, whose insatiable appetite generates a constant demand for goods, and a ceaseless circulation of capital. But De Quincey was an addict and a debtor, whose name was bad credit, whose addiction tormented him, and whose debts forced him into the hidden enclaves of the city, separating him from his family, and compelling him to write for magazines he despised. A reality further from the gleaming economic system in which the omnipotent capitalist controlled the world with the pressure of a finger is hard to imagine. If the addict's desires generate the system, De Quincey is also aware that the addict is the system's casualty.

De Quincey's discourse on political economy spares little time or compassion for the consumer-addict. But he will find another discursive space in which to address these needs—the humane sphere of literature.

3

Reader's Digestion: The Compensations of Literature

> Owing to dyspepsia afflicting my system, . . . and the possibility of any additional derangement of the stomach taking place, consequences incalculably distressing would arise, so much so indeed as to increase nervous irritation, and prevent me from attending to matters of overwhelming importance, if you do not remember to cut the mutton in a diagonal rather than a longitudinal form.
>
> Martha Gordon, citing De Quincey, 1862[1]

In 'Letters to a Young Man whose Education has been Neglected' (1823), De Quincey described his discomfort experienced on entering a library:

In my youthful days, I never entered a great library, suppose of one hundred thousand volumes, but my predominant feeling was one of pain and disturbance of mind,—not much unlike that which drew tears from Xerxes, on viewing his immense army, and reflecting that in one hundred years not one soul would remain alive. To me, with respect to the books, the same effect would be brought about by my own death. Here, said I, are one hundred thousand books, the worst of them capable of giving me some pleasure and instruction; and before I can have had time to extract the honey from one-twentieth of this hive, in all likelihood I shall be summoned away. This thought, I am sure must often have occurred to yourself; and you may judge how much it was aggravated when I found that, subtracting all merely professional books—books of reference, as dictionaries, &c. &c. &c.—from the universal library of Europe, there would still remain a total of not less than twelve hundred thousand books over and above what the presses of Europe are still disemboguing into the ocean of literature, many of them immense folios or quartos. (X: 38)

---

[1] Martha H. Gordon, *Christopher North: A Memoir of John Wilson* (Edinburgh, 1862), i. 157. Cited by Grevel Lindop, *The Opium-Eater: A Life of Thomas De Quincey* (Oxford, 1985), 282.

Faced by an array of books, the infinite source of pleasure it might provide provokes nothing but the misery of recognizing that his life is finite, for the library prefigures his own death. The experience is presented in terms of the mathematical sublime:[2] an object of great magnitude is brought into startling contrast with his own meagre self, undermining him and leaving him only to contemplate death.

De Quincey will tell a similar story in *Suspiria*, in the nightmare of the expanding book order, recounted in Chapter 1. As the cart returns again and again unloading piles of books outside his house, he incurs a debt that is beyond numerical representation, and realizes with horror that his predicament has already been chronicled in the *Arabian Nights*. Swamped beneath a limitless pile of books, economically sunk by an unfathomable debt, his identity subsumed in the fictions of the past, De Quincey's new library narrates the profound horror experienced when subjectivity and identity are dissipated under the weight of the published word.

As we have seen, De Quincey repeatedly worried about the massive expansion of printing and the extended circulation of books and other printed material that took place in the first half of the nineteenth century. One reason for his anxieties was the fact that the expansion of print, coupled with increasing levels of literacy among the working class, enabled the circulation of seditious material, fuelling the rise of popular dissidence and radical activities associated with Chartism. But De Quincey also used the machinery of the printing industry as a metonymy for the processes of industrialization that necessitated changes in the structure of society. In 'Letters to a Young Man', he told of a man who moved from the country to the city and was tormented by a surfeit of books:

in a country town, where, books being few, a man can use up all his materials; his appetite is unpalled, and he is grateful for the loan of a MS., &c. But bring him up to London; show him the waggon-loads of unused stores which he is at liberty to work up; tell him that these even are but a trifle, perhaps, to what he may find in the libraries of Paris, Dresden, Milan, &c., of religious houses, of English noblemen, &c.,—and this same

---

[2] On the mathematical sublime, see Immanuel Kant, *Critique of Judgement*, trans. James Creed Meredith (Oxford: Clarendon Press, 1928), 99–109.

man who came up to London blithe and happy will leave it pale and sad. (X: 40–1)

In De Quincey's imaginative scheme, the mechanization of book production stands for industrialization in general, and the changes in demography and social class with which it was associated. For the man from the country, the fact of industrial production is experienced as a problem of consumer choice. Indeed in the leisured context of *Blackwood's*, all the difficulties of modern life seem to be encapsulated in the confusion of a reader spoilt for the choice of books.

The overproduction of printed material may have caused dissidence among the working class, but according to De Quincey, in the middle-class reader, it provoked a state of insanity. He called it the madness of the miser—a paradoxical condition, since its prevalent symptom was a 'gluttonism' for books (X: 40). His metaphors are confused: unlike the miser for whom any consumption cost too much, the miserly glutton could never consume enough: consumption in this case did not entail expenditure but instead was a kind of hoarding. De Quincey surreptitiously slipped from money to food, from the economy of the market to that of the body. The miser and the glutton shared a refusal of the frenetic circulation of capitalism: if the capitalist is lean, the miser and the glutton were corpulent through hoarding.[3] In the mixture of metaphors, books were compared with both money and food, and reading with hoarding and eating.[4]

Elsewhere in the same essay reading is compared with labour. De Quincey computes a man's life in days reading, his life subjugated to the labour of consuming:

I had myself ascertained that to read a duodecimo volume, in prose, of four hundred pages—all skipping being barred, and the rapid reading

---

[3] Cf. Karl Marx, 'Economic and Philosophical Manuscripts' (1844), in *Early Writings*, trans. Rodney Livingstone and Gregor Benton (Harmondsworth: Penguin, 1975; rev. edn. 1981), 366–7.

[4] Quincey's own peculiar eating habits have been the focus of recent critical attention. See Judith Plotz, 'On Guilt Considered as One of the Fine Arts: De Quincey's Criminal Investigations', *Wordsworth Circle*, 19/2 (1988), 83–8. Plotz speculates that De Quincey provided 'a rare instance . . . of male anorexia' (85). Lindop points out that De Quincey's digestive system was subject to the usual problems inflicted by regular use of morphine: 'Throughout 1842 his gravest problem was not debt or even erysipelas, but constipation', *Opium-Eater*, 346.

which belongs to the vulgar interest of a novel—was a very sufficient work for one day. Consequently, three hundred and sixty-five per annum—that is (with a very small allowance for the claims of life on one's own account and that of one's friends), one thousand for every triennium; that is, ten thousand for thirty years—will be as much as a man who lives for that only can hope to accomplish. (X: 38–9)

The middle-class reader suffers a kind of commodification not dissimilar to that of the worker, whose labour is valued only in relation to the exchange value of the commodity produced.[5] In this case, the labour of reading is comparable with the process of commodification since the former is a task beyond the scope of anyone; the works of Europe are too extensive to be read within a human lifetime, and thus the reader's life is rendered incomplete and consequently meaningless.

The problem of reading repeats the dilemma that De Quincey articulated recurrently in his work: that of the subject's relation to the market, a system too great, too powerful, to be controlled —the juggernaut that stops for no one, rich or poor. In the shifts in the metaphors, the reader is at once the miser who stands outside the market, wishing to evade its unstoppable motions, but also the man caught up within it, whose life is controlled by it. Thus the gluttonous miser's one hope is that his appetite be so gargantuan that he can consume the entire production of the printing presses of Europe. The sole solution to overproduction, the only possibility of controlling the market, lies in the frantic and total consumption of it.[6]

---

[5] See Karl Marx, *Capital: A Critique of Political Economy*, i. trans. Ben Fowkes (Harmondsworth: Penguin, 1976), 283–92.

[6] De Quincey writes elsewhere of extravagant appetites. In his translation of a short story, 'Mr Schnackenberger; or Two Masters for One Dog', first published in the *London Magazine*, May and June, 1823, Mr Schnackenberger's dog is a central figure precisely because she has an insatiable, and thus incurable, hunger. The only solution is for the dog to be killed. In a footnote De Quincey notes the case recorded in a French medical journal, of a man with a similarly boundless hunger, satisfied by neither 'an ounce of opium . . . a stone of beef, or half a bushel of potatoes: all three would not have made him a breakfast' (XII: 356–7, note). Despite the man's protestation that 'I never *do* eat children', De Quincey persists in the belief that he was 'paedophagous or infantivorous', for 'wherever he appeared, a sudden scarcity of children prevailed'. In this bizarre and morbid economy, the man's gargantuan appetite blocks the most profound aspect of reproduction, that is human reproduction. This could of course be read as a description of the appetite of an addict; thus we could interpret De Quincey's

Thus it is ironic, perhaps, that De Quincey considered rapid reading *vulgar*, like eating without masticating; for digestion required time and effort. Writing in haste, on the other hand, was not 'an absolute and unmitigated disadvantage' (X: 53). Indeed, he claimed, 'on no occasion of their lives do men generally speak better than on the scaffold, and with the executioner at their side' (X: 53). At the point of death—at the entrance to a library, perhaps—De Quincey would write, and thereby add another volume to an already death-provoking collection. The response is perverse but none the less familiar, since within the sublime, an act of creative imagination is the required response to a life-threatening event:[7] the excessive production of writing is the conventional outcome of the aesthetic. Instead, De Quincey's anxiety focused on the reading practices that such quantities of writing might incur: reading might be less than exhaustive, something might be wasted, lost before it has been ingested.[8]

De Quincey's justification for writing quickly, in the face of his critique of reading at speed, was expedient for one whose own literary production was excessive, and whose name became by the end of the century a by-word for rapid writing.[9] But the ramifications of his defence resonate beyond personal self-interest. Reading functions as a site in which he can explore the anxi-

aestheticizing of the condition of addiction as the possible means of controlling industrial overproduction. For this, see Ch. 6.

[7] Cf. Neil Hertz's analysis of this moment in the mathematical sublime, which he characterizes as a 'painful pause . . . followed by a compensatory positive movement, the mind's exultation in its own rational faculties, in its ability to think a totality that cannot be taken in through the senses'. See 'The Notion of Blockage in the Literature of the Sublime' in *The End of the Line: Essays on Psychoanalysis and the Sublime* (New York: Columbia University Press, 1985), 40.

[8] Part of De Quincey's dilemma is that time might be wasted reading the wrong books. On this see Margaret Russett's discussion in 'Wordsworth's Gothic Interpreter: De Quincey Personifies "We Are Seven"', *Studies in Romanticism*, 30 (1991), 345–65. She connects De Quincey's conceptualization of reading practices with Wordsworth's comments in the *Preface* to the *Lyrical Ballads* (1800), on 'frantic novels, sickly and stupid German Tragedies, and deluges of idle and extravagant stories in verse' which encourage 'a degrading thirst after outrageous stimulation'. See Wordsworth, *The Prose Works*, eds. W. J. B. Owen and J. W. Smyser (Oxford: Clarendon Press, 1974), i. 128–30, and Russett, 'Gothic Interpreter', 350–1.

[9] See Rev. W. J. Cory's letter to Rev. C. W. Furse, 4 Aug. 1868, in which he writes, 'I had rather write at the level of official style, . . . on topics of real pressing importance, than skim like a De Quincey'. *Extracts from the Letters and Journals of William Cory*, selected and arranged by Francis Warre Cornish, (Oxford, 1897), 238.

eties of an unproductive, consuming middle class in the age of high capitalism. In fact we will discover that literature provides a solution, of a fantasmatic kind, to the problems of industrial over-production. However, to read De Quincey's anxieties about books as merely a response to an economic problem is to forget that he also wrote influentially about literature *per se*. The imbrication of the literary and the economic is such that the two sets of terms can never be entirely separated, nor one subjugated to the other. This chapter will inspect his remarks on reading practices when books are a metonymy for industrial overproduction.

In the previous chapter we saw that in De Quincey's later account of political economy he held the market to be driven by the indestructible desires of the consumer. But these desires left the consumer riven by unpayable debts, for De Quincey's is the economy of addiction. In this chapter I will examine the literary criticism as the place in which De Quincey addressed the prob-lems of the market as they affected the consumer; for him reading was an arena in which the consumer could retrieve some of the powers lost to the market. To this end, he invoked two categories of reader: the general or amateur reader, and the professional reader or critic. The latter worked in the service of the former, assisting in the difficult processes of digestion. But the amateur reader's whole life was constituted through the books he read, and for him the processes of digestion could never be eased enough.

It was in the works of literary criticism that De Quincey devel-oped the terms the 'literature of power' and the 'literature of knowledge'.[10] This chapter will explore these categories, and the particular position they occupy in relation to the market. For De Quincey consumption of every kind entailed a disturbing mixture of gratification and dependency, and the case of the reader, like that of the addict, provides another exemplification of quotidian bourgeois distress. The literature of power would offer some respite from this, for it was constituted as a realm of affectivity in which the alienated consumer could retrieve an emotional dimen-sion to his life. But the feelings to which the literature of power gave expression were archaic and impersonal, and the restoration afforded the consumer was always compromised. The literature

[10] See Introd. n. 13.

of power would offer the reader transcendence—like opium—but this would not entail empowerment in any material sense.

The Literature of Power and the Professional Reader

In 1848 De Quincey published a review article of William Roscoe's 1847 edition of *The Works of Alexander Pope, Esquire,* entitled 'The Poetry of Pope'.[11] Although some twenty-five years after the 'Letters to a Young Man', there were many continuities between the two texts. Both argued that the vast quantity of books presented a problem of choice for the reader, and both suggested that the situation might be relieved by distinguishing between different qualities of literature: between the literature of power and the literature of knowledge. It is important to note that on both occasions, De Quincey articulated these terms in the context of the problems raised by the overproduction of books, for it suggests that for him the economic function of literature was crucial.

The categories 'power' and 'knowledge', terms inherited from Wordsworth, were based on a distinction between the affective and didactic functions of literature.[12] They were defined similarly in both essays, even though the earlier essay adopted a more tentative tone.[13] In 'The Poetry of Pope' he wrote: 'The function of the first [power] is—to *teach*; the function of the second [knowledge] is—to *move*: the first is a rudder; the second, an oar or a sail.

[11] The article first appeared in the *North British Review* in August 1848. It was reprinted by De Quincey in vol. ix of *Selections Grave and Gay* under the title 'Alexander Pope'. Masson gave it its present title.

[12] On De Quincey's explication of Wordsworth's terms, see W. J. B. Owen, *Wordsworth as Critic* (London: OUP, 1969), 191–210. Isobel Armstrong points out that in the early Victorian period, all criticism of poetry was couched in terms of the affective and didactic effects on the reader. Poems were praised for being morally instructive through their capacity to provoke an emotional response, that is, through engendering a notion of sympathy. Despite this, De Quincey shared with other writers of the period a disdain for the didactic mode in poetry. See *Victorian Scrutinies: Reviews of Poetry 1830–1870*, ed. Isobel Armstrong (London: Athlone Press, 1972), 1–14.

[13] See De Quincey's claim in 'Letters to a Young Man', that the word power 'was originally introduced expressly to provide for the case where, though the poem was *not* good, from defect in the *composition*, or from other causes, the stamina and *matériel* of good poetry, as fine thinking and passionate conceptions, could not be denied to exist' (X: 48 n.).

The first speaks to the *mere* discursive understanding; the second speaks ultimately, it may happen, to the higher understanding or reason, but always *through* affections of pleasure and sympathy' [XI: 54]. While the literature of knowledge, or *anti-literature* (X: 49), communicated facts and provided an education, true literature, the literature of power, worked in the realm of the emotions, allowing the reader 'to feel vividly, and with a vital consciousness, emotions which ordinary life rarely or never supplie[d] occasions for exciting, and which had previously lain unwakened, and hardly within the dawn of consciousness' [X: 48]. Thus the literature of knowledge concerned itself with events and issues in the material world,[14] while the sublime literature of power operated within a realm of archaic feelings and transcendent and unchanging values. This was a realm crucially separated from the material world, for he claimed, 'the very *first* step in power is a flight—is an ascending movement into another element where earth is forgotten' [XI: 56].

Thus far the two essays agreed. However, the two essays differed significantly in the relationship they envisaged between the literature of power and the market. In the later essay, the economic function of literature was forged through a certain rhetorical slippage relating to the category of the sublime. In both essays, sublimity was an attribute of the material quantity of books that threatened to swamp him; in the later essay it also became a pleasurable and life-transforming effect of the literature of power. Thus if the physical mass of books, the products and symbols of industrial overproduction, at first constituted a mortiferous phenomenon, through the sublimity of the literature of power, the impact of the sheer mass of volumes was transformed to become a quality of the writing, and a positive and empowering force. The material problems invoked by the overproduction of books had been resolved at a symbolic level, as the capacity to overwhelm became an aspect of textuality.

---

[14] In 'Letters to a Young Man', he asserts that the literature of knowledge would contain 'a dictionary, a grammar, a spelling-book, an almanac, a pharmacopoeia, a Parliamentary report, a system of farriery, a treatise on billiards, the Court Callendar, &c.,... books of voyages and travels, and generally all books in which the matter to be communicated is paramount to the manner or form of its communication' (X: 47).

This was emphasized in the later essay when De Quincey described a scene which evoked the dizzying overproduction of affectivity within the literary text. 'But what are words to thoughts?' he asked,

Every word has a thought corresponding to it, so that not by so much as one solitary counter can the words outrun the thoughts. But every thought has *not* a word corresponding to it: so that the thoughts may outrun the words by many thousand counters. In a developed nature they *do* so. But what are the thoughts when set against the modifications of thoughts by feelings, hidden even from him that feels them, or against the inter-combinations of such modifications with others—complex with complex, decomplex with decomplex? These can be unravelled by no human eye. This is the infinite music that God only can read upon the vast harp of the human heart. [XI: 80–1]

As thoughts outran words, and feelings thoughts, the literary text produced more than it could know. The words of the text contained the multiple traces of feelings, the effects of which were hidden even from the being 'who feels them'. Only God, the cosmic reader, was able to unravel them. In this scenario, which is terrifying for the ignorance it predicates on the part of the subject whose feelings were concealed in words, the massive and uncontrolled overproduction of affectivity is described as 'infinite music'. Once brought into the realm of the aesthetic, figures of overproduction were transformed from sites of terror in which the subject was obliterated or swamped, into a mode of sublime transcendence in which he experienced a naked confrontation with God. In this way, De Quincey reworked the Romantic idea that literature provided a means through which the corrupting influences of industry and capital might be fended off. For him, the literature of power enabled the reader to experience the horrors of industrial process as *pleasure*, through the aesthetic of the sublime.

The potential of literature to harness the disruptive influence of industrial overproduction in the service of the consuming subject was only made evident in the 1848 essay. In the earlier essay, 'Letters to a Young Man', De Quincey answered Coleridge's dictum in the *Biographia*, 'never pursue literature as a trade', in his advice to the fictitious young man of the title. Coleridge had argued that since literature provided a context for independent thought and pure values, it should remain untainted by the demands of the market place; to write commercially would be to abase literature, and pollute it with the interests of the market.[15] In 'Letters to a Young Man', De Quincey maintained Coleridge's sense that literature should be disinterested, but ironically he saw this as a quality that might be utilized by the state, rather than conserved as a quality that enhanced itself as literature. In 1823, he argued, it was no longer expedient to protect literature from the taint of commercial values for its own sake, but instead, literature itself might serve to protect the nation from the relentless onslaught of the market. A professional group of literary men was needed in order to protect Britain from the vulgarities of the *'nation boutiquière'* it was fast becoming.[16] The precise occupation of this group was unclear: he did not distinguish between the processes of writing and reading, regarding them as mutually endorsing activities. The sharp distinction between authorship and interpretation, production and consumption, that would be crucial in the 1848 essay, was not made. In 1823 the category of the literature of power as *fine art* (X: 47) was necessary merely to endorse, on behalf of the nation, his critique of the values of trade and commerce.

By 1848, in 'The Poetry of Pope', the literature of power had been absorbed into the market as a category through which the individual might find empowerment even at the point of obliteration by the processes of industrial overproduction. The professional literary man, who by now was specifically a reader or critic, was crucial to the efficient management of the household economy, and by extension, the smooth running of the market. It was he who would distinguish the literature of power from the literature of knowledge, and perform the necessary task of pre-selecting books for the consumption of the reading public. De Quincey wrote:

As books multiply to an unmanageable excess, selection becomes more and more a necessity for readers, and the power of selection more and more a desperate problem for the busy part of readers. The possibility of selecting wisely is becoming continually more hopeless as the necessity

---

[15] S. T. Coleridge, *Biographia Literaria, or Biographical Sketches of my Literary Life and Opinions*, eds. James Engell and W. Jackson Bate (London: Routledge & Kegan Paul, 1983), i. 223.

[16] De Quincey cites Napoleon I's apocryphal statement, 'L'Angleterre est une nation de boutiquiers.'

for selection is becoming continually more pressing. . . . For, where the good cannot be read in its twentieth part, the more requisite it is that no part of the bad should steal an hour of the available time; and it is not to be endured that people without a minute to spare should be obliged first of all to read a book before they can ascertain whether in fact it is *worth* reading. . . . And thus, as literature expands, becoming continually more of a household necessity, the duty resting upon critics (who are the vicarious readers for the public) becomes continually more urgent. (XI: 52–3)

The point that is repeatedly stressed is that people have not 'a minute to spare'. The reader is the busy man of business, as in the essays on Kant discussed in Chapter 1, without time to fritter, always engaged in purposeful pursuits. The literary critic is thus crucial as the 'vicarious reader for the public'. Reverting to bodily metaphors, De Quincey named critics the 'pregustatores', who carried out preliminary tests for the literary gourmands that constituted the reading public. The critic provided a vital service as a consumer guide, saving time and contributing to good household economy when time meant money.

This notion is borne out repeatedly in 'The Poetry of Pope'. De Quincey recommended that 'it is no longer advisable to reprint the whole of either Dryden or Pope' (XI: 95). The critic-editor's purpose was only to help the reader digest the work of literature. He must not add to the expansion of printed material 'with undigested commentaries'; 'the ideal merit in an annotator' was 'austere instinct of compression and verbal parsimony' (XI: 94). The function of criticism was subjugated to the economy and efficiency of the general reader: combining the attributes of a digestive aid and budget-plan, it directed the reader to the best works and guided him in the processes of reading.[17]

Thus in the 1848 essay, De Quincey had to make a crucial distinction between the literary critic, who was an agent of the

---

[17] John Woolford points out that 'the Victorian aesthetic theorist has, by the 1850s, arrived at the firm belief that popular acceptability formed a text not only of success but even of aesthetic merit', and he cites G. H. Lewes, E. S. Dallas, and Ruskin in support of this claim. See 'Periodicals and the Practice of Literary Criticism, 1855–1864', in *The Victorian Periodical Press: Samplings and Soundings*, ed. Joanne Shattock and Michael Wolff (Leicester: Leicester University Press, 1982), 109–42 esp. 114. This emphasizes the urgency of De Quincey's attempt to control the critical judgements of the reading public, for it could be seen as an attempt to control literary value itself.

market and could translate market values into the language of literary criticism, and the general reader. In addition to his mercantile functions, the literary critic possessed the powers of insight of a mystic. As God was able to unravel the invisible traces of feeling within the literary text, the critic uncovered the marks of quality that were concealed to the popular eye. In a footnote, De Quincey wrote:

> The reason why the broad distinctions between the two literatures of power and knowledge so little fix the attention lies in the fact that a vast proportion of books,—history, biography, travels, miscellaneous essays, &c.,—lying in a middle zone, confound these distinctions by interblending them. All that we call 'amusement' or 'entertainment' is a diluted form of the power belonging to passion, and also a mixed form; and, where threads of direct *instruction* intermingle in the texture with these threads of *power*, this absorption of the duality into one representative *nuance* neutralizes the separate perception of either. Fused into a *tertium quid*, or neutral state, they disappear to the popular eye as the repelling forces which, in fact they are. (XI: 59 n.)

The problem that De Quincey identified was that the publishing outlets of the time, both books and periodicals, required that literature be produced within generic categories that failed to observe a distinction between power and knowledge. As 'history, biography, travels', for example—the genres of much of De Quincey's own literary production—writing may have contained the qualities of both literatures of power and knowledge, but these were concealed within the 'neutralizing' texture of the book or magazine. With his discerning gaze, the literary critic alone was able to unravel the traces of each within the text.

De Quincey's vision of popular literature as a bland arena in which opposing forces were dissipated operates within a structure familiar from his political writings. Here, as we have seen, he suggested that the opposing forces of Whigs and Tories were engaged in a peculiarly undynamic contest which generated and perpetuated the status quo. It is this irresolvable struggle, he argued, that constituted the invisible infrastructure of society. Literature, however, provided a different case, for in it the opposing forces of power and knowledge must be made visible in order for the reader to benefit from their distinct qualities. De Quincey habitually distinguished between political and literary contexts: in this case the evidence of power and conflict within social dynamics must be concealed for the sake of order, but in the transcendent world of literature, power was a quality in which the reader participates.

In this context it is significant that De Quincey used the term *tertium quid* (literally, the 'third thing') to refer to the 'middle zone' book in which the distinctions between power and knowledge were lost. The *tertium quid* appeared to be related to Coleridge's slightly vaguer term, *tertium aliquid* (literally, the 'third something'), which he used in the *Biographia* to refer to the synthetic powers of the creative imagination.[18] For Coleridge and the German writers, such as Fichte and Schelling, whom he emulated, this synthesis represented the highest imaginative powers of the artist.[19] But for De Quincey, the *tertium quid* had been reduced to a publishing strategy that nullified power and created blandness. For him it was the critic who would reconstitute this power, by identifying its traces *in spite of* the dissipation that had taken place. In De Quincey's scheme, the energy and potency of the imagination had been transferred from the poet to the critic. The power of the literary text now depended on the existence of a particular reader, the literary critic.

Between Coleridge and De Quincey of the 1840s, the magnificent powers of the creative imagination had been removed from the work and the writer, and now resided, in diluted form, in the critic's ability to discern the hidden traces of literary power; for it was now the critic who possessed the capacity to lift the veil of textuality that occluded that power. However, De Quincey's concept of the professional reader owed a great deal to Romantic views of writers and readers. The distinction that he drew between the two types of reader, the critic and the general reader, was one which repeated the distinction between the poet and general humanity made by the Romantics. Now the superior talents of the poet had been shifted to the professional literary critic, a move which suggested a surprising complicity between De Quincey's commercially oriented literary context, and the

---

[18] Coleridge, *Biographia Literaria*, i. 300.

[19] On Coleridge's theory of the imagination in relation to the German context, see Jerome Christensen, *Coleridge's Blessed Machine of Language* (Ithaca, NY: Cornell University Press, 1981), 118–85. A good account of Coleridge's relation to the German philosophical tradition is Paul Hamilton's *Coleridge's Poetics* (Oxford: Blackwell, 1983).

realm of pure inspiration of the Romantic poets. Indeed ground had already been laid for the establishment of a distinction between two classes of readers in Romantic works: both Wordsworth and Coleridge had expressed the need for a special group of readers who would be able to assist the public in the reading of great literature, whether in the form of the small band of talented readers who could distinguish the superior value of the *Lyrical Ballads*, or else the clerisy, Coleridge's elected group that would oversee the education of the nation through the management of national literature. If De Quincey's critic inherited the insight of the creative genius, the poet, he was also a version of a Wordsworthian disciple (a role which De Quincey self-consciously played)[20], or indeed a species of the Coleridgean *clerus*.

Important distinctions nevertheless must be maintained between De Quincey's professional critic and Wordsworth's and Coleridge's special readers. The clerisy's moral and social function, to educate the public through literature, was quite different from the purpose of literary criticism outlined in De Quincey's late essay in which stress was laid on economic efficiency, and the smooth running of the market. In his insistence on the disinterestedness of the critic, De Quincey was in fact closer to Wordsworth, who had maintained a notion of absolute literary value that only a talented or chosen reader might distinguish. De Quincey's assumption in 'The Poetry of Pope', that the purpose of the critic was to recognize value that was always present but hidden, was in line with Wordsworth's views expressed in the 'Essay, Supplementary to the Preface' (1815), an essay which was proffered as a rebuke to the critics of the *Lyrical Ballads*, who in Wordsworth's eyes, had failed to assert absolute standards of literary value, and had missed the true value of his work.[21] Wordsworth's aim was to correct the existing situation whereby a work might enjoy instant and long-term popularity, but not necessarily on account of its literary quality. Thus when De Quincey wrote that 'no man escapes the contagion from his contemporary bystanders' (XI: 51), he repeated Wordsworth's assertion that all great works of litera-

---

[20] On De Quincey's self-fashioning as a Wordsworthian disciple, see Russett, 'Gothic Interpreter'.
[21] Wordsworth, *Prose Works*, iii. 62–84.

ture would necessarily receive scanty or derisive notices from their contemporary audience, for 'the qualities of writing best fitted for eager reception are either such as startle the world into attention by their audacity and extravagance; or they are chiefly of a superficial kind'.[22] For Wordsworth the largely unserious and prejudiced reading public produced a situation in which works that had achieved immediate popularity would be quickly supplanted by some new (equally inferior) work. Popular works, Wordsworth argued, were 'essentially different from those by which permanent influence is secured'. While inferior works were always bound to the moment and context of their production, great works transcended time and place, history and culture, both in their production and in their reception; thus great works '[were] most naturally and most fitly conceived in solitude', for the writer had to step outside his historical context in order to produce them.

Wordsworth's eagerness to impugn contemporary critics suggests that his interest lay in distinguishing between the quality of various critical judgements rather than defining literary value itself. In fact the qualities of universality were transferred from the literary text to the critical judgement. Thus he distinguished between aberrant evaluations of literature that were always historically and culturally specific, and correct evaluations that were universally true. Wordsworth used the example of *Paradise Lost*, whose early readers admired it for religious or political reasons; only a few discerning readers responded to its 'poetical merits' and recognized it as a poem 'everywhere impregnated with *original* excellence'.[23] This idea of a hierarchy of readers provided a background to the argument in 'The Poetry of Pope', that it was the responsibility of the talented reader or critic to distinguish true literary value. For De Quincey the talented reader would engage with the text to bring about a recognition, figured as a kind of release, of the correct reading,

---

[22] Ibid. 83.

[23] Ibid. 70–1. Wordsworth's position has changed since the *Preface* to the *Lyrical Ballads* of 1800, which are more democratic in spirit. In them the underlying argument is that under the right conditions, all 'men' are capable of appreciating the poems, and they should judge by their 'own feelings genuinely' (i. 154).

that had 'permanent influence'. Great literature was characterized not by a formal quality but by a union of text with a given class of reader.[24]

When De Quincey called for a class of professional readers to uncover works of real literary value, he consolidated Wordsworth's opinion in the later essay, that value could only be perceived by a particular class of talented readers. Nevertheless, De Quincey's end had to do with economic efficiency, and this was distinct from Wordsworth's concern for literary worth, no matter how self-regarding Wordsworth's interest may have been. For De Quincey, literature was a commodity, and literary criticism, by providing a guide to consumption, facilitated circulation in the market. De Quincey thus proposed the professionalization of criticism, and this marked out his argument from Wordsworth's formulation of the relationship between literature and readers.[25]

For De Quincey, not all readers were critics, for the professional reader always read for another, the general reader. The general reader's relationship with literature was a more complicated one than that of the critic. In the case of the literary critic, reading was an activity segregated from his private life by the exigencies of professionalism. But the general reader's whole life was directed by his reading practices, his consciousness moulded by the literature he had consumed. This troubling intersection of an emergent consciousness with the commodity form, which at one level was a collision of private and public realms, provided, as we shall see, the focus for his critical works, as well as the autobiographies.

---

[24] Cf. De Quincey, in 'Letters to a Young Man', on the derivation of the term *classic*: '[The term] is drawn ... from the political economy of Rome. Such a man was rated as to his income in the third class, such another in the fourth, and so on; but he who was in the highest was said emphatically to be of *the* class, 'classicus', a class-man, without adding the number, as in that case superfluous. Hence, by an obvious analogy, the best authors were rated as classici, or men of the highest class' (X: 49–50 n.).

[25] Cf. T. W. Heyck in *The Transformation of Intellectual Life in Victorian England* (London: Croom Helm, 1982), who argues that the distinction between Romantic and Victorian attitudes towards literature rested on the Victorian view that art was concerned with values extrinsic to it, which he identifies as primarily 'moral-utilitarian', rather than the late 18th-cent. trend of viewing art as an activity produced for itself (43).

The General Reader

In a startling passage in 'The Poetry of Pope' De Quincey compared works of literature with lost childhood memories, thus attributing books' determining significance in a reader's psychic development: 'Let everyone be assured—that he owes to the impassioned books which he has read many a thousand more of emotions than he can consciously trace back to them. Dim by their origination, these emotions yet arise in him, and mould him through life, like forgotten incidents of his childhood' (XI: 59–60). The effects of literature, like those of childhood events, were concealed in the life of an adult, and thus consigned to the depths of the unconscious; they returned, nevertheless, to reverberate in mature life, unseen and unknown.[26]

The image is striking not least because De Quincey was an autobiographer who recurrently narrated the events of his own childhood. His own life was thus textualized in two senses: through his telling of it in literary autobiographies; but also in the sense that, by his account, his life had been constituted through his childhood consumption of literary works. Since literature had an effect similar to the primal events of the past, De Quincey suggested that a private life, even in its most intimate parts, was determined by these public texts. We may well be reminded of the book order episode in *Suspiria*, referred to at the beginning of this chapter, in which the boy De Quincey became aware that his situation had been anticipated by the *Arabian Nights*, and that he was in fact living out a story he had already read. In this context, this is a source of profound anxiety. However, in 'The Poetry of Pope', a similar notion of the determining effects of literature is welcomed as something ennobling. The autobiographical text registered what is fundamentally the same trope—that of the intervention of literature in private life—as a source of terror,

---

[26] Relevant to this discussion is Mary Jacobus's 'The Art of Managing Books: Romantic Prose and the Writing of the Past', in *Romanticism, Writing, and Sexual Difference: Essays on* The Prelude (Oxford: Clarendon Press, 1989), 126–58. Jacobus focuses on De Quincey's outrage in the essay on 'Style', at his landlady's use of the word 'anteriorly'. His anxiety is caused not only by the landlady's precocious vocabulary (on this, see Ch. 4), but an awareness provoked by this word, of the determining influence of writings of the past. Jacobus concentrates on De Quincey's intertextual construction of the historical past; what is interesting here is that he uses a similar model for the individual psyche.

because such an intrusion brought about a loss of autonomy, and an expulsion of the individual self. In the critical text, however, the intervention is expressed as a 'moulding' of subjectivity; the adverse implications of this for the integrity and autonomy of the self are overlooked.

De Quincey's interest in the interrelations between text and reader was shared by his contemporaries. Mid-nineteenth-century writers were particularly interested in states of self-consciousness: the way in which one's comprehension of the external world was affected by modes of perception, and moreover, the ways in which modes of perception were, in turn, moulded by external objects, such as literary texts.[27] The philosopher J. F. Ferrier, for instance, in a number of works, some of which were published in *Blackwood's*, explored the notion that the mind's relation to the external world was like a frame which it was impossible to detach from a picture; knowledge of external objects, he argued, always implied a mind that was conscious of them.[28] Ferrier's work was influential among the writers of the day, including Tennyson.[29] De Quincey referred to Ferrier's work in his essay 'On Wordsworth's Poetry', suggesting a genealogy between Ferrier and the Romantics: Wordsworth's poem 'We Are Seven' had provided Ferrier with evidence that the self could never conceive of its own annihilation.[30] Ferrier implied a similar level of complicity between subject and object as was proposed by De Quincey; but De Quincey's assertion that the subject was moulded by external objects was precisely opposite to the implications of Ferrier's axiom, that all knowledge of the external world was determined by individual consciousness. Indeed De

[27] On Victorian theories of self-conscious response, see W. David Shaw, *The Lucid Veil: Poetic Truth in the Victorian Age* (London: Athlone Press, 1987), 47–74. Shaw refers in particular to J. F. Ferrier, Robert Browning, Arthur Hallam, W. J. Fox, Carlyle, and Keble. See also Armstrong, *Victorian Scrutinies*, 1–31.

[28] J. F. Ferrier's 'An Introduction to the Philosophy of Consciousness' was published in seven parts in *Blackwood's*, vols. 43, 44, and 45, from Feb. 1838 to Mar. 1839.

[29] See Shaw, *Lucid Veil*, 48–53.

[30] De Quincey draws attention to 'a truth on which Mr Ferrier has since commented beautifully in his "Philosophy of Consciousness"' that Wordsworth had expressed in 'We Are Seven', 'viz. that the mind of an infant cannot admit the idea of death, cannot comprehend it, any more than the fountain of light can comprehend the aboriginal darkness' (XI: 301).

Quincey's version of this dialectic relationship implied a world view fundamentally more unstable and disturbing than Ferrier's.

De Quincey and Ferrier both traced their preoccupation with the relationship between individual consciousness and literature to Wordsworth. Wordsworth's interest in consciousness was considered by them to be characteristic of a new, Romantic way of thinking about literature that was closely related to the assumptions of idealist philosophy, and in particular Kant's formulation of the sublime as an attribute of the subject's experience of an object, rather than of the object itself.[31] Mid-nineteenth-century theories of poetry can be seen as developments upon this idea laid down by the preceding generation. Alexander Smith, for instance, writing in *Blackwood's* in 1835 on 'The Philosophy of Poetry', claimed that poetry conveyed 'not information, but emotion'. The emotions with which poetry was concerned were feelings of sublimity and beauty, and, following Kant, these were attributes of the perceiving subject, rather than an observed object, in the same way that heat from a fire would be considered to be an attribute of the sentient body beside it.[32] As Ferrier would later put it, the external world had been internalized to become a quality of the perceiving subject. Thus a poem, in so far as it represented the external world, did so only in the sense that it was a record of the poet's feelings about it. By the same count, literary criticism would provide not an account of the poem itself, but that of the critic's feelings on reading the poem. Aesthetic response had become a record of feeling on the part of the perceiving subject.

Smith's argument was similar to that of other Victorian writers who followed Wordsworth in stressing the centrality of affective response in the definition of poetry. One version of this was the

---

[31] See Samuel Monk, *The Sublime: A Study of Critical Theories in 18th-Century England* (1935; repr. Ann Arbor, Mich.: University of Michigan Press, 1960), 4–9. See also Thomas Weiskel, *The Romantic Sublime: Studies in the Structure and Psychology of Transcendence* (Baltimore, Md.: Johns Hopkins University Press, 1976), 22–33, and Frances Ferguson, 'Legislating the Sublime', in *Studies in 18th-Century British Art and Aesthetics*, ed. Ralph Cohen, (Berkeley, Calif.: University of California Press, 1985), 128–47.

[32] Alexander Smith, 'The Philosophy of Poetry', *Blackwood's*, 38 (Dec. 1835), 827–39. The relevant extracts are reprinted in *The Victorian Poet: Poetics and Persona*, ed. Joseph Bristow (London: Croom Helm, 1987), 45–52. On Smith, see M. H. Abrams, *The Mirror and the Lamp: Romantic Theory and the Critical Tradition* (New York: OUP, 1953), 148–55.

so-called poetry of sensation of the 1830s and 1840s. John Wilson, in an acerbic review of Tennyson's *Poems, Chiefly Lyrical* of 1830, mocked this type of poetry for its excessive emphasis on feeling which displaced external reality as the proper realm of poetry. For him, it undermined the possibility of knowing external reality at all, since the subject's own thoughts and feelings were held to colour perceptions of the world to the extent that one could know only one's own feelings.[33] 'It is well known', he wrote sardonically, 'that we create nine-tenths at least of what appears to exist externally; and that such is somewhere about the proportion between reality and imagination.'[34] In the poetry of sensation, the external world was devoured by individual consciousnesses.

For De Quincey, however, the process worked in reverse: his subject was obliterated in the processes of consumption. His was not a devouring subject, but rather a subject devoured by external objects, for self-knowledge was obtained by picking through the tissues of a public and publicly available literature. De Quincey's formulation of the interactive relationship between subject and object avoided the solipsism with which Wilson charged Tennyson, but it did so at the expense of the autonomy of the subject. Indeed, De Quincey's model of literary consumption was like a form of addiction in which the consumer's identity and autonomy were lost to the objects of consumption; the reader, like the opium-eater, was swallowed up by the very objects he consumed. The scenario is terrifying in its implications for subjectivity, as he would demonstrate in the autobiographies.

In *Suspiria* De Quincey outlined a model of consciousness that was similar to that proposed in 'The Poetry of Pope', in which childhood memories and literature constituted adult consciousness: this model was the palimpsest. The human brain, De Quincey wrote, was like a palimpsest, that is to say, a repository of lost texts; at some traumatic moment, 'some potent convulsion of the system' (C, 146) such as death or the consumption of

---

[33] Wilson, 'Christopher North', review of Tennyson, *Poems, Chiefly Lyrical*, in *Blackwood's*, 31 (May 1832), 721–41. Reprinted in *Victorian Scrutinies*, ed. Armstrong, 102–24.
[34] *Victorian Scrutinies*, 102.

opium, all 'wheels back' to its original state. The image is a recurrent one in his work. In a letter to Robert Blackwood on 16 September 1842, for instance, he explained his self-proclaimedly prodigious political insight by referring to

[the] multitudes of facts and phenomena [that] had even through this period of childish inattention silently deposited themselves in my memory to which in after years growing knowledge had either given me the key or had given hints towards looking for the key. So that for the practical result I might truely assume an experience of 42 to 45 years extent. I had the facts in 1800: I kindled them into life in 1825.[35]

In this case the palimpsest allowed him to operate a kind of post-dating system, and to extend his conscious life backwards to include periods of inattention and unconsciousness. In its suspension of time, the model is not unlike Wordsworth's version of poetry as 'emotion recollected in tranquillity'.[36]

The palimpsest was a frequent metaphor in nineteenth-century writing, and provided a model for subjectivity, history, and epistemology for writers such as Coleridge, Carlyle, Barrett Browning, and Lewes.[37] Palimpsests were in fact invaluable as archaeological sources which philologists and other historians used to reconstruct the lost artefacts of past cultures, for within

---

[35] See letter to Robert Blackwood, 16 Sept. 1842, National Library of Scotland, MS 4060 fo. 262.

[36] De Quincey's palimpsest shares much with Wordsworth's 'spots of time'. See Robert Young, ' "For Thou Wert There" ' in *Glyph Textual Studies*, i, *Demarcating the Disciplines: Philosophy, Literature, Art*, ed. Samuel Weber, (Minneapolis: University of Minnesota Press, 1986), 103–28.

[37] 'I have in vain tried to recover the lines from the palimpsest tablet of my memory', Coleridge, 'The Wanderings of Cain', in *Poetical Works*, ed. Ernest Hartley Coleridge (1912; repr. Oxford: OUP, 1980), 287; 'the whole meaning [of the past] lies far beyond our ken; yet in that complex manuscript, covered over with formless inextricably entangled characters—nay, which is a *Palimpsest* . . .', Thomas Carlyle, 'On History' (1830), in *Critical and Miscellaneous Essays* (London, 1899), 89–90; 'A palimpsest, a prophet's holograph/Defiled . . .', Elizabeth Barrett Browning, *Aurora Leigh* (1856; repr. London: Women's Press, 1978), 64: 'The sensitive subject is no *tabula rasa*; it is not a blank sheet of paper, but a palimpsest', G. H. Lewes, *Problems of Life and Mind*, 1st ser., iii, *The Foundations of a Creed* (London, 1874), 162. For accounts of the palimpsest, see Thomas Reisner, 'De Quincey's Palimpsest Reconsidered,' *Modern Language Studies*, 12/2 (1982), 93–5; and Josephine McDonagh, 'Writings on the Mind: Thomas De Quincey and the Importance of the Palimpsest in Nineteenth-Century Thought,' *Prose Studies*, 10/2 (1987), 207–24. Some of the following discussion derives from that essay.

their surfaces forgotten depths could be excavated.[38] The paradoxical nature of the palimpsest—a two-dimensional surface that nevertheless had depth—captured the imagination of the age, for it was a model that allowed the unification of objects dispersed in history and culture.

For De Quincey the model served to represent the construction of human consciousness through the indelible traces of the past, the process he had figured in 'The Poetry of Pope'. However, the various scenarios which he used to describe this process were particularly violent, representing recollection as a kind of undoing, a non-production, even death:

the footsteps of the game pursued, wolf or stage, in each several chase, have been unlinked and hunted back through all their doubles: and, as the chorus of the Athenian stage unwove through the antistrophe every step that had been mystically woven through the strophe, so, by our modern conjurations of science, secrets of ages remote from each other have been exorcised from the accumulated shadows of centuries. (C, 142–3)

Figured as the pursuer of game, the palimpsest editor becomes a hunter and the original text an animal, which, when discovered, reconstituted and read, will be slaughtered. Interpretation of the text thus constitutes its violation, for the original inscription dies in its unravelling. The model is a troubling one, and nowhere more so than in its insistence on the importance of the material form of writing: it is the indelible nature of the writing that is the cause of awe and terror: 'Alchemy there is none of passion or disease that can scorch away these immortal impresses' (C, 146), he wrote, to underline the point of wonder, that this writing can never be erased. Images of writing infuse the passage at all levels: memory is like writing; death is like writing. As has often been noted, De Quincey's model of the mind as a palimpsest is close to Freud's model of the mind as a mystic writing pad, a model of infinite depth and 'perfectly superficial exteriority', that allows

[38] The most famous archaeologist of palimpsests was Cardinal Angelo Mai. See C. W. Russell, 'Palimpsest Literature and its Editor, Cardinal Angelo Mai' in *Afternoon lectures on Literature and Art* (London, 1899), 83–95. On the importance of palimpsest for 19th-cent. philologists, see H. Pedersen, *Linguistic Science in the Nineteenth Century: Methods and Results*, trans. J. W. Spargo, (Cambridge, Mass.: Harvard University Press, 1931).

both forgetting and the retrieval of memories.[39] In his essay, 'Freud and the Scene of Writing', Jacques Derrida suggests that the metaphorical inscription of memory as writing makes a fundamental attack on the autonomy of the subject. De Quincey's *Suspiria* displays symptoms of this condition, for it is an autobiography that tells the story of the loss of self, focusing continually on points at which the individuated self is under threat whether from reading the *Arabian Nights*, or, for instance, from experiencing grief on the death of a sister. This notion of loss of control is built into the very structure and style of the work, as he explains in the extended metaphors of the introductory section which are presented to exemplify his point that 'the whole course of this narrative resembles, and was meant to resemble, a *caduceus* wreathed about with meandering ornaments' (C, 93).[40]

If in the autobiographical text the loss of self is connected with writing as a metaphor for consciousness, it is significant that in 'The Poetry of Pope' the metaphor is literalized. Here the subject is constituted by the consumption of literary texts: memories of childhood are no longer *like* texts, but *are* in fact texts, the texts of childhood consumption. In this essay, the process is clearly ennobling and the distress that scars the autobiographical text is no longer there. It is as though the subject can take refuge and find empowerment of an obscure and mystified kind in the impersonal works of great literature; in the literature of power. As the expression of feeling, the literature of power enables the reader to share in the realm of affectivity. Nevertheless, these feelings are curiously impersonal; they have neither subject nor object, and take place in a transcendental arena beyond material space and time.

---

[39] See Sigmund Freud, 'Note upon the "Mystic Writing-Pad" ', *Standard Edition of the Complete Psychological Works*, trans. James Strachey (London: Hogarth Press, 1961), XIX, 223–32. The citation is from Jacques Derrida, 'Freud and the Scene of Writing' in *Writing and Difference*, trans. Alan Bass, (London: Routledge & Kegan Paul, 1978), 196–231, esp. 224. The relationship between De Quincey's and Freud's models of the mind is explored by Robert Maniquis in 'The Dark Interpreter and the Palimpsest of Violence: De Quincey and the Unconscious' and Charles L. Proudfitt, 'Thomas De Quincey and Sigmund Freud: Sons, Fathers, Dreamers— Precursors of Psychoanalytic Development Psychology' both in *Thomas De Quincey: Bicentenary Studies*, ed. Robert Lance Snyder (Norman, Okla.: University of Oklahoma Press, 1981), 109–39 and 88–108.

[40] The caduceus was Mercury's wand, and it was frequently represented entwined by two serpents.

This is made clear in 'On Wordsworth's Poetry', when De Quincey made the remarkable assertion that 'heretofore . . . I have never undertaken an examination of any man's writings'. Since by this time he had written essays on Shakespeare, Milton and Goethe, numerous pieces on the Lakeland poets, and moreover the essays on 'Style' and 'Rhetoric', the admission is puzzling. Masson interpreted the claim, arguing that De Quincey meant that he had never written on the entire body of works by a particular writer (XI: 294 n. 2); but it is apparent from the essay that this was not the point De Quincey wished to make. Rather he made a distinction between 'sketches of personal recollection' and 'critical sketches'. The writing of the former, he claimed, was simpler, but nevertheless burdened by 'painful scruples': 'Of books, so long as you rest only on grounds which, in sincerity, you believe to be true, and speak without anger or scorn, you can hardly say the thing which *ought* to be taken amiss. But of men and women you dare not, and must not, tell all that chance may have revealed to you' (XI: 294–5). Although his apparent highmindedness may have appeared insincere given his reputation for revealing the unseemly secrets of his contemporaries' private lives,[41] it is nevertheless significant that he wished to claim for literary criticism a freedom to speak a truth beyond the compromises imposed by a consideration for particular human feelings. Since truth is not always compatible with feeling, the literary critic must dissociate his feelings for the author from the evaluation of texts: objectivity demands the expulsion of personality from the critique of literature. The claims are remarkable from the pen of a man who had made his living from occasionally scandalous sketches of prominent writers.

Nevertheless, De Quincey's literary criticism remained a commentary on feeling. The 'great distinction' of Wordsworth, the poet, and not the man, was 'the extent of his sympathy with what is *really* permanent in human feelings, and also the depth of this sympathy' (XI: 321). Feeling had been detached from personality:

---

[41] Among the secrets De Quincey told were Coleridge's opium addiction, his plagiarism, and details of his marriage. On this see Lindop, *Opium-Eater*, 314–18. Nevertheless he was quick to accuse others of scandalmongering. See for instance his gossipy essay on Samuel Parr, whom he accuses of being a 'lithping slandermonger, and retailer of gossip' (V: 18). See 'Dr Samuel Parr; or Whiggism in its Relations to Literature' (1831), V: 9–145.

poetry spoke of free-floating and subjectless feelings in a peculiarly amorphous realm of abstraction in which emotion was deep
and permanent but without subject or object.

In the opening passages of *Suspiria*, De Quincey wavered between the two incompatible uses of the term critic which obtain
even now: the critic as the fault-finding reader, and the critic as
the professional reader of higher insight.[42] The contradiction that
the term embraces is perhaps a comment on the ambiguous relationship that literature comes to occupy in relation to capital,
being at once a refuge from and defence against the encroachment
of industrialization and capital, but also complicit with the values
and interests of industry and commerce. By the 1840s, De Quincey
uses the term the literature of power, a term with a strong Romantic heritage, in order to attempt some kind of reconciliation of the
two, a reconciliation of a contradiction so severe that it can only
ever be in effect an effacement of differences: the literature of
power becomes a realm for the expression of feeling, but feelings
that are fundamentally impersonal.

We shall return to the consumer in his various guises in Chapter 6, for he is the subject of De Quincey's autobiographical writings. Through the idea of consumption, De Quincey tackled the
problems of subjectivity faced in the modern world, after the
certainties of the old, traditional world had been lost. But he did
not always address these problems from the point of view of the
consumer: he was also concerned with the social ramifications of
this situation. The chaos he perceived to abound in society was
closely connected to the alienation experienced by the consumer,
as both its cause and effect. Much of his work was an attempt to
restore social order in the light of the lost agency of the subject,
significantly through a particular form of representation. In the
following chapters we shall consider this form of representation
as it is worked out through his aesthetics of murder and his gothic
fictions, but first through his theory of language.

[42] See Raymond Williams, *Keywords: A Vocabulary of Culture and Society*
(London: Fontana, 1983), 84–6.

4

Style Slaves: The Labour of Language

The horny substance, which encrusts my feet increases continually: and the torpor of the circulation is so great—that
with every exertion I cannot execute the 5th part each day of
what I could have done 18 months ago.

De Quincey, letter to Robert Blackwood, 15 April 1843[1]

The Politics of the Study of Language

In *Confessions*, De Quincey described an unlikely encounter with
a Malay who called at his house in Westmorland, possibly, he
surmised, en route to Liverpool. So as not to lose face with his
neighbours and servants who reckoned him to be a master of
obscure and rare languages, De Quincey, possessing in fact but
two words of Arabic, addressed the stranger with lines from the
Iliad. Luckily the Malay responded: with oriental circumspection,
he 'worshipped [him] in a most devout manner, and replied in
what [De Quincey] suppose[d] was Malay' (C, 57).

In the early decades of the nineteenth century, De Quincey's
choice of ancient Greek as an approximation to Malay was not as
preposterous as all that. De Quincey selected it because Greek
'came geographically nearest to an Oriental [language]', and he
speculated that, on account of this, there may have been some
affinity between them.

The idea that different languages might be related to each other
in terms of idiom, syntax, etymology, and grammar, as though
they were members of an extended family, was the underlying
principle of the major works of linguistic scholarship of the period, subscribed to by philologists such as William Jones, J. C.
Adelung, Jacob Grimm, Rasmus Rask, Franz Bopp, and Friedrich
Schlegel.[2] Much of this work was rooted in the study of oriental

---

[1] National Library of Scotland, MS 4065 fo. 172.
[2] See Hans Aarsleff, *The Study of Language in England, 1780–1860* (London:
Athlone Press, 1983), 115–61.

languages, in particular Sanskrit, which was considered to have been the origin of Greek, Latin, and all Germanic languages. William Jones's 1786 lecture, 'On the Hindus', which celebrated the 'wonderful structure' of Sanskrit, 'more perfect than the Greek, more copious than the Latin, and more exquisitely refined than either', asserted that the three must have derived from a common source which 'perhaps no longer exists'.[3] The study of ancient and foreign languages not only offered an important source of historical and anthropological information about oriental cultures, but more importantly, it told Europeans about their own pasts and origins.[4] De Quincey, in his 'Letters to a Young Man', mused that the theory of the affinity of languages had 'furnish[ed] the main clue for ascending, through the labyrinths of nations, to their earliest origins and connections' (XI: 34). And in a review of Colonel Vans Kennedy's *Researches into the Origin and Affinity of the Principal Languages of Asia and Europe* (1828), which appeared in the *Edinburgh Literary Gazette* in 1829, he wrote

The ancient language of Hindustan, the Sanskrit, bears in roots, as well as in grammatical form, a striking analogy to Greek and Latin, nay, to Icelandic, Slavonic, and German. Hence we infer, with the highest degree of certainty, that those nations, though living at so great a distance for more than three thousand years, must once have lived in a close relation, and at some very remote period, in all probability, spoken the same tongue.[5]

If Hindustanis and Slavs once spoke the same tongue, why not an exiled Malay and an Ancient Greek poet?

The philologists' theory of the affinity of languages, which, as an organic, all-embracing system, was particularly attractive to De Quincey, was in tune with much of the contemporary thinking of the time, in particular the Romantic quest for the origins of European culture and its privileging of the primitive and natural

[3] Cited by Raymond Schwab in *The Oriental Renaissance: Europe's Rediscovery of India and the East 1680–1880*, trans. Gene Patterson-Black and Victor Reinking (New York: Columbia University Press, 1984), 41. See also Aarsleff, *Study of Language*, 133, and Edward Said, *Orientalism* (1979; repr. Harmondsworth: Penguin, 1985), 77–9.

[4] See Said, *Orientalism*.

[5] David Groves ascribes this essay to De Quincey in 'Thomas De Quincey and the *Edinburgh Literary Gazette*, and the Affinity of Languages', *English Language Notes*, 26/3 (1989), 55–69, esp. 60.

over the corrupt and alienating modern political and social world. For Romantic philosophers and poets, language was one domain in which one might attempt to recuperate a natural, original state. Rousseau, in *Essai sur l'origine des langues où il est parlé de la mélodie et de l'imitation musicale* (1754), and Herder, in *Über den Ursprung der Sprache* (1772),[6] had written influentially on the origin of language. Both argued that language originated on the first occasion on which primitive man expressed his desires and passions. For Rousseau, this meant that the first language was figurative. 'Proper meaning', he argued, 'was discovered last. One calls things by their true name only when one sees them in their true form. At first only poetry was spoken....'[7] To explain this claim, he used the example of the savage and the giant. Seeing a man of whom he was afraid, the savage called him *giant*; when that fear was conquered, he called the man *man*, and 'le[ft] *giant* to the fictitious object that had impressed him during his illusion'.[8] Thus language originated in passion and fantasy, and to recover that language was to find words that referred not directly to objects, but to the desires of a vulnerable savage groping his way through a world of his own narcissistic and paranoid imaginings.

Herder, too, located the first language in passion. Much of his argument was directed towards current theories of the divine origin of language, in particular the work of Süssmilch.[9] Like Rousseau, Herder argued that language emerged as an aspect of relations between people, and that its origin was social rather than God-given. In the opening passage, he wrote

A suffering animal, no less than the hero Philoctetus, will whine, will moan when pain befalls it even though it be abandoned on a desert island, without sight or trace or hope of a helpful fellow creature. It is as though it could breathe more freely as it vents its burning, frightened spirit. It is as though it could sigh out part of its pain and at least draw in from the empty space new strength of endurance as it fills the unhearing winds with its moans, so little did nature create us as severed blocks of rack, as egotistic monads![10]

---

[6] Both essays are reprinted in *Two Essays on the Origin of Language*, trans. John H. Moran and Alexander Gode (Chicago: University of Chicago Press, 1966).
[7] Rousseau in *Two Essays*, 12.
[8] Ibid. 13.
[9] See Herder in *Two Essays*, 92–9.
[10] Ibid. 87.

No 'egotistic monads', people were social beings and language was an expression of their identifying social desires. As the suffering individual 'sigh[s] out part of its pain', language participated in a cathartic process of exchange in which language replaced suffering, and established bonds between people. A complex economy was thus established in which pain would be expunged by language. For both Herder and Rousseau, language marked the origin of society.

Claims that language originated in deeply felt emotion lay behind the work of the poets of emerging Romantic movements across Europe; one aspect of the project of such poetry was the reconstitution of the spirit of this primal language of passion. In Britain, the clearest expression of the view that poetic language had sprung from emotion was Wordsworth's assertion that poetry was 'the spontaneous overflow of powerful feelings';[11] his attempt to find this in the 'language of men', the rural peasants of the *Lyrical Ballads*, provided just one example of the way in which particular groups of language-users were implicated in this ideal category. As we have seen, De Quincey's idea of literature as impassioned prose owed much to these beliefs. However, the philologists' empirical work on oriental languages suggested another answer to the question that had been addressed by the poets. For them, the original language could be reconstituted through tracing the ancestry of modern languages in the manuscripts of past and foreign literatures.

Comparative philology dominated the study of language in Europe at the beginning of the nineteenth century. Despite its nostalgic impulse to retrieve the origins of language, it was nevertheless fundamentally a synchronic science, which compared the structures of different languages. Rather than addressing problems of reference to the exterior world, the focus of previous linguistic enquiry, it devoted its attention to the internal mechanisms of language. Language itself was now the object of study and this self-reflexive turn within philology identified it for Foucault as one of the three defining discourses of the nineteenth century. For him, philology occupied the new space of representation, which was also occupied by political economy and

---

[11] Wordsworth, *The Prose Works*, ed. W. J. B. Owen and J. W. Smyser (Oxford: Clarendon Press, 1974), i. 148.

biology; each was a self-referential discourse which explored its own workings as though they were the internal organs of a living being.[12] However, comparative philology never gained the ascendancy in Britain that it enjoyed elsewhere in Europe. While some intellectuals in Britain, such as Max Müller, practised influentially as philologists, more generally people were worried by its purported atheistic tendencies and by what they considered to be its too ambitious scope.[13] De Quincey voiced this opinion in 'Letters to a Young Man', when he advised his pupil that, although a philologist should 'examine the structure of as many languages as possible; gather as many thousand specimens as possible', for the amateur linguist, 'the act of learning a language is in itself an evil' (X: 34). '[I]n the study of language,' he continued, 'all is arbitrary', and thus, 'by its lifeless forms, [it] kill[s] and mortif[ies] the action of the intellect' (X: 35). In Britain, another branch of the study of language more suited to the amateur scholar would develop: this was the study not of all languages, but of English in particular; not of dead languages, but of a living one. The object of study would be the history of the English language, for by scrutinizing its development more could be learnt about the language as a living organism. It is clear from the extract from the 'Letters to a Young Man' that such a discipline would hold advantages for De Quincey, and indeed his essay on the English language, published in 1839, is singled out as seminal among the first works in this new discipline, the history of the language.[14]

Unlike comparative philologists, historians of the English language focused on the differences rather than the continuities between different languages. They were interested in the ancestry of modern English only in so far as it underlined its special and individual qualities, for, as Crowley writes, this new discipline carried with it an important nationalist project. As historians of the language celebrated the glories of English, the language became a repository of national values shared by all its native users. Crowley argues that the history of the language was a discourse

---

[12] See Michel Foucault, *The Order of Things* (London: Tavistock, 1970), 280–300. See also Tony Crowley, *The Politics of Discourse: The Standard Language Question in British Cultural Debate* (Basingstoke: Macmillan, 1989), 14–39.

[13] See Crowley, *Politics of Discourse*, 20–6.

[14] Ibid. 31–4 and 39–42.

set up in response to the social antagonism engendered by Chartism in the 1830s and 1840s, through which the nation might be reunified and consolidated. Following Gareth Stedman Jones, in 'Rethinking Chartism', he argues that the state's strategies for dealing with Chartism shifted in the late 1830s from a policy of overt repression, whereby the government implemented measures such as 'the New Poor Law, the Municipal Corporations Act, opposition to factory legislation, attacks on trade unionism and the extension of the police force', to more latent processes of education and reform.[15] Crowley argues that among the many responses to Chartism, the formation of the new discipline of the history of the language was 'one of the most important of the cultural and educational responses, and one with far-reaching effects'.[16]

This argument is persuasive, and suggestive for thinking about De Quincey's other writings on language. De Quincey's almost obsessional interest in these matters is evident from the numerous digressions and notes on questions of etymology and grammar that litter his essays. In this chapter I will explore his ideas about language, nation and labour as they interact in his essays, by focusing on his sustained writings on language, namely, pieces in the 'Notes from a Pocket Book of a Late Opium Eater' (1823–4), the essay on 'Style' (1840–1), as well as 'The English Language'.[17]

In the 'Notes', we will see that De Quincey's early thinking about language took place in the context of an unequivocal rejection of Romantic primitivism, at the same time paradoxically as he boasted an intimacy and identity with the central figures of the British Romantic movement. The most helpful context in which to understand this is the heated debates about the moral, political and economic issues of slavery that continued throughout De Quincey's life. High Tories such as De Quincey, who tended to speak for the interests of the West Indian traders, had experienced the abolition of the slave trade in 1807 as the cause of economic

---

[15] Gareth Stedman Jones, 'Rethinking Chartism', in *Languages of Class: Studies in English Working-Class History, 1832–1982* (Cambridge: CUP, 1983), 90–178; Crowley, *Politics of Discourse*, 43.

[16] Crowley, *Politics of Discourse*, 46.

[17] Also relevant are his essays on 'Rhetoric', published in 1828 in *Blackwood's*, and 'On the Present State of the English Language', published in 1857 in *Hogg's Weekly Instructor*, neither of which will be discussed in detail here.

and social turmoil. Thus the intensified activities of the anti-slavery lobby in the 1820s and 1830s, campaigning for the complete outlawing of not only the trade in slaves, but of the practice of slavery itself in British colonies and elsewhere, were a persisting source of consternation. The scale of these activities was large and they were well organized: the Emancipation Society was established in London in 1823, and this was followed by the establishment of similar societies throughout Britain; the first World Anti-Slavery Convention took place in London in 1840; and, as Linda Colley has pointed out, the abolition movement motivated the biggest petitioning campaign ever to have taken place in Britain.[18] The Emancipation Act of 1833 ostensibly put an end to Britain's part in slavery, but, nevertheless, Britain continued to trade with countries in which slavery persisted. In 1843 the *Eclectic Review* computed that there were still over six million slaves in countries under 'nominally Christian government': North America, the countries of South America, and Spanish, French, Danish, Dutch, and Swedish colonies in the West Indies. Moreover it claimed that 450,000 slaves continued to be bought and sold each year.[19] The periodical literature of the time attests that slavery continued to be a live issue well beyond 1833.

For the High Tory, pro-slavery writers, the moral issues of slavery were an inconvenience to be circumvented. As a commentator in *Fraser's Magazine* observed in 1830:

We have no intention of entering into the question of the legality or illegality of slavery, either as respects the laws of God, or the abstract rule of moral right, or the existing institutions of this country. . . . [The Anti-Slavery Society is] the great enem[y] of the West Indian proprietors, a body of great wealth and influence in this country, which draws its principle of vitality and action through the medium of commerce. As the

---

[18] On slavery see James Walvin, *England, Slaves, and Freedom* (Basingstoke: Macmillan, 1986); Duncan C. Rice, 'Controversies over Slavery in Eighteenth- and Nineteenth-Century Scotland', in *Anti-Slavery Reconsidered: New Perspectives on the Abolitionists*, ed. Lewis Perry and Michael Fellman (Baton Rouge, La.: Louisiana State University Press, 1979), 24–50, and *The Scots Abolitionists, 1833–1861* (Baton Rouge, La.: Louisiana State University Press, 1981). See also Linda Colley, *Britons: Forging the Nation, 1707–1837* (New Haven, Conn.: Yale University Press, 1992), 350–60. Colley argues that the passing of the Emancipation Act in 1833 is a crucial element in the formation of national consciousness that is often overlooked (324).

[19] 'The Present State of the Anti-Slavery Cause', *Eclectic Review*, NS, 13 (June 1843), 673–90.

West Indian proprietors are the grand prop of the prosperity of our colonies across the Atlantic, their actual condition, whether prosperous or adverse, is a matter of some consequence to every true politician and lover of the international grandeur of Great Britain.[20]

For this group, the wealth and consequently the very stature of the nation depended on the continuation of slavery abroad; the glory of the nation rested on the invisible labour that supported and created it, just as domestic comfort required the concealed work of good gardeners and servants. De Quincey voiced opinions similar to these in the *Edinburgh Saturday Post*, in a pair of essays published in June 1828 on West Indian property.[21] In these, he argued that abolition of slavery would be an affront to the West Indian property owners; that slavery was a form of labour that had been 'sanctioned' by 'so many industrious statesmen, and . . . a long line of kings, parliaments, councils, and courts of national justice';[22] that Africans would be happier if they were free from responsibilities of property themselves; and that slavery did not degrade, but, in fact, ennobled their 'savagery'. Behind these assertions, in addition to a set of economic factors that required the continuance of slavery in the colonies, lay an ideological commitment to slavery as a form of labour that approximated the kind of social relations for which De Quincey was nostalgic. As an increasingly disgruntled working class voiced their political demands and attracted the attention of the political nation, the idea of slavery presented a form of labour which was in many ways preferable to the troubling manifestations of the industrial working class.[23] For De Quincey, slavery was not a moral sore, but a benignly paternalistic form of labour.

Chartism, then, is one context for understanding De Quincey's writings on language. But it is not the only one, for the interests

[20] 'The Anti-Slavery Society', *Fraser's Magazine for Town and Country*, 1 (June 1830), 610–22 esp. 610.

[21] 'West India Property', pts. 1 and 2, repr. in *New Essays by De Quincey: His Contributions to the Edinburgh Saturday Post and the Edinburgh Evening Post, 1827–1828*, ed. Stuart M. Tave (Princeton, NJ: Princeton University Press, 1966), 358–83.

[22] Tave, *New Essays*, 369–70.

[23] This position should be contrasted with that of Coleridge and Robert Owen, who both considered slavery to be a sign of the problems in industrial labour at home. See Catherine Gallagher, *The Industrial Reformation of English Fiction: Social Discourse and Narrative Form, 1832–1867* (Chicago: University of Chicago Press, 1985), 10–12.

and rhetoric of the slavery debates were intricately entwined with debates about labour at home.[24] De Quincey's works are informed by a complex network of ideas about labour that were held by other reactionary thinkers of the time. Sharing Carlyle's disturbance at the Chartists' 'inarticulate uproar, like dumb creatures in pain',[25] De Quincey saw slavery as a viable and acceptable alternative—a form of labour, indeed, that in many ways replicated the relations of a paternalistic feudal society, the nostalgic fantasy that underpinned his political rhetoric. It will be no surprise then to find that De Quincey's ideal style of language use was based on a model of slavery: for him, words should be the slaves of style, and he their sovereign master.

Language and Racial Determinism

During 1823–4, while still mainly residing in Dove Cottage, and directly following his success with *Confessions*, De Quincey published a series of short pieces on subjects as diverse and inconsequential as 'Proverbs', 'Madness', and 'Superficial Knowledge', in a frequently pompous and brash tone.[26] Throughout, he boasted intimacy with the literary great and good: he mentioned a projected collaboration between himself, Wordsworth, Coleridge, and John Wilson, and, with studied casualness, cited anecdotes recounted to him by Coleridge. In the piece on 'Superficial Knowledge' he noted how, coincidentally, Schiller happened to

[24] Gallagher maps the complex array of positions adopted on the slavery issue in *The Industrial Reformation*, 3–35.

[25] See Thomas Carlyle, 'Chartism', reprinted in *Selected Writings*, ed. Alan Shelston (Harmondsworth: Penguin, 1971), 155. De Quincey, however, distances himself from Carlyle's position in a letter to Robert Blackwood, dated 30 June 1840: '[Carlyle] and others are affirming that something must be dreadfully amiss in our social condition; and, when you look into the nature of the grievance it turns out to be nothing special to us and our age,—but only the external facts of poverty etc. . . . And even those, who adopt his views as a handle of change, admit that he is very obscure when it comes to remedies.' National Library of Scotland, MS 4051 fo. 133.

[26] 'English Dictionaries' includes a note on the common misuse of the word 'nice', in 'an objective instead of a subjective sense', which De Quincey names 'the most shocking of the unscholarlike barbarisms' (X: 433 n. 1). The same point is made by Henry Tilney, in Jane Austen's *Northanger Abbey* (1818). In this text, the example serves to emphasize the pomposity of its male lead. See *Northanger Abbey*, ed. A. H. Ehrenpreis (Harmondsworth: Penguin, 1972), 122.

express an opinion similar to his own in the *Aesthetic Education of Man*. The dramatis personae of Romanticism loomed large and proudly in these essays. But there were aspects of Romanticism from which De Quincey was keen to disentangle himself, particularly the implications of Rousseauian primitivism that celebrated the noble savage. Thus in 'False Distinctions', as we shall see, De Quincey laid out a programme for the racial cleansing of the Romantic imagination, and in 'English Physiology', he asserted the superiority of the English through the scientific discourse of physiology. This, then, is the context of his first essay on the English language, 'English Dictionaries', which, like the later essay, called for an English dictionary which would 'tell the history of each word' (X: 430). The project is a corrective one designed to protect the purity of the language from the contaminations encouraged by misuse. It was another appeal to origins, but this time to the origin of proper, civilized Englishness, as a stable point in a deteriorating world of sloppy language use.

The stated purpose of 'False Distinctions' was to make the Kantian point that the imagination and the understanding were integrally related, and to correct a popular misapprehension that they existed in isolation from each other. De Quincey did so by redressing three common errors: '*That women have more imagination than men*' (X: 440), '*That the savage has more imagination than the civilized man*', and '*That Oriental nations have more imagination (and according to some, a more passionate constitution of mind) than those of Europe*' (X: 443). The force of his argument was less that a categorical error had been made, than that this error had led to these misattributions of the great Romantic faculty, the imagination. In De Quincey's eyes, the imagination was a faculty reserved for the white man. The essay was a controversial one triggering a correspondence in subsequent editions of the *London Magazine* on 'female genius', as 'the champions of the female sex [rose] *en masse* against XYZ'.[27] However, the letters touched on only the charge of discrimination against women, suggesting that while an emergent feminist consciousness existed among the readers

---

[27] The words here are those of the editor, John Taylor. See *London Magazine*, 10 (1824), 3. For the correspondence, see *London Magazine*, 10 (1824), 53–5, 184–8, and 333.

of the *London Magazine*, statements of racial prejudice might go unnoticed.

In the present context, the second and third points—redressing the misapprehension that savages and orientals are more imaginative than 'civilized' Europeans—are interesting because they constituted an explicit rejoinder to various tenets of Romantic philosophy—but curiously a rejoinder in its own terms. Implicitly recalling Rousseau's claim that the first language was a poetic one, De Quincey wrote:

As to savages, their poetry and their eloquence are always of the most unimaginative order: when they are figurative, they are so by mere necessity; language being too poor amongst savage nations to express any but the rudest thoughts, so that such feelings as are not of hourly recurrence can be expressed only by figures. Moreover, it is a mistake to suppose that merely to deal in figurative language implies any imaginative power; it is one of the commonest expressions of the overexcitement of weakness. (X: 443)

Without referring directly to Rousseau, De Quincey argued against Rousseau's claim that all language, in its origin, was figurative. For De Quincey, figurative language was an embellishment of normal language, which was non-figurative or literal. Savages used figurative language only when their own language failed them; thus for them, embellishment was rooted in necessity not luxury, which was another sign of the impoverishment of their language. Moreover figurative language in itself was not a sign of the deep and profound workings of the true imagination, but a superficial decoration from the weak and over-excitable. The case against the poetic prowess of savages was conclusive. The chief distinction between De Quincey's and Rousseau's texts was that, while for Rousseau the savage was the primitive version of all men, for De Quincey, who spoke of 'savage nations', a clear division existed between 'civilized' and 'savage' peoples. 'Savages' lived somewhere else, had different modes of existence, and shared no continuities whatsoever with European men, although they did share the imaginative deficiencies of European women.

He continued: if the savage was unimaginative, the oriental was less than imaginative, for 'the [o]riental nations betray the *negative* of that power (= −imagination)' (X: 444). The oriental imagination tended to concretize, while the authentic imagination abstracted. De Quincey had in mind the fascination with the orient shown by Romantic poets, not least Coleridge in, for instance, 'Kubla Khan'. But he used Coleridge's own terms from the *Biographia Literaria* to provide evidence that the oriental imagination was but a poor semblance of the authentic imagination. Commenting on an image in the Koran that compared the pen of God with a race-course that was so long that 'an Arabian courser . . . would not be able to gallop from one end to the other in a space of 500 years', he wrote, 'the imagination seeks the illimitable; dissolves the definite; translates the finite into the infinite. But this Arabian image has, on the contrary, translated the infinite into the finite' (X: 444).[28] Throughout, De Quincey's aim was to protect Romantic philosophy from the implications of its own enthusiasms, for in its celebration of the imagination, and its mistaken belief that the imagination was distinct from the understanding, it had falsely equated the imagination with savages and so on. For De Quincey, this idealization of savages, orientals and women was a risky business, because these were categories of people who had disruptive political and social demands.

In 'English Physiology', De Quincey found 'scientific' support for his ideas about the inequalities between races. Referring to the work of William Lawrence, the physiologist and translator of Johann Friedrich Blumenbach,[29] De Quincey claimed that the very shape and construction of Caucasian and Negro skulls indicated the intellectual superiority of the Caucasian. Lawrence's work provided an early example of the 'scientific' explanations for racial (and sexual) inequalities that gained in popularity throughout the century, in particular through the 'science' of craniology, outlined in the works of S. G. Morton, *Crania Americana* (1839) and *Crania Aegyptiaca* (1844). At this point, De Quincey found in Lawrence's work justification for a celebration of the 'lower' qualities of Negroes:

[28] Cf. S. T. Coleridge, *Biographia Literaria, or Biographical Sketches of my Literary Life and Opinions*, ed. James Engell and W. Jackson Bate (London: Routledge & Kegan Paul, 1983), i. 304: 'It dissolves, diffuses, dissipates, in order to re-create; or where this process is rendered impossible, yet, still at all events it struggles to idealize and to unify.'

[29] See J. F. Blumenbach, *A Short System of Comparative Anatomy, With Additional Notes and an Introductory View of the Classification of Animals, by the Translator*, trans. William Lawrence (London, 1807). Coleridge studied under Blumenbach in 1799.

But it is in a high degree unphilosophic to suppose that Nature ever varies her workmanship for the sake of absolute degradation. Through all differences of degree she pursues some difference of kind which could not perhaps have coexisted with a higher degree. If, therefore, the negro intellect be in some of the higher qualities inferior to that of the European, we may reasonably presume that this inferiority exists for the purpose of obtaining some compensatory excellence in lower qualities that could not else have existed. (X: 448)

This patronizing resignation to the existence of natural racial differences was a position assumed frequently at this time by both the political Right and Left. De Quincey's assertion of the different capacities of racial groups lent scientific grounds to his support of slavery.

In 'English Dictionaries', De Quincey returned to the role of disciplinarian which he adopted in 'False Distinctions'. This time his aim was to save the English language from 'faulty evolutions' (X: 431). Invoking once more the authority of Coleridge, he called for an English dictionary to chart the history of each word as a check on present usages.[30] 'The original and primitive sense of the word', De Quincey claimed, 'will contain virtually all which can afterwards arise: as in the *evolution*-theory of generation the whole series of births is represented as involved in the first parent' (X: 431). But that is not to say that evolutions would always be natural and wholesome; quite frequently words would develop in an aberrant way under the pressure of subversive social forces (such as, we will see, the Catholic Church or the newspaper press). The role of the 'original and primitive' moment in this was always retrospective: no longer the source of wonder and the true outlet of the imagination, the original state of language was significant as a checking point that could be mobilized against possible deviancy, a fount of traditional values to weigh against the corruptions of the modern world.

To demonstrate his thesis, De Quincey presented examples of words which had been subject to 'faulty evolution'. The word he focused on was 'implicit': in this case, the correct meaning was an unspoken action; the incorrect, 'a vague rhetorical word which

---

[30] On Coleridge's theory of desynonization, see Paul Hamilton, *Coleridge's Poetics* (Oxford: Blackwell, 1983), 62–88.

expresses a great *degree'* (X: 431). His examples of 'correct' usage included the following:

Q. Had he expressed any contempt for your opinion?
A. ... not explicit contempt, I admit, for he never opened his stupid mouth; but implicitly he expressed the utmost that he could: for when I had spoken two hours against the old newspaper, and in favour of the new one, he went instantly and put his name as a subscriber to the old one. (X: 432)

The 'aberrant' usage of 'implicit'—as the needless repetition of words—laid stress on language itself; the 'correct' usage, however, drew on meanings outside language, for it refers to quite literally that which was not spoken ('he never opened his stupid mouth'), but performed. The example is apposite because it offered a commentary on the impoverished state into which De Quincey feared the English language was falling; it demonstrated the new ineffectualness of language, a symptom of modern corruption, that should be checked. Reclamation of the correct meaning of 'implicit' entailed abandoning rhetorical excess for a sparse but effective language in which deeds would speak louder than words.

According to De Quincey, the Roman Catholic Church was to blame for the corruption of the word. In an attempt to popularize its difficult doctrines which could not be understood by uneducated people, the church attributed the people with *implicit* faith; ignorant of theological arguments, they believed *implicitly*, without learning. The Protestant Church saw the existence of large numbers espousing a faith they could not understand as a sharp indictment of Catholic doctrine. In response, the Catholics cannily corrupted the meaning of the word, claiming now that '*implicit* faith' meant a 'strong faith'. However, it was not only religious prejudice that motivated De Quincey; here and elsewhere he expressed an antipathy to a situation in which the meanings of words might change under popular pressure. For him, the assigning of meaning was the prerogative of a particular class of people, and not to be made available to the masses. The Catholics' redefinition of the word in a sense gave it to the people, because now 'implicit' accurately described their uncomprehending and incorruptible faith.

Later on in this chapter we will see that his notion of good style developed from the same premiss—that language had to be defended against the abuses of subordinates: working-class women and journalists. In the essay, 'Style', however, rather than abandoning words for deeds as in 'Notes', De Quincey argued that words should be transparent to the thoughts of the writer or speaker.

The End of Language

By the time De Quincey wrote 'Style', he had already published 'The English Language'. In the latter he repeated his call for a history of the language made earlier in 'Notes', for the purpose of correcting aberrant language use, as he saw it in 1823; in 1839 this history was designed as a work of patriotism that would honour and celebrate the achievements of the nation. However, the intricacy of the imagery suggests that the relationship between the language and nation was a complex one. The essay contains a series of rhetorical ploys to endorse this relationship and to assert the purity of both the English language and nation. However, a reading of the essay will reveal an awareness that the nation's greatness derived from its position as a trading nation, and that its wealth had been built on the labour and materials plundered in distant parts. In 'The English Language', we see the beginning of an argument developed more fully in 'Style', namely, that language, at its best, is founded on the idea of concealed labour that is realized in slavery.

The term 'nation' is emphasized throughout 'The English Language', and this distinguishes it from the earlier essay. A history of the language, De Quincey claims, would complete the project of national literature which was to record all aspects of national life and achievement. The language was a 'capital' subject, since its growth not only recorded, but also mirrored, the development of the nation itself, 'from its earliest rudiments, through all the periods of its growth, to its stationary condition' (XIV: 149). As a 'monument of learning and patriotism', it would be the final exhibit in a museum of national culture. As Crowley has argued, De Quincey's call was answered many times by Victorian linguists such as Skeat and Trench, whose considerable works contributed to a history of the English language established on such lines.[31]

---

[31] Work on what would be known as the *Oxford English Dictionary* began in the late 1850s.

De Quincey's essay conveys the greatness of the nation through the grand sense of an ending that it constructs. Not only is the projected history of the language to be the final insertion in an exhibition of national accomplishments, but it is also an artefact in itself complete and ready for retrospective celebration. This is curious since elsewhere De Quincey held a more fluid notion of language, declaring that 'no language is stationary, except in rude and early periods of society' (X: 246). But to declare that the language is a finished artefact, as he does here, lends the argument ideological force: given the analogous relation posited between language and nation, not only does the statement foreclose any question of future linguistic and social change, but asserts that the present state of language and society is the culmination of a process of steady refinement and improvement, and represents the epitome of civilization.

The dominant imagery throughout is to do with rivers and water—organic imagery suggesting processes of natural growth and maturation, events in the unstoppable flow of nature. However, as frequently happens in De Quincey's work, the imagery is overly complex and muddled. It is most effective when he uses the idea of the mechanism of the tides—another example of the organic machine—as a metaphor for describing the relationship between language and its social contexts. National, or in his terms, *human*, consciousness is like a tidal force that pulls water into the channels, which represent aspects of national culture. The tide, or national consciousness, is powered by two machines, one hydraulic, the other hydrostatic:

Long after the main highway of waters has felt the full power of the tide, channels running far inland, with thousands of little collateral creeks, may be still under the very process of filling; for two powers are required to those final effects of the tide,—the general hydrostatic power for maintaining the equilibrium, and also hydraulic power for searching narrow conduits. On the same analogy many human interests . . . may long linger unnoticed, and survive for a time the widest expansion of intellectual activity. Possibly the aspects of society must shift materially before even the human consciousness, far less a human interest of curiosity, settles upon them with steadiness enough to light up and vivify their relations. (XIV: 146–7)

Hydrostatic power is produced by the pressure of the water gained through depth, and it sets the hydraulic power in motion.

The hydraulic power is a lateral process, and accumulates as the water moves through the channels and conduits. The hydraulic power needs the fundamental resource of hydrostatic power, but it assumes its own momentum through lateral movement. The relationship between the two is not determining, although one initiates the other.[32] The analogy that De Quincey draws between these machines and the production of the history of the language is an intricate one. The hydrostatic power represents the shift in material circumstances; it is this that motivates the hydraulic power, or 'human consciousness', to move out and fill existing but invisible channels of 'human interests' (like the language) and write their histories. The relationship between material change and national consciousness, like that between hydrostatic and hydraulic powers, is a flexible one: consciousness is dependent on material circumstances, but not absolutely determined by it. The crucial point is that, in De Quincey's account, neither material conditions nor consciousness affect 'human interests'; these have an existence prior to and independent of either power. The 'human interests' are the cultural artefacts that will become the subject of new histories, and in this account they stand unsullied by the material conditions of their existence. Thus De Quincey separates the language and its history from material circumstances and human consciousness: reflecting the glories of the nation, the English language stands beyond all material concerns and outside historical process.[33]

While the project of writing the history of the language takes place in the wider context of material change, the forces at work in the development of language itself tend to be located within the internal structures of the language. De Quincey isolates three causes that account for linguistic change:

first, the instinct of abbreviation, prompted continually by hurry or by impatience; secondly, the instinct of *onomatopeia*, or, more generally, the instinct of imitation applied directly to sounds, indirectly to motion, and

---

[32] Cf. the distinction De Quincey made between the two uses of the word *determine*, in his economic works. See Ch. 2, n. 32.

[33] Crowley focuses on this point. See Crowley, *Politics of Discourse*, 32–41. Crowley suggests that there are continuities between the thinking of De Quincey, Marx, and Foucault. But it should be remembered that for De Quincey, language exists outside historical process, and this marks the limits of these relationships.

by the aid of analogies more or less obvious applied to many other classes of objects; thirdly, the instinct of distinction, sometimes for purposes of necessity, sometimes of convenience. (XIV: 158) '

The surprising feature of all three causes is their common reliance on phonological and linguistic concerns. De Quincey again breaks the link between materiality and language by privileging internal above social causes for the development and change of language. If the social is reinstated, it is only in the third cause, 'the instinct of distinction, sometimes for purposes of necessity, sometimes of convenience'; but it becomes clear that 'necessity' and 'convenience' concern articulation and pronunciation rather than social needs for new words and categories. To explain his point he provides the following examples:

from *propriety* . . . was struck off, by a more rapid pronunciation and a throwing back of the accent, the modern word *property*, in which the same general idea is limited to appropriations of pecuniary value . . . So, again, *major* as a military designation, and *mayor* as a civil one, have split off from the very same original word by varied pronunciations. (XIV: 158–9)

The meanings of the words alter in response to almost casual changes in pronunciation; the social dimension of language is now merely the toy of arbitrary shifts in vocalization.

At this point De Quincey returns to questions of nationality. The *number* of different words that any nation develops is a marker of that nation's sophistication:

these divergencies into multiplied derivatives from some single radix are, in fact, the great source of opulence to one language by preference to another. And it is clear that the difference in this respect between nation and nation will be in a compound ratio of the complexity and variety of situations into which men are thrown . . . —in the ratio, we say, of this complexity on the one hand, and, on the other, of the intellectual activity put forth to seize and apprehend these fleeting relations of things and persons. Whence, according to the vast inequalities of national minds, the vast disparity of languages. (XIV: 159)

De Quincey makes a neat link between the sophisticated society and the scope of its language, as the variety of situations in advanced societies calls for a wider range of words to articulate them. The level of sophistication achieved by a language is the combined result of the variety of situations to be met in that nation, and the national intellect with which these are 'seized'. In the end De Quincey returns to the idea of national inequality to account for differences in languages. Just as he claims that language develops under the pressure of internal causes such as vocalization, he adduces the notion of innate national superiority to account for the glories of England, its language and its people.

The particular greatness of English, De Quincey claims, comes from its 'special dowry of power in its double-headed origin', that is, its roots in Germanic and Romance languages. This is surprising, since, given De Quincey's alignment of language and nationality, to invoke these 'double-headed origins' calls into doubt the racial and cultural purity of English and the English. In a contradictory footnote, he qualifies this idea of the double origin. While the German language's adaptation of French and Latin 'embroideries' is a ludicrous process of 'denationalization', the double origin of English is a thorough mixing of languages which reinforces its nationality. In a complex manipulation of a rhetoric that denigrates a 'mixed origin', De Quincey legitimates the ancestry of English by marrying its parents:

The peculiar, and without exaggeration we may say the providential, felicity of the English language has been made its capital reproach—that, whilst yet ductile and capable of new impressions, it received a fresh and large infusion of alien wealth. It is, say the imbecile, a 'bastard' language, a 'hybrid' language, and so forth. And thus, for a metaphor, for a name, for a sound, they overlook, as far as depends on *their* will they sign away, the main prerogative and dowry of their mother tongue. (XIV: 150–1)

With due filial respect, and invoking a confusing mixture of familial relations, De Quincey rejects the claim that his 'mother tongue' is a 'bastard'; rather its parents are joined in respectable matrimony, enjoying a 'dowry' of special powers. Through the codes of marriage, he legitimates the 'natural' supremacy of English.

The purity of English is compromised throughout, not only by its 'double-headed origins', but also through the large number of 'borrowed' words it incorporates. De Quincey rationalizes these through the use of a rhetoric of trade: indeed the superiority of English derives from its ability to receive the 'new impressions' of 'a fresh and large infusion of alien wealth'. If England is the market place of the world, the English language is the market place of words. He goes on: 'Let us recognize with thankfulness that fortunate inheritance of collateral wealth which, by inoculating our Anglo-Saxon stem with the mixed dialect of Neustria, laid open an avenue mediately through which the whole opulence of Rome, and ultimately of Grecian, thought plays freely through the pulses of our native English' (XIV: 151). Naturalized through the use of the botanical image of inoculation, language is figured as the instigator of a trade route, through which the products of classical history might be imported into England.

There is another sense in which English operated as the facilitator of trade, of which De Quincey was surely aware. As the most important commodity of export to the colonies, the English language functioned as an instrument of compliance and co-operation, a means of deculturating indigenous peoples, imposing and managing racial inequalities, and thus, indirectly, a tool for procuring materials and cheap labour in the great workshops of the world.

The England that the English language commemorates is the great trading nation, whose wealth and glory comes from its commercial transactions in the world. The point is perhaps a strategic one in 1839, because it refutes Chartist rhetoricians who argued that Britain's greatness derived from its capacity as a *producing* nation.[34]

In 'Style', published the following year, this point is developed further. Now he argues that the precarious state of the nation might be saved through a particular use of language—and the form he prefers is one built on a model of slavery. Embedded in his writings on language we will find a belief that slavery offers a resolution to the problems caused by industrial labour at home, that threaten the fundamental stability of the nation.

Organology and the Defence of Language

There are three things wrong with England, claimed De Quincey wryly, at the beginning of the essay, 'Style': the fashion for wearing turbans, the impoverishment of British music, and the tendency 'to set the matter above the manner, the substance above the external show' (X: 137). The last is the most serious fault, and

---

[34] See Stedman Jones, 'Rethinking Chartism'.

to be witnessed most often in relation to language in an inattention to style. A detailed survey of classical and English literature follows as he expiates upon the deficiencies of contemporary styles of writing and oratory in both eloquence and effect. While in past societies the place of good style was in political debate, now Parliament is preoccupied with the tawdry business of economics, and there are no occasions for the exercise of the skills of fine rhetoric. By implication the new institutional home for good style is literature, and thus it is no surprise that he calls on Wordsworth's 'Essay on Epitaphs'—in which Wordsworth had written that words should be the incarnation rather than the clothing of thought—as the key to good style.[35] Good style for De Quincey occurs when language and thought, words and their referents, enjoy organic cohesion. The idea is at the heart of his theory of the literature of power, and of impassioned prose.

In the context of his previous writings on language, his return to Romantic theories of language and the imagination is surprisingly uncritical. For instance, he writes,

originally, and whilst man was in his primitive condition of simplicity, it must have seemed unnatural, nay an absurd thing to speak in prose. For in those elder days the sole justifying or exciting cases for a public harangue would be cases connected with impassioned motives . . . Hence the necessity that the oracles should be delivered in verse. (X: 171)

The idea that primitive language is poetry because it arose from passion clearly derives from Rousseau. The occasion of this first, impassioned, utterance is the 'public harangue'. This underlines a second point: there is a political project attached to De Quincey's idea of good style, but it is not the one we might expect from this association with Rousseau.[36] Much of the essay is a call for the revival of the art of rhetoric, adumbrated earlier in his review essay of Richard Whately's *Elements of Rhetoric* published in *Blackwood's* in December 1828. Both of these essays express a view that is by now familiar in his writings: that the use of language has

---

[35] Wordsworth, 'Essay on Epitaphs, III', in *The Prose Works*, ed. W. J. B. Owen and J. W. Smyser, 3 vols. (Oxford: OUP, 1974), ii. 84.

[36] Cf. Hugh Cunningham, in 'The Language of Patriotism, 1750–1914', *History Workshop Journal*, 12 (1981), 8–33, for an account of the conservative co-option of Rousseau in 19th-cent. Britain.

deteriorated in the modern world under the pressures of business, industry, and, in particular, the mechanization of the printing press which has led to widespread literacy and the greater availability of reading material. The revival of the art of rhetoric is a way of both defending language against the appalling attacks carried out by modern social and literary subversives, and of maintaining a traditional social order through language use. Thus, in 'Style' we shall see that newspapers are the source of linguistic contamination. Compared with the press of the 1830s, which disseminated political ideas and information to a radical and working-class readership, 'the public harangues' envisioned by Rousseau as the originary moment of language suggested a desirably contained public arena.

If the recourse to Rousseau in this essay appears to suggest an uncharacteristic approval of the association between impassioned language and civil dispute, it does so in order to idealize the imagined disputes of a traditional society in comparison with the anarchic expressions of self-interest that characterize contemporary political life. His praise of Burke as the best of recent rhetoricians brings to mind the distinction that Burke made in the *Reflections on the Revolution in France* (1790) between the silent cattle of tradition, and the grasshopper Jacobins.[37] Burke had in mind the revolutionaries' self-conscious use of rhetoric, which he claimed was noisy and troublesome, but, in his opinion, destined to be ineffective. Following Burke, De Quincey reclaims the art of rhetoric for a conservative politics, claiming that true rhetoric will be, as Burke supposed his language to be, natural, organic, and supportive of a traditional order.[38] In 1841, then, De Quincey can align Rousseau with Burke, and see a primitive language as an emblem of a paternalistic and intransigently hierarchical social organization.

---

[37] See Edmund Burke, *Reflections on the Revolution in France*, ed. C. C. O'Brien (Harmondsworth: Penguin, 1969), 181: 'Because half a dozen grasshoppers under a fern make the field ring with their importunate chink, whilst thousands of great cattle, reposed beneath the shadow of the British oak, chew the cud and are silent, pray do not imagine, that those who make the noise are the only inhabitants of the field.'

[38] On Burke's organicism, see Ronald Paulson, 'Burke's Sublime and the Representation of Revolution', in *Culture and Politics from Puritanism to the Enlightenment*, ed. Perez Zagorin (Berkeley, Calif.: University of California Press, 1980), 244–69.

It is important to bear in mind, however, that De Quincey was not in search of an original language *per se*, but a *style* of language use that recalls this primal state. As Mary Jacobus has demonstrated, this was in the mode of the Romantic desire to maintain the authority of the 'voice of the living Speaker',[39] which resulted in the privileging of the spoken over the written language, and, as she points out, a recurrently articulated anxiety about the effects of literacy. However, for the Romantics, these effects were felt more frequently as philosophical problems of subjectivity, as the worries of a subject faced by an ineluctable abyss of language that had its own histories and meanings. While De Quincey was caught within these Romantic anxieties of influence and determination, as Jacobus and other commentators have usefully shown,[40] for him, concerns about literacy also had direct ramifications within the political and social world. It is important not to underestimate the significance of the political context of De Quincey's work, which was substantially different from his Romantic forebears. Thus when he searched not for an authentic language, but for a style that gave the appearance of one, it was as though he recognized the futility of the Romantic quest, but also its political expediency at the present time. To achieve his objective De Quincey invoked another version of his frequent trope: the organic machine. The work of this machine was, as we shall see, beset with problems which emphasized the difficulty of his political task.

According to De Quincey, the word 'style' had two meanings, but in each case it referred to a system of relations. In the first, 'the narrow meaning', it referred to 'the syntaxis or combination of words into sentences'; the other 'express[es] all possible relations that can arise between thoughts and words—the total effect of a writer as derived from manner' (X: 163). The first meaning thus denoted the relationship between words and other words, the second between words and thoughts. These two definitions

---

[39] H. Blair, *Lectures on Rhetoric and Belles Lettres* (1783), ed. H. F. Harding, 2 vols. (Carbondale, Ill.: Southern Illinois University Press, 1965), ii. 136. Cited by Mary Jacobus, *Romanticism, Writing, and Sexual Difference: Essays on* The Prelude (Oxford: Clarendon Press, 1989), 129. For discussion, see Jacobus, 'The Art of Managing Books: Romantic Prose and the Writing of the Past' in *Romanticism, Writing and Sexual Difference*, 126–58.

[40] See, for instance, Arden Reed, 'Abysmal Influence: Baudelaire, Coleridge, De Quincey, Piranesi, Wordsworth,' *Glyph*, 4 (1978), 188–206.

corresponded with a distinction he made between two 'sciences of style', mechanology and organology: loosely speaking, the former concerned grammar, the latter concerned thoughts. The two were not mutually exclusive, for any piece of language use would have both functions. He compared language with a human body that was organic, in so far as it had organs, and mechanic, in so far as it was exercised: language therefore was the organic machine. Similarly, he wrote, 'the use of words is an organic thing, in so far as language is connected with thoughts, and modified by thoughts. It is a mechanic thing, in so far as words in combination determine or modify each other' (X: 164). Ruled by thought, language was organic; ruled by the laws of language itself, it was mechanic. In this organic scheme, thought was given the absolute priority of the life force of the body. However, although the mechanic functions were as necessary as bones and muscles, they were also dangerous because as words 'determine or modify each other', they tended to make their own meanings independent of the thought that preceded them. Grammar was like an inspirited automaton, capable of usurping organic life and living for itself.

Although mechanic and organic functions were coterminous, the best style was that in which mechanic functions remained minimal and invisible, and thought was conveyed without impediment. Nevertheless there were various modes of 'artificial machinery' for 'maintaining the integrity of the sense against all mistakes of the writer' (X: 165). This amounted to dangerous and paradoxical advice: to annul the effects of machinery, use more machinery; to find the authentic, use the artificial. Among the recommended mechanical aids he listed punctuation, the 'excrescence' of the footnote, and, in the case of the Roman writer, even 'the exquisitely artificial structure of the Latin language' (X: 165). But each carried its own risks. De Quincey's own writing, elaborately footnoted and punctuated, is hardly uncontaminated by mechanical taints, and in these circumstances it is impossible to imagine a style that is.

The full subversive potential of these devices is implied in a discussion of punctuation:

Punctuation . . . was the product of typography . . . Previously a man was driven to depend for his security against misunderstanding upon the pure virtue of his syntax. Miscollocation or dislocation of related words disturbed the whole sense; its least effect was to give *no* sense,—often it gave a dangerous sense. Now, punctuation was an artificial machinery for maintaining the integrity of the sense against all mistakes of the writer; and, as one consequence, it withdrew the energy of men's anxieties from the natural machinery, which lay in just and careful arrangement. (X: 164–5)

If punctuation distracts a writer from the pursuit of a pure organic style, the problems of an unpunctuated style are nevertheless significant: slips in syntax produced either '*no* sense', or at worst, 'a dangerous sense'. However, in a footnote (a dangerous place itself), which he appended to the revised edition of 1859, he wrote of the 'false prejudicating effect' of punctuation which had led lawyers to abandon it altogether:

All punctuation narrows the path, which is else unlimited; and (*by* narrowing it) may chance to guide the reader into the right groove amongst several that are *not* right. But also punctuation has the *effect* very often (and almost always has the power) of biassing and predetermining the reader to an erroneous choice of meaning. (X: 164–5, note)

Every device for containing interpretation lay writing open to even more possibilities of misinterpretation. Formulated for the clarification of authorial meaning, these devices marked only the point at which authorial control receded, giving way to the autonomous work of mechanical language.

The difficulties of organology demonstrate the limits of the organic machine. Indeed they indicate the problems De Quincey faced in trying to establish his ideal social conditions through the effects of language, problems that were not surprising given that in the previous essay he had asserted the separateness of language from consciousness and material conditions. Thus he looked elsewhere for his ideal society. Luckily for De Quincey there was still one residual group of language users untainted by the demands of sophisticated society and mechanized language use: a certain class of women who spoke from pure sentiment. His account of the female speaker, with its emphasis on the excess of feeling, is strikingly similar to that of the primitive man, taken from Rousseau and Herder:

From the greater excitability of females, the superior vivacity of their feelings, they will be liable to more irritations from wounded sensibilities. . . . Now, there is not in the world so certain a guarantee for pure idiomatic diction, without tricks or affectation, as a case of genuine excitement. . . . No woman in this world, under a movement of resentment from a false accusation, or from jealousy, or from confidence betrayed, ever was at leisure to practise vagaries of caprice in the management of her mother tongue. (X: 144–5)

Feminine language thus originated in authentic sentiment and a sense of natural justice. Herder, too, identified the heightened sensitivity that could be witnessed in women, children and the sick as the condition for authenticity in language, claiming that 'they all accomplish a thousand times more than truth itself'.[41] Although decorative, Herder's hyperbole was nevertheless double-edged, and indicated a distrust of sensitive language users of such exaggerated accomplishment that was reminiscent of Rousseau's famous admonition of the deceitful Sophie in *Emile, ou de l'Education* (1762). De Quincey's attitude towards female language users was similarly ambiguous. If women were the best speakers, they were also the worst: the prime offenders of language abuse being women who were professional writers, landladies and apple-sellers. Being a good language user depended on more than gender, but also on education, class and profession: 'if they happen to move in polished circles, or have received a tolerable education, they will speak their native language of necessity with truth and simplicity' (X: 144). Although vulnerable to 'monstrous and fanciful' 'name-inventions', due to strong 'sentiment or romance', these women nevertheless provided the best source of the national language.

In a passage remarkable for its voyeurism, he recommended breaking open mail bags and stealing glances at the intimate correspondence between women:

Would you desire at this day to read our noble language in its native beauty, picturesque from idiomatic propriety, racy in its phraseology, delicate yet sinewy in its composition, steal the mail-bags, and break open all the letters in female handwriting. Three out of four will have been written by that class of women who have the most leisure and the most interest in a correspondence by the post: that class who combine more of intelligence, cultivation, and of thoughtfulness, than any other in Europe—the class of unmarried women above twenty-five—an

---

[41] Herder, in *Two Essays*, 98.

increasing class; who, from mere dignity of character, have renounced all prospects of conjugal and parental life, rather than descend into habit unsuitable to their birth. (X: 145)

With its 'native beauty', being 'picturesque from . . . propriety', 'racy', 'delicate' and 'sinewy', idiom is equated with sexuality, and De Quincey becomes a peeping Tom taking pleasure in his illicit gaze. In accordance with the codes of feminine respectability, these women are chaste, for the purity of their language becomes an aspect of their 'honour'. Linguistic terms are added to the familiar mixture of the social and sexual, so that a social descent, a sexual 'fall', and a deterioration of idiom would be one and the same event. The association of a loss of sexual honour and a fall in standards of language use resonates throughout the essay. As the Romantics had located a 'fall' of language with the advent of writing, for De Quincey too a 'fall' took place, not with writing itself, but specifically with print, publication and circulation of literature.[42] Thus he focused on women—lady novelists and female readers of newspapers—who lost their honour like the fallen forms of literature; merely by association, female readers and writers circulated like printed works and prostitutes.

The disease that threatened language was 'bookish idiom': 'This is one form of the evil impressed upon our style by journalism: a dire monotony of bookish idiom has encrusted and stiffened all native freedom of expression, like some scaly leprosy or elephantiasis, barking and hide-binding the fine natural pulses of the elastic flesh' (X: 149). 'Bookish idiom' attacks 'native freedom of expression', the legacy of the pure 'mother tongue' that is embedded in the letters of the uncontaminated language users. The carriers of this journalistic disease are old mangy women. 'Every old woman in the nation now reads a vast miscellany in one volume royal octavo', he tells us. 'Any old apple-woman' might regularly use phrases such as 'I will *avail myself* of your kindness' (X: 149). The symptom of their contamination is a large

---

[42] On Rousseau and the fall of language, see Jacques Derrida, *Of Grammatology*, trans. Gayatri Chakravorty Spivak (Baltimore, Md.: Johns Hopkins University Press, 1976), 165–268, and Paul de Man, *Allegories of Reading: Figural Language in Rousseau, Nietzche, Rilke, and Proust* (New Haven, Conn.: Yale University Press, 1979), 135–59. See also *Romanticism and Language*, ed. Arden Reed (London: Methuen, 1984).

and pretentious vocabulary; and it is contagious, for their logorrhoea is a kind of gonorrhoea that threatens to infiltrate the once chaste body politic. It is not the misuse of words that affronts De Quincey, but instead the accuracy and accomplishment of these precocious language users:

> But observe, as a point which took away any gleam of consolation from the case, the total absence of all *malaprop* picturesqueness that might have defeated its deadly action upon the nervous system. No; it is due to the integrity of *her* disease, and to the contemplation of *our* suffering, that we should attest the unimpeachable correctness of her words, and of the syntax by which she connected them. (X: 152)

Lacking '*malaprop* picturesqueness', the new literate working-class woman resisted her traditional role as the butt of comic opportunities. What concerned De Quincey was the unprecedented and, in his eyes, excessive education of the working class, a point he returned to again and again in his attacks on newspapers and the press. Like whores, newspapers respected no social boundaries, and spread their contaminated knowledge greedily and unreservedly. 'The evil of this,' he wrote, sustaining a vocabulary of the morally inflected disease, 'as regards the quality of knowledge communicated, admits of no remedy. Public business, in its whole unwieldy compass, must always form the subject of these daily chronicles' (X: 149). A politically informed public was as irredeemable as a venereally infected, disease-ridden people.

This is the context of organology. Its political programme was redemptive and nostalgic, an attempt to stop the pollution of social disorder both represented and inspired by the unprecedented spread of literacy. When De Quincey recalled Wordsworth's distinction between language as the dress of thoughts and the incarnation of thoughts, he surely remembered that it was as the dress of thoughts that language was 'a counter-spirit, unremittingly and noiselessly at work to derange, to subvert, to lay waste, to vitiate, and to dissolve'.[43] Writing in 1840, De Quincey saw a direct analogy between these linguistic categories, which Wordsworth had invoked to engage with ontological problems of

---

[43] Wordsworth, *Prose Works*, ii. 84.

subjectivity,[44] and groups of language users that existed, or had existed, or might have existed, in the social world. For De Quincey, the counter-spirit was an unruly mob of bad stylists subverting and dissolving social hierarchies and traditions.

When De Quincey defined the sciences of organology and mechanology, he used some striking and unusual terms: 'By organic, we mean that which, being acted upon, reacts, and which propagates the communicated power without loss. By mechanic, that which, being impressed with motion, cannot throw it back without loss, and therefore soon comes to an end' (X: 163–4). Invoking economies of loss and renewal, and notions of power and motion, style was like a force of energy, that in the first case was renewable, in the second extinguished. The vocabulary incorporated a range of scientific referents from botany to physics, which added a sense of empirical certitude to his argument. It also invoked a context of industry and technology that De Quincey, with his dislike of the mechanic, wished to avoid by promoting 'organology'. More than this, however, as he emphasized the idea of energy and power, the coining of the terms organology and mechanology concealed an argument about two kinds of labour: on the one hand, labour that was always renewable without loss, on the other, labour that incurred loss. That is to say, organic style was the style of labour under feudalism, or in a more readily available contemporary form, perhaps slave labour; such labour was always renewable, and organic in the sense that the slave and his labour were identified as one. Mechanic style was like the labour of the industrial working class that not only incurred loss in the form of remuneration or wages, but also the considerable losses of social stability as the working class, identifying itself as a particular class with shared interests sought political representation for those interests, and spoke about them loudly and unremittingly in the press.

It was not merely rhetorical prowess that attracted De Quincey to the great orators of Greece and Rome. Supported by the labour of slaves and the wealth of invaded colonies, he saw these as ideal societies in which orators could address themselves calmly to great moral and political issues of democracy and justice in the

---

[44] See Frances Ferguson, *Wordsworth: Language as Counter-Spirit* (New Haven, Conn.: Yale University Press, 1977), 28–34.

luxury of an economically and politically stable society. In the essay on 'Rhetoric' (1828), he claimed, 'the case of Roman rhetoric, . . . proclaims at least a quiescent state of the public mind, unoccupied with daily novelties, and at leisure from the agitations of eternal change' (X: 97). Supported by 'the plunder of conquest', Rome was free of economic problems of business, the rantings of an unruly proletariat, the disease of bookishness. Organology, then, was like slavery because it liberated thought from the encumbrances of language. No Hegelianism this; the ideal organologist was a master uncompromised by the bondage of words.

We might add organology to the history of the language, as another of the responses to Chartism that Crowley discussed. For this is a use of language which maintained social hierarchies, a use of language dependent on the silent submission of the working class. However, organology alone, as De Quincey knew, was ineffective. It only worked when those hierarchies were established and secure. In the modern mechanized, industrialized, and reluctantly democratized world, organology was not much more than a turban in polite society; a sign of a certain longing, a certain ideological commitment, a stylistic identity with a certain class.

De Quincey did not believe that cultural processes alone were sufficient for enforcing and policing the society he desired. There is a strong thrust in his writing that suggests that he would like to evade language altogether, and find more direct means of social control through forms of physical coercion. Paradoxically, this desire is at the heart of the form of representation—the aesthetic of force—that characterizes a large part of his writing, and it is this that is the subject of the next chapter.

5

The Violence of Aesthetics and the Comedy of Murder

> The dwarf Opium-Eater ... lives here in lodgings, with a wife and children living or starving off the scanty produce of his scribble, far off in Westmorland. He carries a laudanum bottle in his pocket; and the venom of a wasp in his heart. ... If I could find him, it would give me a pleasure to procure him one substantial beef-steak before he dies.
>
> Thomas Carlyle, 1829[1]

In the last chapter, we saw how De Quincey considered the English language to offer some source of order and cohesion in the disintegrating body of the nation. Mooting a particular use of language as a civilizing and socializing force, he recognized the ideological force of representations, their stabilizing function within the social order.

If De Quincey saw inscribed in the English language the power of the state over the populace, elsewhere he was preoccupied with another form of power in its relation to representation: the self-empowerment that is to be gained and lost through one's own acts of expression and self-representation. The dilemmas that result from this lead to his most compelling narratives—and some of his best jokes. Such as, for instance, the one about the transvestite nun, a woman imprisoned in the trajectories of her own misrepresentations whose story he told in 'The Spanish Military Nun' (1847). In this playful translation of the picaresque adventures of Catalina de Erauso, recounted first earlier that year in the *Revue des Deux Mondes*, the nun, disguised as a soldier, inadvertently committed daring and violent crimes, and unwittingly se-

---

[1] Cited in *Thomas De Quincey: An English Opium-Eater*, Introduction and notes by Robert Woof (Cumbria: Trustees of Dove Cottage, 1985), 96.

duced ladies unsuspecting her true sex.[2] A victim of circumstances beyond her control, Catalina is destined to a life evading the consequences of acts that are of her own accidental making. Her fate is analogous to that of a misread book that must bear the responsibilities of others' misprisions.

The idea that a subject's agency would be compromised by the promiscuities of representations had many sources for De Quincey, but one was undoubtedly a network of problems that emerged from Kant's transcendental philosophy, and in particular his work on aesthetics, *The Critique of Judgement*. For Kant, aesthetics completed his philosophical system, mediating between the separate realms of cognition and ethics; the faculty of pleasure formed a bridge over the 'great gulf' that separated understanding and desire.[3] However as Lacoue-Labarthe and Nancy have argued, rather than a bridge, the third critique in fact opened up an abyss; they observe that the subject, who functioned as the lynchpin of Kant's system, was irredeemably fractured by the incompatible demands that it made, and thus the system could never achieve the unity it required.[4]

In this chapter I will argue that much of De Quincey's work can be understood as a response to the problems of subjectivity that are thrown up by Kant's transcendental system. However, this situation is complicated by the fact that De Quincey, at one with many of his contemporaries, also held industry and capital responsible for the problems experienced by the subject, who always had to submit to the greater powers of machinery and the market. Thus the troubling implications of Kantian philosophy, in which aesthetic representation was offered as insufficient resolution to the problems of the subject, were always enmeshed, indeed identified with, those of industrial production and its social consequences. Thus we will find strongly articulated in De

---

[2] De Quincey's 'The Spanish Military Nun' was first published as 'The Nautico-Military Nun of Spain' in *Tait's*, NS, 14 (May, June, July 1847), 324–33, 369–76, and 431–40. On its sources, see Albert Goldman, *The Mine and the Mint: Sources for the Writings of Thomas De Quincey* (Carbondale, Ill.: Southern Illinois University Press, 1965), 129.

[3] Immanuel Kant, *The Critique of Judgement*, trans. J. C. Meredith (Oxford: Clarendon Press, 1928), 14.

[4] Philippe Lacoue-Labarthe and Jean-Luc Nancy, *The Literary Absolute: The Theory of Literature in German Romanticism*, trans. Philip Barnard and Cheryl Lester (Albany, NY: State University of New York Press, 1988), 29–30.

Quincey's work the sense that if one could control the meanings of one's acts of representation, one might control the social world at large.

However, De Quincey is notoriously the least empowered and most frustrated of writers of the period, continually inscribing in his lengthy and digressive writings an inability to take control of his pen or his life. This aspect of his style, his 'wandering musical variations upon the theme . . . those parasitical thoughts, feelings, digressions, which climb up with bells and blossoms round the arid stock' (C, 94), have been the focus of much critical attention. But there is another side to his style that demands consideration. Another aesthetic is at work alongside this, a form of representation that seeks control for the subject no matter the cost, an aesthetic of force that inscribes only the will of the writing subject.

This structure of representation replicates his political desires, in which the social body would be controlled despite the clamourings of the mob and the compromises inflicted on the state by liberal reformers wishing to do away with the institutions that in De Quincey's eyes, made his country great. Diminutions of the nation, such as the abolition of slavery or the separation of Church and State, happened in a context in which competing representations—those of the radical press, for instance—circulated too freely; a context in which even the right of political representation would be claimed by the working class. The aesthetic of force was thus a mode of representation constituted in order to block the promiscuous circulation of representations; it would provide a context in which a man could say what he meant and mean what he said without interruption from below or wilful misinterpretation.

In this chapter I will trace the development of this aesthetic by focusing first on De Quincey's gothic fictions of the 1830s.[5] 'The Household Wreck' (1838) is particularly interesting here because anxieties about lost agency in the social world are expressed in terms of a man's inability to control the misrepresentations of his wife which circulate freely with tragic consequences. The private realm of the family is seen as a special but threatened enclave in

[5] On the writing of De Quincey's fictions, see Edmund Baxter, *De Quincey's Art of Autobiography* (Edinburgh: Edinburgh University Press, 1990), 93–6.

which a man may enjoy the control that is beyond him in the
public sphere.

In an earlier story, *Klosterheim* (1832), the reconstitution of the
family had been presented as the basis of social order. However,
what is significant in *Klosterheim* is the curious way in which this
order is implemented. The family functions as a spectacle of social
order, and, rather than an organic emanation from the social
body, order is imposed from elsewhere. This can be identified as
the structure of the aesthetic of force: representation is a tyrannical spectacle that commands a repetition of itself in the social
world. The clearest statement of this aesthetic is to be found in De
Quincey's free translation of Lessing's *Laocoön* (1826), but the
most complex is in the essays 'On Murder considered as one of
the Fine Arts' (1827, 1839, 1854). Here murder is offered as a mode
of protecting a social context in which agency might be retained.
To consider murder as a fine art, however, is a joke at Kant's
expense, for within the sphere of aesthetics, the empowerment
that is claimed through the act of murder is dissipated. Kant's
moment of aesthetics generates in De Quincey a moral panic, and
he delineates instead a form of representation that replicates the
domination of murder: rather than considering murder as an
aesthetic thing, as he claims to do, he implies an aesthetic that is
a murderous thing. The power relations that this aesthetic establishes mirror those required by the English language if it is to
function as a civilizing force. We might say then that De
Quincey's aesthetic of force is his crude account of the process of
ideology.

Kant's Critique of Judgement

In order to understand De Quincey's aesthetics in the context of
Kant's transcendental philosophy, we need to return briefly to
Kant's system, which defined the great philosophical project of
the nineteenth century, namely the attempt to reconcile notions of
free will and determinism. A cursory account is all that is required at this stage.[6] In the *Critique of Pure Reason*, Kant explained

[6] The most useful accounts of Kant's system are Gilles Deleuze, *Kant's Critical
Philosophy: The Doctrine of the Faculties*, trans. Hugh Tomlinson and Barbara
Habberjam (London: Athlone Press, 1984); Ernst Cassirer, *Kant's Life and Thought*,

that we are able to know the empirical world because natural phenomena are the effects determined by a transcendental principle [God]. But the question posed by the *Critique of Practical Reason* was, how can we make ethical choices if we exist in a world determined by some prior principle? For we must assume that, as ethical beings, we are free to exercise the faculty of desire, which is grounded in Reason. The concept of determination that underpins cognition, it seems, is anathematic to the realm of Reason. In Kant's words:

Concepts of nature contain the ground of all theoretical cognition *a priori* and rest . . . upon the legislative authority of understanding.—The concept of freedom contains the ground of all sensuously unconditioned practical precepts *a priori*, and rests upon that of reason. Both faculties, therefore, . . . have . . . their own peculiar jurisdiction in the matter of their content.[7]

In the *Critique of Judgement*, Kant identified a middle ground between them in the faculty of pleasure. Aesthetic judgements, he claimed, are disinterested: in them, the subject considers a phenomenon apart from its cause which determines its place in the empirical world. That is to say, it is perceived from the point of view of *form*. A representation (*Vorstellung*) in nature and art that is judged to be beautiful has within it a harmony of form that satisfies the mind and liberates the imagination to the pleasures of free play. By a kind of projection, the imagination sees within the form of the object a freedom that mirrors the freedom of the ethical subject. The final harmony of the beautiful object suggests that there is an end in nature that conforms to the ends of Reason, and implies a continuity between Pure and Practical Reason.

This continuity depends on the perceptions of the subject. But for all this, the position of the subject is complicated by the fact that aesthetic judgements are necessarily both subjective and universal. They are subjective because in essence they are descriptions of the subject's feelings about objects rather than statements about qualities in the objects themselves; 'so purely subjective'

trans. James Haden (New Haven, Conn.: Yale University Press, 1981); Donald W. Crawford, *Kant's Aesthetic Theory* (Madison, Wis.: University of Wisconsin Press, 1974), and Terry Eagleton, *The Ideology of the Aesthetic* (Oxford: Blackwell, 1990), 70–101.

[7] Kant, *Critique of Judgement*, 15.

that they are unaffected by idiosyncracy or prejudice and are thus universal.[8] It is this that allows Kant to presume the notion of a community of taste,[9] that supplies a means of integrating the individual into a group. The aesthetic is thus ideologically effective,[10] but none the less constructed on the basis of a subject that is at once all-important and totally effaced. Lacoue-Labarthe and Nancy describe the subject of Kantian aesthetics as a convenience of the system, a point within its logic that is emptied of any content or coherence of its own.[11]

Such problems occur within aesthetic judgements when the formal harmony of the beautiful object lends a sense of completion that allows the subject to perceive an independence and consequent freedom which replicates its own. But when confronted by an object that is formless and chaotic, the predicament of the subject is acute. The aesthetic judgement that responds to such situations is that of the sublime. For Kant there are two types of sublime, the dynamic and the mathematic: the first occurs in response to objects of immense power, the second to those of inestimable size or quantity, but they function similarly.[12] In the mathematical sublime, for instance, the subject encounters an object of infinite proportions, and in the confusion caused by his inability to comprehend the infinite and unrepresentable object, he loses his sense of himself. Thrown into chaos, the boundaries of his subjectivity crumble as he recognizes the limits of his own imagination.

At this point, however, there is what Neil Hertz describes as a moment of blockage, a point of recovery, at which, acknowledging the limits of his imagination, he glimpses the idea of Reason existing beyond himself, and yet nevertheless existing in Nature.[13]

---

[8] Eagleton, *Ideology*, 93.

[9] On the *sensus communis*, see Kant, *Critique of Judgement*, 150–4.

[10] Eagleton argues that the aesthetic, since it proposes referential statements concealing feeling, is similar to ideology itself. Thus, he claims, aesthetics is both the condition of, and the aporia within, bourgeois society.

[11] *The Literary Absolute*, 31–3. Cf. Eagleton, 'The subject lives . . . at the aporetic intersection of [understanding and reason], where blindness and insight, emancipation and subjection, are mutually constitutive' (80).

[12] See Kant, *Critique of Judgement*, 90–117.

[13] Hertz, 'The Notion of Blockage in the Literature of the Sublime' in *The End of the Line: Essays on Psychoanalysis and the Sublime* (New York: Columbia University Press, 1985), 40–60. Cf. Deleuze: 'When imagination is confronted with its limit by something which goes beyond it in all respects it goes beyond its own limit itself,

The sublime thus invokes a 'discordant accord'.[14] In the recovering moment of self-consciousness, the subject moves into a 'supersensible substrate', so that he is able to represent to himself his relation to the infinite. That is, he can rationalize his inability to comprehend by representing this lack. The sublime brings about the ascendancy of the rational over the sensual, but it cannot compensate for the subject's fundamental deficiencies that are exposed in the face of the unrepresentable object. The sublime is empowering in the sense that it enables the reinstatement of subjectivity in the wake of its dissolution, but only through the inscription of lack in the representation of the subject.

Order and coherence in the philosophical system are always at the expense of order and coherence in the subject. It is this that lays fertile soil for the creative work of Romanticism. The Romantic fixation with questions of subjectivity, the overweening powers of the poet's imagination, the self that can create and devour whole worlds—all these familiar motifs of Romanticism could be seen as compensation for this 'weakening of the subject'.[15] It is also in this philosophical context that autobiography as a genre takes root. De Quincey's own autobiographical obsessions, his repeated return, between *Confessions* and *Suspiria*, to earlier and still earlier moments of infancy can be understood in the context of the Kantian sublime: confronted by the formlessness of his life, he is compelled to return to the earliest point in a vain endeavour to find order and meaning. On each return, however, he is always riven by the competing demands of knowledge and desire, the unencompassable rift between himself as a determined being and a rational, free subject, between the written and the writing self.

As I have already pointed out, De Quincey frequently articulated his anxieties concerning lost agency in the context of scenarios of mechanical reproduction, as in the Piranesi episode in the *Confessions* discussed in Chapter 4. Indeed this is a recurrent theme of Victorian literature: writers from Karl Marx to Charles Dickens and Thomas Carlyle complained of the suffering of indi-

---

admittedly in a negative fashion, by representing to itself the inaccessibility of the rational Idea, and by making this very inaccessibility something which is present in sensible nature.' *Kant's Critical Philosophy*, 51.

[14] Deleuze, *Kant's Critical Philosophy*, 51.
[15] Lacoue-Labarthe and Nancy, *The Literary Absolute*, 31.

viduals under the new industrial modes of production in similar terms. Frequently the subject's relation to industry and capital was expressed in terms of the sublime, thus compounding a coincidence between philosophical and social critiques that are otherwise distinct. Faced by the inexhaustible production of machinery and an endlessly self-motivating economy, the subject is confounded by his inability to comprehend the magnitude of industry and capital.

For Marx, the analogy stopped here, for the only satisfactory resolution of an individual's alienation was the collective overthrow of the entire system. But for writers such as Carlyle, another kind of reconciliation was possible. In line with the Kantian sublime, Carlyle located a moment of blockage and recovery, that delivered the individual from his modern distress. The locus of this moment of self-consciousness would be aesthetic representation. Thus in his essay, 'Signs of the Times' (1829), Carlyle figured the problems induced by mechanical production in terms of a proliferation of systems of symbolic representation in the fields of politics, religion, education, and so on. These could only be alleviated when the subject took stock of himself: 'To reform a world, to reform a nation, no wise man will undertake; and all but foolish men know, that the only solid, though a far slower reformation, is what each begins and perfects on *himself*.'[16] Carlyle was writing in the context of agitation for parliamentary reform, and his recourse to the individual self, whose interstices would be explored in the space of literature, marks a refusal of the democratizing spirit of the reform movement.

Similarly, Arthur Hallam, in his 1831 review of Tennyson's *Poems, Chiefly Lyrical* (1830) saw the new poetry of sensation as the place for restoring order to the decaying body politic in which '[t]he whole system no longer worked harmoniously, . . . but there arose a violent and unusual action in the several component functions, each for itself, all striving to reproduce the regular power which the whole had once enjoyed.'[17] The poetry of sensa-

---

[16] Carlyle, *Selected Writings*, ed. Alan Shelston (Harmondsworth: Penguin, 1971), 85.

[17] Hallam, 'On Some Characteristics of Modern Poetry,' *Englishman's Magazine* 1 (Aug. 1831), 616–28. Reprinted in *Victorian Scrutinies. Reviews of Poetry 1830–1870*, ed. Isobel Armstrong (London: Athlone Press, 1972), 84–101 (91).

tion offered a moment of recovery that would repair at least the individual in the face of the sublimely chaotic system. For both Carlyle and Hallam, restoration of the subject and the system depended on the projection of aspects of the individual subject onto the social system: for Carlyle this would be the spiritual life of the individual, for Hallam, his sentient body.

De Quincey subscribed to similar beliefs: the literature of power, as we have seen, was developed as a refuge from capital and industry. However, as I argued in Chapter 3, the literature of power is a complex and profoundly compromised category, administering a loss of self and expunging of personality that always takes place in the realm of the aesthetic. In De Quincey's gothic tales this loss of agency is the source of terror that constitutes the horror of the story. But another aesthetic will emerge in them to act against the problems presented by the Kantian scheme.

The Family and the Aesthetic of Force

Amid the flow of capital there was one place in which a man could still possess and exercise agency: this was the family. As Marx and Engels wrote in the *German Ideology*, in the family a man could own and command his wife and children as his slaves.[18] Indeed, Walter Benjamin has argued, the thick, lush fabrics that draped the interiors of the Victorian home demonstrated a man's power within his own private space. The soft interiors of the bourgeois home provided surfaces on which the inhabitants could display and confirm their agency. Benjamin writes, 'Living means leaving traces. In the interior, these were stressed. Coverings and antimacassars, boxes and casings, were devised in abundance, in which the traces of everyday objects were moulded. The resident's own traces were also moulded in the interior.'[19] The bourgeois home provided a context in which the very act of living was represented at the moment of its happening, supplying a man with a sense of control over his immediate circumstances.

---

[18] 'Private Property and Communism' in *The German Ideology*, ed. C. J. Arthur (London: Lawrence & Wishart, 1970), 52–7.
[19] Walter Benjamin, *Charles Baudelaire: A Lyric Poet in the Era of High Capitalism*, trans. Harry Zohn (London: New Left Review, 1983), 169.

His life assumed meaning since every action had a direct material consequence: its inscription in his furnishings. If the products of his labour outside the home were put into circulation, dispersed in the flow of exchange, in the home his very being made an effect that was always visible, for his agency was represented and constantly on display.

The need for these direct displays of presence indicates the precarious nature of the control that was to be gained in the home, for the family was always under threat from the public sphere, the world outside. It is hardly surprising that the recurrent theme of Victorian novels was the imminent breakdown of the family.[20] De Quincey's gothic fictions are no exception in that they too are preoccupied with the vulnerability of the domestic enclave. In his short melodrama, 'The Household Wreck, or the Juggernaut of Social Life', the narrator's domestic idyll is dramatically disrupted when his wife is wrongly implicated in the theft of some lace.[21] As the plot unfolds, it is clear that the woman has been duped by a lascivious shopkeeper who plans to blackmail her into submission to his lecherous desires through a brush with the law. The case, however, exceeds the shopkeeper's control, and an incident that was meant merely to scare and humiliate a respectable wife results in her long-term imprisonment, during which the narrator suffers a long illness, his baby son dies, and, after her escape from prison, the wife also dies.[22]

---

[20] On the family and the novel, see Nancy Armstrong, *Desire and Domestic Fiction: A Political History of the Novel* (Oxford and New York: Oxford University Press, 1987), ch. 2.

[21] According to W. J. B. Owen, the story is based on the case of a Mrs Perrot, who was similarly charged with shoplifting in Somerset in 1799. See W. J. B. Owen, 'De Quincey and Shoplifting,' *Wordsworth Circle*, 21/2 (1990), 72–6.

[22] There are a number of interesting readings of 'The Household Wreck': V. A. De Luca, in *Thomas De Quincey: The Prose of Vision* (Toronto: University of Toronto Press, 1980), reads the story as a tragedy of 'human impotence' (52); Grevel Lindop, in 'Innocence and Revenge: The Problem of De Quincey's Fiction' in *Thomas De Quincey: Bicentenary Studies*, ed., Robert L. Snyder (Norman, Okla.: University of Oklahoma Press, 1985), 213–39, provides a biographical reading, exploring the point raised by a number of commentators, that the story coincided with the death of De Quincey's own wife; see also Eve Kosofsky Sedgwick, *The Coherence of Gothic Conventions* (1976; repr. London: Macmillan, 1986), 50–1, 77–82, which presents a psychoanalytic reading of the text in the context of a discussion of De Quincey's gothic as an exploration of repression, in which the repressed material is an anxiety concerning the arbitrariness of language.

The story begins with the pessimistic truism that 'to be weak is to be miserable', where strong means the possibility of taking control amid the never-ending stream of life's 'mutabilities'. The greatest weakness of all, however, is to assume that one can take control, for no one can evade the wheel of the juggernaut, the social system, or the flow of capital, that stops for no one, rich or poor.[23] 'This trite but unwearying theme,' he writes,

this impassioned commonplace of humanity, is the subject in every age of variation without end, from the poet, the rhetorician, the fabulist, the moralist, the divine, and the philosopher. All, amidst the sad vanity of their sighs and groans, labour to put on record and to establish this monotonous complaint, which needs not other record or evidence than those very sighs and groans. (XII: 157–8)

All writing encodes nothing more than man's inability to command the external world. This is a version of the sublime, but one in which the individual is overwhelmed by his own incapacity to take control. Discourses from poetry to philosophy proliferate, but each one inscribes nothing more than man's impotence. 'The Household Wreck' is such a document, for it can encode only the narrator's powerlessness. But in this case, the man's predicament is exacerbated by the woman—the impossible object of his representation.

This is a tale of sexual harassment, but more particularly it is a story of the systematic and varied misrepresentations of a woman who never corresponds to the definitions attributed to her. Grevel Lindop has noted that De Quincey was fascinated by physically large women, but in this story Agnes is a big woman whose power is consistently withdrawn from her.[24] Referring to her large stature, De Quincey writes that 'though in the first order a tall woman, yet . . . she seemed to the random sight as little above ordinary height' (XII: 165). If to strangers she appears 'command-

---

[23] The *Juggernaut* was the Hindu god whose enormous car was dragged before processions as devotees threw themselves beneath its wheels, to be crushed to death. De Quincey's figurative use of *juggernaut*, as an institution in which individual agency is lost, predates the example from 1854 which is cited in *OED* as its first use.

[24] Lindop, *The Opium-Eater: A Life of Thomas De Quincey* (Oxford: OUP, 1985), 327.

ing,' to her husband she possesses a 'childlike innocence' and 'feminine timidity'. She is the perfect wife, the beautiful, de-sexualized child-woman, who '[in] perfect womanhood . . . retained a most childlike expression of countenance, so even then in absolute childhood she put forward the blossoms and the dignity of a woman'. Neither child nor woman but a mixture of both, her most striking feature is her unstable identity, which gives the sense that she is always transgressive and disruptive. As the narrator constantly refers to her as his Eve, once even his Pandora, he ominously misses the implications of her less than perfect mythic sisters.

In the power relations of the family, the man's inability to represent his wife becomes his inability to control her; this power is lost entirely when she enters the marketplace. Described as a child in the home, she appears sexless; but in the outside world, she is attributed a rampant and uncontrollable sexuality that is desired by all men and possessed by none. The shopkeeper's trick, which aims to harness the seductive commodity that she so unwittingly flaunts, fails because his misrepresentation is circulated publicly. As the woman is taken into circulation and is misrepresented by the husband, the shopkeeper, and the law, the husband loses all semblance of agency, relinquishing himself to fate and the prophecies of a Hungarian fortuneteller. Finally Agnes is imprisoned, and we have the feeling that this is as much for her transgressive nature as for her part in an alleged crime. When her husband visits her in prison, he finds,

> her beautiful long auburn hair had escaped from its confinement, and was floating over the table and her own person. She took no notice of the disturbance made by our entrance, did not turn, did not raise her head, nor make an effort to do so, nor by any sign whatever intimate that she was conscious of our presence . . . Her breathing, which had been like that of sinless infancy, was now frightfully short and quick; she seemed not properly to breathe, but to gasp. (XII: 209–10)

Sexuality and madness combine as her unbound hair is a sign that marks her unbridled passion, released as she escapes the confines of her socialization. Like that of Bertha Mason in *Jane Eyre*, Agnes's madness is a visible indication of her active sexuality; having lost her state of childlike innocence, Agnes must gasp and pant like an aroused woman.[25] Although guilty of no indiscretion, Agnes has become a fallen woman, for her sexuality has been acknowledged and publicly circulated. If in the family the husband's control was gained only through the effacement of her sexuality, the public acknowledgement of her sexuality suggests the possibility of a promiscuity that is the fundamental threat to the family. The only control that remains is her imprisonment, a physical incarceration that is in fact more effective than the restraints of the family.

There are thus two points to be drawn from this story: first, the man loses agency when representations of his wife are removed from the private sphere and brought into public circulation, when he no longer enjoys the control that is afforded by the marks of presence available in the home; and second, it is the woman, whom he is never able accurately to define or represent, who implicitly causes this breakdown of family life. Agnes is certainly not the only literary woman to threaten a man's agency, but the significant point about this scenario is the way in which representation and control are so closely allied. The family is to be sustained in order to protect the context in which a man can make his mark. But the subtext of 'The Household Wreck' is that the family is a hopelessly vulnerable institution.

The family plays a crucial function in De Quincey's earlier novel, *Klosterheim, or the Masque*, published in 1832. This is the most sustained of his gothic stories, and is interesting because it dramatizes the consolidation of the family as a social unit as the means of re-establishing public order in a time of war and general chaos. The title of the novel, *Klosterheim*, which is also the name of the city in which the story takes place, means literally the cloister-home, or the home as a sacred place, and underlines the significance that the domestic sphere will hold. Placing such emphasis on the family is hardly extraordinary. What is significant is the way in which the idea of the family is used to impose order as an act of force rather than of consent.

---

[25] On Bertha Mason, see Sandra Gilbert and Susan Gubar, *The Madwoman in the Attic: The Woman Writer and the Nineteenth-Century Imagination* (New Haven, Conn.: Yale University Press, 1979), 356–62, and Elaine Showalter, *A Literature of Their Own* (London: Virago, 1982), 118–22. On the collusions between the constructions of femininity and madness, see Elaine Showalter, *The Female Malady: Women, Madness and English Culture 1830–1980* (London: Virago, 1987).

The story is set in the south of Germany during the Thirty Years' War (1618–48). The ancient city of Klosterheim is besieged on all sides: the arrival of Swedish troops is imminent, but the citizens of Klosterheim fear also that their imposter ruler, the Landgrave, will betray them to the enemy. The hero of the novel, Maximilian, disguised as a Masque, carries out a campaign of terror which forces the enemies to give way. Maximilian is revealed as the true Landgrave of Klosterheim, and the imposter dies of a nervous illness, having mistakenly condemned his own daughter to death. The events of the novel are recognizably gothic: military conflicts, whose aims and causes are never clarified, are exacerbated by civil disturbances as wild bandits lurk in the secret corridors of ancient gothic buildings and the dark corners of forests, and insidious foreigners scheme and politic. Such events form an unsettling backdrop to the appearances of the Masque. For most of the novel the Masque appears to defy the laws of nature, appearing as if from nowhere to haunt the inhabitants of Klosterheim; its silent footsteps tread a path of murder and destruction leaving only cryptic notes as a memorial of its presence. Only in the heavy-handed final chapter, when the events of the novel are brought to an abrupt close, is the identity of the Masque revealed.

Throughout the novel, attention is focused on architectural imagery, and the home as an architectural space. Outside the city walls lies the dangerous forest from which the city must be protected. The forest is represented as forming another kind of architecture, with ubiquitous 'alleys, arched high overhead, and resembling the aisles of a cathedral, . . . stretching away apparently without end, but more and more obscure, until impenetrable blackness terminated the long vista' (XII: 25). At all costs, the home must be protected from the encroachment of the sprawling architecture of the gothic. The suspense of the novel is thus realized in the various attacks on homes that abound. These range from the invasion of family hearths by the supernatural Masque, to the displacement of narrative attention from cosy domestic buildings to unwieldy gothic structures, such as castles, abbeys, abandoned palaces, and a network of secret tunnels, and the grotesque perversion of the domestic interior by events and images that turn the familiar and comforting into the horrific and threatening.

In time-honoured tradition, the plot is resolved when Maximilian marries his lover, the beautiful and noble Paulina, 'who stood equally related to the Imperial house and to that of her lover' (XII: 153). This is not merely a love match, for Paulina's royal status satisfies obscure laws of dynastic inheritance, resolving external conflict as well as re-establishing domestic harmony. The novel betrays an unusual concern for reconciling public and private spheres, for it is the relation between the two that lies at the heart of this text. The private world of the family is offered as a model for social order, but the implementation of this model is troubling. There are two points in the novel at which we can observe the model in operation, and these provide a dramatization of the aesthetic of force.

The first point occurs in the opening pages of the novel. A picture is presented of all-encompassing public disorder; the specificities of the conflict are never given, as all differences seem to be erased in the face of total chaos:

[the] system of warfare [which] now swept over Germany in full career, threatening soon to convert its vast central provinces—so recently blooming Edens of peace and expanding prosperity—into a howling wilderness; and which had already inverted immense tracts into one universal aceldama or human shambles, reviving to the recollection at every step the extent of past happiness in the endless memorials of its destruction. (XII: 5)

In this scene the differences between factions are overlooked: it is a 'system', spreading limitless chaos. However this system of decay is not dissimilar to the former 'system' of prosperity that it displaces: the 'blooming Edens' of 'expanding prosperity' turn into a 'howling wilderness' in an inversion that turns one positive totalizing system into its antithesis. In fact, the two appear to merge into each other, as the negative always signifies its opposite: as it 'revives . . . recollections' of former prosperity, destruction represents the lack of past happiness, which in its turn becomes a 'memorial' to destruction, a kind of representation of destruction. In this circular process of signification, the terms of order (prosperity) and disorder have no meaning outside each other and tend to become conflated. By merging opposites, the war brings not just physical destruction but an epistemological crisis as well.

The intervention of the domestic scene in the narrative presages a change in the situation. Harsh weather conditions force people to retreat into their families, and the consequent domestic pleasures arouse 'the natural hopefulness of the human heart' for the prospect of 'permanent pacification' (XII: 6).

Winter, which by its peculiar severity had created the apparent necessity for an armistice, brought many household pleasures in its train—associated immemorially with that season in all northern climates. The cold which had casually opened a path to more distant hopes was also for the present moment a screen between themselves and the enemy's sword. And thus it happened that the same season which held out a not improbable picture of final restoration, however remote, to public happiness, promised them a certain foretaste of this blessing in the immediate security of their homes. (XII: 6)

The cold acts as a 'screen' in a number of senses, protecting the people from external attacks, allowing domestic pleasures within the confines of the home, but also, importantly, screening people from all forms of public life. This prohibition is more significant than it might at first appear. In the absence of political life, small-scale family harmony acts as a specularization of public harmony, a metonymic projection of social order. The weather, as a figural screen, functions as the site of representation of a public life that, paradoxically, as a screen-fence, it materially denies.

The social and epistemological collapse experienced in time of war is thus repaired in domestic confinement, as the family prefigures and *represents* harmony to the public sphere. But this is problematic: the representation of a harmonious social order is in fact achieved through the denial of public life. It overlooks real political conflict, and constitutes a form of public life that is incohesive and fragmented since it is based on the idea of division and confinement. Thus the family can only form the basis of public order, in effect, by a rhetorical trick: under the guise of an organic emanation, the family restores order in fact by a wilful imposition from outside. This then is the first enactment of the aesthetic of force.

The second such enactment occurs towards the end of the novel. The agent of peace in the novel is Maximilian, in his disguise as the Masque. But before he establishes the new order, he spreads chaos and disruption on a grand scale, his disruptive effect being gained as much from his mystery as from his violent acts. His anonymity and cryptic notes leave no clues as to his motives or identity: 'Landgrave, beware! henceforth not you, but I, govern in Klosterheim' (XII: 77), he writes, a declaration as bewildering as the terror inflicted by the imposter Landgrave himself. The Masque strikes in the heart of the home: 'the seclusion of a man's private hearth, the secrecy of bedrooms, was no longer a protection. Locks gave way, bars fell, doors flew open' (XII: 78). The home is opened up and privacy dissolved.

This is the scenario that the Masque must repair in the denouement of the plot. He does so by stage-managing a kind of pageant, an intricate succession of public unveilings. The true identity of the Masque is revealed at the same time as the Landgrave is exposed as an imposter and Maximilian, the Masque, the rightful ruler. Simultaneously a large curtain is lifted to reveal the presence of thousands of imperial troops that have secretly and silently entered the Abbey. Although undeniably contrived, this theatrical display of military force splendidly inaugurates the re-establishment of social order. The tableau repeats the structure of the earlier moment, yet more emphatically. If the cold functioned as a metaphorical screen on which was projected the new social order in the form of the spectacle of the family, here another spectacle, that of the troops concealed behind the curtain, impels the establishment of new order. This time the sheer force of the spectacle is compounded by the military power of the soldiers.

The structure of the aesthetic of force should be clear from these two examples. There are two defining points. First, the spectacle has no history; it appears from nowhere, hidden behind a curtain. Second, the spectacle functions by compelling conformity to itself in the social world; it is a form of representation that demands submission on the part of its audience. It performs symbolic violence, both in the site of representation and in the broader social context in which it operates. The spectacle is a recurrent motif particularly in De Quincey's later writing: for instance, in the revised *Confessions*, the 'spectacle of a happy marriage' (III: 244) provides the best discipline for wayward servant girls; and in his 1840 essay on the Opium War, he claims that the spectacle of the British army, which unequivocally conveys the message of military superiority, compels the Chinese to comply with British wishes.[26] In *Klosterheim*, as elsewhere, the aesthetic of force provides a source of discipline in a world of disintegrating order.

In the gothic fictions, De Quincey saw the family as crucial to the establishment of social order. But as an organic unit, the family was inadequate to protect society from the encroachment of disorder. In the broader context in which De Quincey wrote, the effects of capital and industry, the agitations of the mob, or the desires of women were the contagions from which the family needed protection. To maintain its integrity as a unit of social organization, the family had to be bolstered by acts of force. We know from the political writings that De Quincey had no compunction about endorsing acts of state violence at home, or imperial violence abroad, in order to maintain the sanctity and security of the family as the organ of traditional values. *Klosterheim* is important because it demonstrates the process of a form of representation, the aesthetic of force, that is congruent with this. As meanings are conjured from behind veils, the aesthetic of force is fundamentally antidemocratic in structure, and, it should be noted, strongly militates against the popular call for parliamentary reform. We can trace the development of the aesthetic of force elsewhere in De Quincey's work, but most clearly in his free rendering of Lessing's *Laocoön*.

Between 1826 and 1827 *Blackwood's* published De Quincey's loose translation of Lessing's *Laocoön* as part of a series projected by De Quincey on topics from German literature and philosophy that would be of interest to its audience. *Laocoön: or, on the Limits of Painting and Poetry* is a significant work because it argued for the importance of genre in the consideration of works of art, and laid the ground for a criticism that would give appropriate weight to the formal aspects of representation. It has subsequently been held up as a founding work in the distinctively German critical tradition.[27] However, it is not clear from De Quincey's translation

[26] For discussion of this essay, see Ch. 6, pp. 170, 176–8, 183.

[27] For the German, see *Laokoön: oder über die Grenzen der Malerei und Poesies* in Gotthold Ephraim Lessing, *Werke*, vi., ed. H. G. Gopfert (Munich: Carl Hanser Verlag, 1974). For a full translation, see W. A. Steel, 'Laocoön', in *German Aesthetic and Literary Criticism: Winckelmann, Lessing, Hamann, Herder, Schiller and Goethe*, ed. H. B. Nisbet (Cambridge: CUP, 1985), 58–133. Lindop refers to De Quincey's translation as 'a minor literary landmark, for the *Laocoön*, one of the liveliest and most stimulating of all Romantic essays in aesthetics, had never before been seen

that he recognized the significance of the work; his stated reason for selecting it is the ease with which he might extract from it, for 'whilst the subject is one of popular interest, no great demand is made upon [the reader] for continuous attention' (XI: 162). Only as a rather dismissive afterthought does he add that Kant and Schlegel felt that the work did an important 'negative service' in 'clear[ing] up the boundaries of the different species' (XI: 163). Ostensibly De Quincey used *Laocoön* as a vehicle through which to introduce Lessing's work to a British readership; but it is also the case that he used the translation as a medium for exploring his own ideas about representation. Thus there are aspects of Lessing's work that interest him, some that he misrepresents, and some he plainly disagrees with or forgets to mention. My interest is not in comparing the two texts, but rather in the point that De Quincey's version of *Laocoön* presents a theoretical outline for the aesthetic of force that was in operation in *Klosterheim*.

Lessing's objective is to distinguish between painting and po-etry. Painting represents objects in space, and uses natural signs that accurately reproduce spatial relations. Poetry, on the other hand, uses language which functions temporally and is made up of arbitrary signs that bear no natural correspondence to the spatial relations between objects. Thus while painting represents bodies in space, poetry represents bodies in process: De Quincey's translation distinguishes between painting that '*represents*', and poetry that represents with the additional anthropomorphizing function, of making an object 'live'. It is this definition of poetry that fascinates him, for it contains the basis of his notion of organic style discussed in the previous chapter.

Lessing's comparison of Homer's and Virgil's descriptions of the sword of Achilles provides De Quincey with an early oppor-tunity to explore the idea of organic and mechanic writing. De Quincey translates: 'Homer describes the shield not as a thing

in English'. See Lindop, *Opium-Eater*, 282. Lessing's work's importance is recorded by Robert Philimore: 'The effect of the *Laocoön* in Germany was marvellous; while on the continent it was very great. It is hardly too much to say that what Adam Smith did in the domain of Political Economy by his *Wealth of Nations*, Lessing did in the domain of Art and Criticism.' See Philimore, 'Introduction', *Laocoön*, trans. Philimore (London, 1874), 17. On the substance of the work, see David Wellberg, *Lessing's 'Laocoön': Semiotics and Aesthetics in the Age of Reason* (Cambridge: CUP, 1984).

finished and complete, but in the stages of its growth. Here . . . he has . . . converted the inert description of a fixed material object into the living picture of an action. It is not the shield that we see, but the divine artist in the act and process of making it' (XI: 211). The complaint against Virgil's shield is based on the fact that its construction is not represented, so that its ornaments are not fully incorporated in the unity of the object. It is deemed 'a pure mechanic interpolation, contrived with no other view than that of flattering the Roman pride' (XI: 212). For language to be *poetic* or organic, it must present a hermetically sealed system which will disguise its own processes of representation; ironically, it does so by representing its own processes of production. It must make no reference to any other medium or genre; nor, more importantly, must it refer to any social or material context other than that imagined in the text. De Quincey shifts the emphasis in Lessing's text and focuses not on the relations between genres but instead on the difficult relationship between aesthetic representation in general and the social context in which it belongs or which it envisages. Lessing addresses these points too; indeed *Laocoön* contains seminal discussion of the role of the arts in the formation of national consciousness. De Quincey's remarks owe something to Lessing, but also diverge significantly from him. Primarily he sees in Lessing's work a strong statement of the official function of art within the state, which he will refine, but not dismiss.

De Quincey is most open about his difference from Lessing in a 'Postscript' appended to the translation of *Laocoön*, in which he takes issue with Lessing's assertion that, 'the didactic poet . . . wherever he is strictly didactic, . . . is in fact no poet' (XI: 213). The grounds for his objection are that didacticism requires the subjugation of the objects of representation to some other function beyond the aim of poetry, which is to represent a living whole in the self-referential terms of poetic language; merely by referring to a non-aesthetic function, in this case the moral, poetry fails in its true purpose. De Quincey, however, argues that didactic poetry can be poetic *in spite of* its didacticism. Any subject, he argues, once it is represented in aesthetic terms, necessarily transcends its moral, social or economic function. He gives the example of washing clothes, the basest of all human activities, as it is an action subjugated to human need; aesthetic representation of such labour 'would at once disarm the inherent meanness in the subject of all power to affect unpleasurably' (XI: 218–19), for in aesthetic representation all existing social meanings are erased.

What is at stake then is the place of the aesthetic in relation to the social. For De Quincey the role of aesthetics is in one sense much stronger than for Lessing since it has the power to efface social context. De Quincey constructs an aesthetic arena that will transcend the social world.

De Quincey also takes issue with Lessing's assertion that government or state intervention is necessary for the control of the arts. Lessing argues that in the case of science, which produces truth, state intervention is both unnecessary and inadmissible. In the case of the arts, which produce not truth but pleasure, the state can and should administer control, for the pleasure obtainable from the arts is instrumental in the formation of 'national character'. For Lessing, the arts, or aesthetic representation, therefore have a significant role in the production and reproduction of society and social values. Thus he writes, 'When beautiful men fashioned beautiful statues, these in their turn affected them, and the state had beautiful statues in part to thank for beautiful citizens',[28] establishing a context in which art and society are involved in mutual production. Lessing extends the point further. He gives the example of six mothers of heroes, who, during pregnancy, share a dream of adultery with a serpent. 'The serpent was a symbol of deity, and the beautiful statues and pictures of Bacchus, an Apollo, a Mercury and a Hercules were seldom seen without a serpent. The honest women had by day feasted their eyes on the god, and the bewildering dream called up the image of the reptile.'[29] Lessing's point is not that these symbols have a role in biological reproduction, but that they have a function in the unconscious reproduction of cultural values, and consequently make particular material effects.

De Quincey however refuses to accept the dynamic capacity of cultural representations to intervene in the material world. He does not include the passage, cited above, concerning the mutually productive relation between the men and statues, and his translation of the passage about the pregnant women is significant since it accounts for the phenomenon in terms of the 'fancy'

---

[28] Steele, 'Laocoön', in *German Aesthetic and Literary Criticism*, 64.
[29] Ibid. 64.

of the women who, 'reproduced in the confusion of dreams this symbolic image as an associated circumstance' (XI: 173).

In a footnote, De Quincey argues against Lessing's justification of state intervention in the arts. De Quincey claims that there is no necessity for state control of the arts precisely because the arts transcend social and political issues. However, the arts do have a significant investment in the social realm, for their transcendent values are instrumental in the construction of that society's values. For instance, discussing the difference between science and the arts, he denies that science is in any way more 'indispensible': indeed, without the arts, 'the gifts of Science would be a most dangerous possession for any nation which was not guided in the use of them by a moral culture derived from manner, institutions, and the arts' (XI: 173 n.). Thus art not only controls science, but also constitutes 'moral culture'. Echoing Kant, he claims that 'the true object of the Fine Arts' is not pleasure but 'the sense of power and the illimitable incarnated as it were in pleasure' and

their final purpose therefore, as truly as that of Science and much more directly, the exaltation of our human nature; which, being the very highest conceivable purpose of man, is least of all a fit subject for the caprices or experiments of the scoundrel magistrate. (XI: 173 n.)

The argument is arcane but familiar. The power of art is to transcend the social context, and its purpose, to inculcate the best values of human nature which lie beyond the whims of the 'scoundrel magistrate'. The social content of aesthetic representation is effaced, as we have already seen; instead, aesthetic representation brings to bear on society itself values that are formulated outside the bounds of culture and society. From behind a veil of mystification, they present themselves like the troops in *Klosterheim*, a conservative heavy mob impelling order within the social body by the mere spectacle of themselves.

De Quincey gives no clues here as to the content of the values he has in mind here, and indeed that is not really the point in question. What is interesting is the structure of the relation between the aesthetic and the social, for it resembles that implicit in the moments of pageantry in *Klosterheim*. For De Quincey, fine art functions as the spectacle of social order. It is the aesthetic of force.

Murder

In his translation of *Laocoön*, De Quincey proposed the idea that moral concerns are erased in aesthetic representation. Such a proposition derives from his reading of Kant. But he was clearly perplexed by the implications of this notion, and it becomes the starting point for a series of essays entitled, 'On Murder Considered as one of the Fine Arts' published between 1827 and 1854.

De Quincey was obsessed by the idea of murder. In 1818, as editor of the *Westmorland Gazette*, to the bemusement of his local readership, he had filled the paper with lurid accounts of assize proceedings, frequently at the expense of domestic and agricultural news.[30] His justification for this was twofold: first, reports of murder educated the working class who learned by example about the punishment that is the inevitable result of crime; and second, such accounts represented the state of the nation's morals to the ruling class, which could be moved to check any significant decline.[31] At this stage, murder constituted an untroubled site of representation which worked to sustain a particular class structure. Nine years later, in 1827, after extensive reading in German philosophy and in particular Kant, and in the context of the burgeoning political crisis associated with Catholic emancipation, De Quincey published the first of his essays 'On Murder Considered as one of the Fine Arts', which was followed by a second essay by the same title in 1839 and a 'Postscript' in 1854.[32] Kant's philosophy had demonstrated to De Quincey that aesthetic representation, while offering personal empowerment and control, in fact brought about a loss of control, and a disruption of subjectivity. Even murder, the ultimate bid for control, once it has been represented as an aesthetic object, marked only a man's loss of power, his inability to control the consequences of his actions and the meanings of his acts of representation.[33] It thus precipitated a

---

[30] Lindop, *Opium-Eater*, 228–9. See also Charles Pollitt, *De Quincey's Editorship of 'The Westmorland Gazette', July, 1818 to November, 1819* (Kendal: Atkinson & Pollitt, 1890).

[31] Pollitt, *De Quincey's Editorship*, 11.

[32] See also his 'Murder as a Fine Art—Some Notes for a New Paper' in *Posthumous Works*, ed. Alexander H. Japp (London, 1891) i. 77–84.

[33] For discussion of De Quincey's murder essays as a commentary on the ethical problems raised by Kantian aesthetics, see Joel Black, *The Aesthetics of Murder: A*

breakdown in the social order that had been sustained by his pre-Kantian representations of murder in the *Westmorland Gazette*.

'Everything in this world has two handles,' quipped De Quincey. 'Murder, for instance, may be laid hold of by its moral handle . . . ; or it may also be treated *aesthetically*, as the Germans call it—that is, in relation to good taste' (XIII: 13).[34] Only a murder yet to take place can have a moral aspect, he argued, for once perpetrated, there would be no possibility of intervening. In his contorted logic, he declared that since morality and aesthetics are mutually exclusive zones, a man could only have a moral response to a situation or an idea if he had the possibility of acting upon it. The argument is clearly ludicrous, but buried within it is the persistent worry that acts of representation incur a loss of agency.

Throughout his works, De Quincey was tantalized by Kant's idea that transcendent values are to be glimpsed in aesthetic experience, but the difficulties this system presented to the subject troubled him. As a writer, he knew that rather than find empowerment, he was destined to be lost and confused in his endless processes of self-representation. Hence his interest in the moment of death, for this was the point at which he might have access to self-knowledge: if he could represent his death, then he would have certain control over his life. 'To hear people talk,' he wrote, 'you would suppose that all the disadvantages and inconveniences were on the side of being murdered, and that there were none at all in *not* being murdered' (XIII: 42). The advantage of being murdered was that you would have consciousness of your own death. Of course the joke is that such knowledge would not be much good to you once you were dead. Making the preposterous claim that all philosophers since Descartes had been the victims, rather than the perpetrators, of an attempted murder, De Quincey spun an elaborate joke about the necessity of representing death in a philosophical system in which self-consciousness, and consequently self-representation, were acts of self-affirma-

Study in Romantic Literature and Contemporary Culture (Baltimore, Md.: Johns Hopkins University Press, 1991), 12–17, 29–103.

[34] Hugh Sykes Davies claimed that De Quincey's was the first English usage of the word 'aesthetic'. See John Whale, *De Quincey's Reluctant Autobiography* (London: Croom Helm, 1984), 46.

tion. As Descartes thought in order to be, gaining self-affirmation through self-consciousness, the greatest self-affirmation was reached through consciousness of the limits of his own existence.

De Quincey proposed that an intellectual shift concomitant with the work of Descartes was manifested in the history of representations of murder. Indeed the same point has been made less frivolously and more recently by Francis Barker in *The Private Tremulous Body*.[35] Barker points out that this shift occurred at the same time as significant political and social changes which announced the construction of the new, bourgeois subject, and he provides a reading of *Hamlet* to demonstrate the beginnings of an interiorizing of the subject in a movement away from 'the corporeal order of the spectacle' of Jacobean drama.[36] The all-important first murder, the death of the king and the father, pre-empts the drama, but within the course of the play it is represented many times: once by the ghost, once by the dumb show preceding the play in Act 3, again in the play, and then again in the murders at the end. There is perhaps no better example of a burgeoning mass of aesthetic representations that come to supplement the unrepresented murder, the primal death.[37]

According to De Quincey, another intellectual shift had occurred with Kant, which had also been marked in the history of murder. Kant did not experience his own murder, De Quincey argues; instead his would-be murderer chose to kill a small child. The attainment of self-consciousness was thus never achieved, and Kant remained oblivious to the whole affair. The explanation is curious: ironizing Kant's scrupulous morality, De Quincey claimed that the murderer's motives were moral, for he thought that an old philosopher 'might be laden with sins', and concluded that it was less morally damaging to condemn to death a child who was blameless than a man who had yet to atone for his many

---

[35] Francis Barker, *The Tremulous Private Body: Essays in Subjection* (London: Methuen, 1984).

[36] Ibid. 25–40.

[37] Cf. Freud, *Totem and Taboo: Some Points of Agreement between the Mental Lives of Savages and Neurotics* (1912–13), *Standard Edition of the Complete Psychological Works of Sigmund Freud*, trans. James Strachey, 24 vols. (London: Hogarth Press, 1953–74), xiii. 1–161, in which the primal parricide is never known but endlessly represented in religious and unconscious ideation; for example in the Oedipus complex.

sins. But then again, the motives might have been aesthetic: to murder old Kant would provide no satisfaction, for 'there was no room for display, as the man could not possibly look more like a mummy when dead than he had done when alive' (XIII: 35). This disturbing and anarchic moment which precipitated the murder of a child, is the moment of aesthetics: for Kant, the realm of the aesthetic occurs at the point at which self-knowledge is rendered unobtainable. But more than this, the aesthetic marks the breakdown of economics, the law, culture, in fact all modes of symbolic representation. For all its disturbing implications, this is a potentially radical and liberating moment, for it opens the possibility of stepping beyond the strictures of society, a moment of transcendence and empowerment.[38]

However, in these essays, this unstable moment is always recovered in a way which allows the deeper inscription of conservative values; murder is a powerful display of violence and force, and it is used to enforce existing social relations. Rather than transcendence, a step beyond culture, we will see that murder is used to bring about the blockage in the circulation of representations and the preservation of a particular social order. Thus considering murder as a fine art begins as a joke derived from an anxiety about the loss of agency incurred by representation; but a transformation occurs in the essays whereby murder comes to offer a solution to those very problems. Another aesthetic based on the idea of murder—the murderous aesthetic of force—will restore to De Quincey the lost agency of the Kantian aesthetic.

In the course of the essays, the context of murder comes to hold particular importance and it is significant that De Quincey considered the most interesting murders to be those that took place in domestic situations. Walter Benjamin has argued that the traces within the domestic interior which display the power and control

---

[38] Cf. Angela Carter in *Sadeian Woman: An Exercise in Cultural History* (London: Virago, 1979), who finds in the work of de Sade a similar liberating moment that, she claims, works in the interests of women. I discuss this further in another version of this chapter: see Josephine McDonagh, 'Do or Die: Questions of Agency and Gender in the Aesthetics of Murder', *Genders*, 5 (1989), 120–34. Mario Praz in *The Romantic Agony*, trans. Angus Davidson, (1933; London: Collins, 1960), 113–214, discusses the influence of de Sade in 19th-cent. European writing, and proposes some links with De Quincey.

of the inhabitant when his agency is lost in the public sphere, are the basis of the detective story.[39] As the detective retraces the traces of the murderer to discover the scene of the crime, the first trace is the wound, the deathly mark of the murder. Like the marks of the interior, the wound is the mark that displays the agency and power, the force of the murderer. Murder is the mark of power whose meaning for the perpetrator does not alter in circulation, a display of force more powerful and more permanent than the marks in a flimsy piece of velveteen. Murder is indeed a form of representation that makes an unmistakable bid for control.

Thus for De Quincey, the perfect murder was one that obliterated an entire household: the murders with which he was most fascinated were those that involved the massacre of a family complete with servants. As De Quincey's writings constantly display anxieties concerning the imminent and inescapable collapse of the family, murder becomes an expression of power and agency in the face of this breakdown of social order.

The murderer to whom he returned most obsessively was one John Williams, who, 'during the winter of 1812 . . . in one hour smote two houses with emptiness, exterminated all but two entire households, and asserted his own supremacy above all the children of Cain' (XIII: 74).[40] Williams's own tangential position in relation to the family is always emphasized: he is a traveller, a sailor who has no family nor home of his own, but lives in a hostel with other sailors of mixed nationalities: his own birth place, writes De Quincey, 'was certainly not known' (XIII: 116). His foppish appearance is often referred to, his unnatural and 'unmanly' interest in clothing, and hair which was often of 'the most extraordinary and vivid colour,—viz. bright yellow, something

---

[39] Benjamin, *Charles Baudelaire*, 169: 'The detective story appeared, which investigated these traces. [Poe's] *Philosophy of Furniture*, as much as his detective stories, shows Poe to have been the first physiognomist of the interior.'

[40] For a full account of the Williams' murders, see T. A. Critchley and P. D. James, *The Maul and the Pear Tree: The Ratcliffe Highway Murders, 1811* (London: Constable, 1971). Albert Goldman is struck by the accuracy of De Quincey's account. See Goldman, *The Mine and the Mint*, 143. On the other hand, A. S. Plumtree, in 'The Artist as Murderer: De Quincey's Essay "On Murder considered as one of the Fine Arts"', in *Bicentenary Essays*, ed. R. L. Snyder (Norman, Okla.: University of Oklahoma Press, 1985), 140–63, writes that 'it is remarkable how much De Quincey distorted or embroidered the facts of the case' (156).

between an orange and a lemon colour' (XIII: 77). His synaesthetic hair colouring is a legacy of trips to India, where 'it is notorious that in the Punjab horses of a high caste are often painted—crimson, blue, green, purple' (XIII: 77). Such curious details confirm his position in relation to the family, the home, and the nation, for he is tainted with all things that mark their boundaries. Nevertheless, the casual reference to Indian caste indicates an interest in the preservation of particular hierarchical values that might not always be protected in the family. In this case, India seems to imply not the undermining and threatening Orient, but the existence of a jealously preserved set of social relations which are at risk in the 'democratic' west.

The families that Williams selects to murder significantly already show signs of being under threat from such a breakdown in social order. The first family, the Marrs, employ a maid who exists in sisterly relation to the wife, thus usefully inscribing relations of labour into the family. At the time, however, De Quincey tells us, 'a great democratic change is . . . passing over British society. Multitudes of persons are becoming ashamed of saying "my master" or "my mistress": the term now in the slow process of superseding it is "my employer" ' (XIII: 82). Protection for the Marr family from the democratic change that promises to revolutionize the power relations of society, we suspect is only temporary, for De Quincey describes a tide that is sweeping over the entire nation; their only certain escape from this is death. The other family, the Williamsons, are the keepers of a hostelry 'on an old patriarchal footing', in which 'although people of considerable property resorted to the house in the evenings, no kind of anxious separation was maintained between them and the other visitors from the class of artisans or common labourers' (XIII: 97–8). Once again, relations of labour are naturalized and effaced. However, like the Marrs, the Williamsons cannot guarantee the continuation of this arrangement. By annihilating them, Williams protects them from the inevitability of a collapse in social relations.

In his own iconoclastic way, like the subsequent murderers, Peter Sutcliffe, the Yorkshire Ripper, who claimed 'I were just cleaning up streets', or Jack the Ripper who was 'down on prostitutes', Williams is the ultimate guardian of the family, a force of conservatism and conservation.[41] In De Quincey's text, to protect the family is to maintain the context in which a man can possess agency and control, in which he can mean what he says and say what he means and is not at risk from the misrepresentations of circulation. Significantly, the Williamsons, the victims of his second murders, are in name his own family, the family of his son. If the family offers the conditions for control and the expression of agency, De Quincey, who recognizes the precarious nature of the family, presents murder as the one act of total and individual control. To kill his son is to kill the trajectory of his own actions, his own being: it is to control the circulation of his own representations.

It is therefore significant that, according to De Quincey, Southey considered the Williams murders pre-eminent for they, 'ranked amongst the few domestic events which, by the depth and expansion of horror attending them, had risen to the dignity of a *national* interest' (XIII: 124 n.). Murder makes the private public; it is an act of representation whose meanings will not change in circulation. But, De Quincey observes, to kill a public figure is self-defeating, since no one would believe he had done it: the representations of public figures are already in circulation and therefore cannot be controlled. He gives two examples: the Pope, who 'has such a virtual ubiquity as the father of Christendom, and, like the cuckoo, is so often heard but never seen' (XIII: 47), and Abraham Newland, the man whose name appeared on all bank notes: one cannot stop the circulation of money by murdering the man whose name was 'a shorthand expression for paper money' (XIII: 47 n.).[42] If a position in the public realm offers immunity from murder, it is only because, in relation to them, agency and control had already been lost: murder has nothing to retrieve outside the home.

The issue of the murder of public figures, or assassination, is raised early in the first essay, in a discussion of its significant difference from other kinds of murder: 'Assassination is a branch of the art which demands a separate notice; and it is possible that

---

[41] See Deborah Cameron and Elizabeth Fraser, *The Lust to Kill: A Feminist Investigation of Sexual Murder* (Oxford: Polity Press, 1987), 123.

[42] De Quincey added the footnote in the revised version in 1854.

I may devote an entire lecture to it' (XIII: 22). This lecture, however, was never produced. Tracing the etymology of the word 'assassin', De Quincey follows Skeat to link it to the Arabic *Hashishin*, or 'hashish-drinkers', 'from the fact . . . that . . . when [they] were detached on their murderous errands, went forth nerved for the task by the intoxication of *hashish*, or Indian hemp' (XIII: 22 n.).[43] Perpetrated in drug-induced stupor, assassination of a public figure could never constitute a display of will or power in the same way as the domestic murders. De Quincey claims that the most recent assassination was the death of Wallenstein in 1634 during the Thirty Years War—thirty-four years after *Hamlet*, three years before the publication of Descartes's *Discourse on Method*. Public assassination gave way to private murder at around the time of the establishment of the family as the primary social, moral, and economic unit, and the constitution of the free-thinking, self-determining Cartesian subject.

De Quincey's family murders are not transcendent acts but displays of violence and force strategically constructed in culture to halt a process of social democratization. His murderer is the guardian of a nostalgic world of hierarchical social relations, the keeper of a precapitalist idyll, and murder an act constituted as an attempt to stop the circulation of representations.

We can understand why De Quincey, whose obscurantist political views we have already discussed, should be so attracted to the idea of murder. Murder is the best possible model for the aesthetic of force. The murderer, concealed in the shadows of the home, leaping out as if from nowhere, is the most extreme violator whose will is always felt, whose absolute power never passes without acknowledgement.

Curiously though, De Quincey, the opium-eater and assassin of public reputations in his biographical sketches, resembles the assassin more closely than the domestic murderer.[44] His writings are always ambiguous: while he develops the aesthetic of force to counter the problems of lost agency, nevertheless, as his opium

[43] Likewise, this note was added in 1854.

[44] He did not, however, take hashish. Lindop notes that in 1854 De Quincey claimed, 'I, for my part, have tried everything in this world except "bang" [hashish], which I believe to be obtained from hemp'. According to Lindop, he later reported that he had 'received from a young friend a present of *bang*', but that he did not leave an account of its effects. See Lindop, *Opium-Eater*, 368.

confessions attest, he enjoys the intense masochistic pleasures of losing control. In the next chapter we will explore the pleasures and pains of addiction in the context of Britain's troubled relations with the East, by focusing on opium. As the source of both his sublime pleasures and physical pains, the cause of his literary success and his financial ruin, and, in the Opium War with China, a tool of imperial aggression, and a spot of economic vulnerability in an increasingly precarious world, opium plays an important role in De Quincey's imaginative topography.

6

Opium-Eaters: The Addict, the Imperialist, and the Autobiographer

I wish he was not so little.

Robert Southey on De Quincey, 1805[1]

The essays on murder detailed the social functions of the murderer. But throughout, De Quincey's attention was continually drawn back to the victim, and his or her thoughts at the dreadful moment before the murderer strikes his deathly blow. In his essay 'On the Knocking on the Gate in Macbeth' (1823), De Quincey demonstrated that this sublime moment of suspense and uncertainty, the point at which death is glimpsed, is a key one in the construction of a work of art. Much of his own best work is a response to the question posed in 'The English Mail Coach' (1849), 'What is to be thought of sudden death?' (C, 209). The visions he describes in this work occur at that point of suspended time at which, facing death, he wallows in the 'luxury of ruin' (C, 212). The 'dreadful ulcer, lurking far down in the depths of human nature' (C, 211) is the intense pleasure which is to be gained from the contemplation of one's own end.

Critics have agreed with De Quincey that 'The English Mail Coach' ranks among his finest works and belongs to the category of 'impassioned prose' or the literature of power. In Chapter 3, I suggested that works within the literature of power tend to witness a loss of agency and identity on the part of the writer, a beautiful expunging of personality. The visions of death in 'The English Mail Coach' clearly show the way in which his own lost potency, his own imminent death, can be the subject of his best prose. De Quincey's other works within the literature of power, most notably *Confessions* and *Suspiria*, as autobiographical works, appear, on the face of it, to be works of self-affirmation; however,

---

[1] Cited by Masson, V: 19 n.

as I have already suggested, De Quincey's autobiographies also narrate tales of lost agency and the relinquishing of power.

In the last chapter I delineated the emergence of the aesthetic of force, a mode of representation that counters the sense of disempowerment experienced in society and culture. The 'impassioned prose' and the autobiographies, in particular, are interesting because, on the contrary, they inscribe the pleasures of lost agency, the 'luxury of ruin'. That a writer should propose two such different forms of writing, two opposing aesthetics, is irregular and puzzling. In this chapter I explore the relationship between the two and suggest that the logic that sustains this contradictory situation is drawn from a discursive economy which aims to separate aesthetic from political writing.

The focus of discussion here will be the autobiographical work. This is a genre to which De Quincey repeatedly returns throughout his life, but there are significant differences between the early and late works. It is possible to chart an endeavour to demote opium from its role as 'the true hero of the tale' in *Confessions* in 1821, to the position of the 'ugly pole ... there only for support' (C, 94) in *Suspiria* in 1845. Indeed, his own literary reputation appears to have shifted at around the same time from that of the popularizer of opium to that of a significant contributor to the broader fields of philosophy, literature, and political economy. While in the 1820s and 1830s most critical discussion of his works centred on the medical, psychological, and moral issues raised by opium addiction, from about 1840 writers such as George Gilfillan and Francis Jacox considered De Quincey as a more serious literary and philosophical writer, while McCullogh and J. S. Mill responded to his economic works as fellow economists.[2] This change in the position of opium in his own estimation and in

---

[2] The early reviews are listed in H. O. Dendurent, *Thomas De Quincey: A Reference Guide* (Boston: G. K. Hall, 1978). Typical is the review in *Eclectic Review*, NS, 19 (April 1823), which regards the work as 'medically worthless' yet 'morally affecting'. See Dendurent, *Reference Guide*, 3. For an account of the reviews, see John O. Hayden, 'De Quincey's *Confessions* and the Reviewers', *Wordsworth Circle*, 6 (1975), 273–9. In contrast to the morally condemnatory tone that prevails in the early reviews, critics such as Gilfillan and Jacox adopt a more indulgent attitude towards his works and draw attention to their humour and eccentricity. See for instance Jacox, 'The English Opium-Eater', *People's and Howitt's Journal*, 8 (1849), 217–21, and Gilfillan, 'Thomas De Quincey', *Eclectic Review*, 27 (Apr. 1850), 397–408.

the evaluation of his works by others mirrored a shift in the social reputation of opium between 1820 and 1840 that has been documented by Virginia Berridge and Gareth Edwards in their social history of opium, *Opium and the People*. The awed curiosity that the drug inspired early in the century turned by mid-century into disapproval and uncertainty as to its effects.[3]

One of the factors that affected the popular representation of opium was the outbreak of war against China in 1839 provoked by the attempt on the part of the Chinese government to stop the importation of opium by British merchants.[4] In his political essays, De Quincey voiced strong opinions in support of Britain's brutal military campaign in the Opium War (1839–1842), and described the unscrupulous deviousness of the Chinese.[5] This position is predictable given De Quincey's High Tory political beliefs, but surprisingly for a renowned opium-eater, he appears to despise the Chinese for their opium consumption. This contradiction opens up his work in interesting ways. In this chapter I will suggest that opium itself functions as a bridge between the writer of 'impassioned prose' who, like an addict, relinquishes agency to enjoy the 'luxury of ruin', and the High Tory political writer who recommends the repressive control and subjection of other people through violence and intimidation. We will see that opium has crucial links with the two forms of representation that De Quincey invokes, and these are played out with astonishing effects in the different contexts presented by his various works. It is both a crucial commodity for export in the British economy and a means of the impoverishment and subjugation of the Chinese

---

[3] V. Berridge and G. Edwards, *Opium and the People: Opiate Use in Nineteenth-Century England* (New Haven, Conn.: Yale University Press, 1987).

[4] On the events of the Opium War, see Immanuel C. Y. Hsü, *The Rise of Modern China*, 2nd edn. (New York: OUP, 1975), 220–49, and *The Cambridge History of China*, x, *Late Ch'ing, 1800–1911*, pt 1, ed. John K. Fairbank (Cambridge: CUP, 1978), 163–212. See also *The New Cambridge Modern History* x, *The Zenith of European Power, 1830–70*, ed. J. P. T. Bury (Cambridge: CUP, 1960), 685–92, and Brian Inglis, *The Opium War* (Sevenoaks: Hodder & Stoughton, 1976).

[5] See 'The Opium and the China Question', *Blackwood's*, 47 (June 1840), 717–38 and 'Postscript on the China and Opium Question', *Blackwood's*, 47 (June 1840), 847–53, reprinted as 'The Opium Question with China in 1840' and 'Postscript on the Duke of Wellington's Views' in XIV: 162–218; 'Canton Expedition and Convention', *Blackwood's*, 50 (Nov. 1841), 677–88; and *China, by Thomas De Quincey: A Revised Imprint of Articles from 'Titan', with Preface and Additions*, (Edinburgh, 1857).

people, but it is also an agent of extraordinary pleasures and devastating pains in his own fragile body.[6]

Autobiography

De Quincey's autobiographical writings form a disorganized and incomplete group of works. His first major work, *Confessions of an English Opium-Eater*, was initially published in two parts in the *London Magazine* in 1821, reprinted many times in book form, and later revised and substantially enlarged by De Quincey in volume five of his *Selections Grave and Gay* which appeared in 1856. *Suspiria de Profundis*, billed as the sequel to *Confessions*, appeared in *Blackwood's* in 1845. He did not reprint this in its entirety in *Selections Grave and Gay*, but incorporated sections from it in the volumes entitled *Autobiographic Sketches* (1853–54). The bulk of material in these volumes came from the *Tait's* essays, 'Sketches of Men and Manners from the Autobiography of an English Opium-Eater' and the 'Lake Reminiscences', which were published between 1834 and 1841.

Despite the fact that most of the work was produced in the 1840s and 1850s, towards the end of his life, he left his later years conspicuously undocumented, and returned obsessively to the events of early childhood. Moreover the works themselves are full of unfulfilled plans and projections. *Suspiria*, for instance, includes a scheme for a larger work that is not realized, and the revised *Confessions* promises additional dreams that are never incorporated.[7] Thus the works are neither complete as an account of his life story, nor indeed are they finished in a formal sense, as works of literature.

The *Autobiographic Sketches* in *Selections Grave and Gay* present more problems, for here autobiographical essays merge with biographical pieces such as his 'Lake Reminiscences' of Wordsworth, Coleridge, and Southey. At a particular point in his early

---

[6] On De Quincey and addiction, see Michael G. Cooke, 'De Quincey, Coleridge, and the Formal Uses of Intoxication,' *Yale French Studies* 50 (1974), 26–40. See also John Frederick Logan, 'The Age of Intoxication,' ibid., 81–94.

[7] For his intentions for *Suspiria*, see C,153; and for the revised *Confessions*, see III: 221–2.

adulthood, his autobiography became absorbed into literary history, as though his own identity were somehow fused with the identity of other, more central figures. In the introduction to *Selections Grave and Gay*, De Quincey distinguished between these essays and the *Confessions* and *Suspiria*, claiming that the former were literary 'amusement[s] . . . thoughtfully and faithfully related', and the latter, the greater and more substantial 'impassioned prose'.[8] He claimed for the former a greater sense of historical accuracy than was possible or even desirable in the latter group, for the subject of impassioned prose transcended historical circumstance. The consequence of this was that self-identity was forsaken in the pursuit of historical accuracy, fractured and dispersed as autobiography gave way to biography. De Quincey's works illustrate Paul de Man's point, that historical and aesthetic discourses collide over the autobiographical terrain.[9]

In De Quincey's case, this collision of the historical and the aesthetic produced a fractured and eccentric body of writing: autobiographies that are also drug narratives, that relinquish centre stage to opium, that subside into biography, that obsessively document memories of infancy, that incorporate elaborate dream sequences, and so on. This has had an effect on their long-term critical assessment. Despite recent developments in the theory of autobiography, De Quincey's works are rarely included in critical discussions of the genre, such as Olney's *Metaphors of Self* (1972), Fleishman's *Figures of Autobiography* (1983), or indeed Lejeune's ground-breaking work on the theory of autobiography.[10] The omission of De Quincey is curious since his autobiographical

---

[8] *Selections Grave and Gay* (Edinburgh, 1853–6), vol. i, pp. x–xi.

[9] Paul de Man, 'Autobiography as Defacement' in *The Rhetoric of Romanticism* (New York: Columbia University Press, 1984), 67–81.

[10] James Olney, *Metaphors of Self: The Meaning of Autobiography* (Princeton, NJ: Princeton University Press, 1972); Avrom Fleishman, *Figures of Autobiography: The Language of Self-Writing in Victorian and Modern England* (Berkeley, Calif.: University of California Press, 1983); de Man, 'Autobiography as Defacement'; Philippe Lejeune, 'The Autobiographical Pact', in *On Autobiography*, ed. P. J. Eakin, trans. Katherine Leary, (Minneapolis: University of Minnesota Press, 1989), 3–30. Elizabeth W. Bruss's *Autobiographical Acts: The Changing Situation of a Literary Genre* (Baltimore, Md.: Johns Hopkins University Press, 1976) is noteworthy as an extended study of De Quincey's autobiographies in the context of other Victorian autobiographies.

writings have generally been highly rated as *literary* works, and their confessional form would appear to place them squarely in the main tradition of autobiographical works that includes St Augustine's and Rousseau's confessional writings.

The exclusion might be explained, at least in part, by the fact that these are drug narratives as well as autobiographies. But their unconventional form also presents a particular challenge to theorists of autobiography. Although such theorists have focused on the fracturing of self that occurs in autobiography—from Olney's creation of split personality, Fleishman's production of a new organic being, to de Man's formulation of autobiography as defacement—all tend to retain some notion of a stated or understood principle of unification in the works. This point is usefully illustrated by Lejeune's contention that a work of autobiography generally includes a fictional contract between the writer and reader, that the work will present an authentic representation of the writing subject.[11] De Quincey's autobiographies present a difficult case, for their dogged incompleteness and notoriously digressive style complicate all claims to unity. Indeed *Confessions* is prefaced with the comment that 'my self-accusation does not amount to a confession of guilt' (C, 2), a claim that disrupts any semblance of a coherent statement of a rhetorical contract to offer an authentic and stable representation of himself as a unified subject.

Nevertheless De Quincey did not neglect all attempts to unify his writings or his representation of himself. Paradoxically, the one constant thrust of his autobiographies is towards unification. Even the structurally fragmented and obscure *Suspiria* is motivated by a pursuit of unitary coherence; although he never realized his own structural plan, the strange and highly stylized prose passages that interrupt the linear narrative of his childhood were nevertheless intended to create unity out of the random fragments of his life. Indeed the very fascination with childhood was a frantic search for some originary event around which his subsequent experiences might be organized and comprehended. Thus although the works clearly lack cohesion and unity, this

---

[11] See Joshua Wilner, 'Autobiography and Addiction: The Case of De Quincey', *Genre*, 14/4 (1981), 493–503, for a reading of *Confessions* based on Lejeune's theoretical work.

does not appear to derive from a want of will or desire to have them so.

The pursuit of unity in his works is in fact conducted with such vigour that some critics have pointed to the schematic and highly aestheticized nature of his writings as the feature that subverts their claim to personal authenticity.[12] The devices he used to create aesthetic unification, it is said, are too prominent, and conceal elements of randomness and fracture which are the evidence of lived experience. Although this criticism is based on a confused belief that realism might be achieved through the representation of a raw experience beyond writing, it none the less demonstrates how De Quincey's autobiographies upset the extraordinarily fine balance between randomness and order that is expected of a convincing representation of a life.

Too ordered and yet not ordered enough, De Quincey's autobiographies fail to comply with the usual requirements of the genre. To add to the difficulties of the situation, the differences between early and late works make generalization difficult. The earlier work does not consider the unification of either the work or the autobiographical subject to be as urgent or imperative as does *Suspiria*. *Confessions* lacks the stylistic devices, such as the lyric passages of *Suspiria* which present various motifs to hold the work together, like 'The Palimpsest' and 'The Brocken Spectre', and is consequently, in some senses, a more discontinuous and disrupted narrative. Divided into two uneven parts, it is composed of rambling and bathetic linear narratives leading from and to absence and loss. The clearest example of this is the trip to Oxford referred to in Chapter 2. De Quincey travels to meet an aristocratic friend to gain surety for a loan; the friend cannot be found; he is refused the loan; and the adventure leads only to the loss of his companion, Ann, a loss that reverberates throughout the *Confessions*, as her absence becomes a recurrent feature of his dreams. The idea of an absent centre is in a sense a structural principle of the *Confessions*, producing an incomplete and digressive narrative that defies all semblance of unity. The final passages, 'The Pains of Opium', are presented as the discontinuous jottings of a tormented mind, and eventually take the form of the

---

[12] Bruss, *Autobiographical Acts*, 96, and Grevel Lindop, *The Opium-Eater: A Life of Thomas De Quincey* (Oxford: OUP, 1985), 382.

scattered entries of a diary. The fragmented narrative is appropriate, for it is supposed to be the work of the tortured and distracted mind of the autobiographer in the torment of addiction. For critics who distrust the highly stylized form of *Suspiria*, this text offers a greater sense of realism, in that the mode of representation is fitting for the subject who represents and is represented.

As already suggested, one significant factor in the comparison of the early and late works is the different emphasis placed on opium. In *Confessions*, opium is offered as the unifying principle of both his life and his autobiography—the agent of 'the most exquisite order, legislation, and harmony' (C, 40); it usurps the subject of the autobiography to become 'the true hero of the tale . . . the legitimate centre on which the interest revolves' (C, 78).[13] In *Suspiria* it is just one of many contributing influences on his life, and De Quincey even suggests that he was subject to opium dreams long before his first taste of the 'celestial drug' in early childhood.[14] As I have suggested, this alteration in the status of opium is consistent with a wider shift in the social reputation of the drug, and implies that differences between De Quincey's autobiographies of the 1820s and 1840s are symptomatic of a range of issues intricately focused around opium.

In *Confessions*, then, opium brings 'order' and 'harmony'. The person who consumes opium experiences an extended state of composure in which 'the diviner parts of his nature are paramount', for 'opium always seems to compose what had been agitated, and to concentrate what had been distracted' (C, 41). While '[W]ine robs a man of his self-possession: opium greatly invigorates it' (C, 40). However, the later part of the text, 'The Pains of Opium', works specifically to undermine these claims, as opium is blamed for his distracted and tortured state of mind. Indeed, De Quincey's comparison of opium with alcohol suggests that we regard his claims for opium cautiously since laudanum,

---

[13] On opium and self-possession, see Edmund Baxter, *De Quincey's Art of Autobiography* (Edinburgh: Edinburgh University Press, 1990), 33–5.

[14] See *Suspiria*, C,106–7. For discussion, see Martin Bock, 'De Quincey's Retrospective Optics: Analogues of Intoxication in the Opium-Eater's "Nursery Experiences"' in *Bicentenary Studies*, ed. R. L. Snyder (Norman, Okla.: University of Oklahoma Press, 1985), 72–87. Of course, as a child De Quincey was likely to have ingested opium, as it was a constituent of a great many conventional medicines for a wide variety of complaints.

the form in which he consumed opium, was a mixture of varying parts of alcohol and opium. M. H. Abrams has speculated that at the height of his consumption, De Quincey drank more than a pint of alcohol with his daily opium.[15] It therefore seems difficult to corroborate his claims to know the distinct qualities of each substance.

Such empirical evidence from De Quincey's life is not without relevance to the text, for throughout he seems confused as to opium's effects. Even in his exultations of the pleasures of opium, his celebration of its power to harmonize all disparate feelings leads on to descriptions of scenes remarkable for their disharmony and strangeness. For example, in 'The Pleasures of Opium', he celebrates the power of opium to reconcile his sensitive emotions to both the wealth and poverty of others. 'Opium', he writes, '. . . can overrule all feelings into a compliance with the master key' (C, 47): opium ensures the elision of difference, so that opposite events provoke the same response. In the description of his nightly excursions in the streets of London discussed in Chapter 2, he indicates how opium also has the capacity to elide temporal and cultural difference, for it expands his sense of time and space. However, as he describes a landscape that is as opaque as an impenetrable text, comprised of 'problems of alleys', 'enigmatic entries', and 'sphynx's riddles of streets', it is as though his own confused mind has been projected onto the landscape of London, which becomes as alien as the undiscovered world. Rather than elide difference, in this case opium has uncovered difference, not only in a familiar city, but also in his unknown self. The alien landscape represents his own mind, and De Quincey stands as the intrepid explorer, on the brink of colonizing himself. The interiority of the experience, in which he is both the alien land and the colonizer, crucially fractures his subjectivity. Opium has not found harmony, but disrupted his selfhood and his relation with the world.

Suspiria looks elsewhere for the harmony and unity that opium offers, yet withholds, in *Confessions*. This work proposes that

---

[15] M. H. Abrams, *The Milk of Paradise: The Effect of Opium Visions on the Works of De Quincey, Crabbe, Francis Thompson, and Coleridge* (1934; repr. New York: Harper & Row, 1970), 67 n. 35. Lindop, in *Opium-Eater*, 203, cites Sara Hutchinson's observation that De Quincey 'doses himself with opium and drinks like a f[ish]'.

unity will flow not from the consumption of opium, but rather from the consumption of both the autobiography and the auto-biographical subject as aesthetic objects. In *Suspiria*, reading and interpretation take the place of opium-eating, and writing is substituted as the sublime agent of order.

In *Suspiria*, temporality fractures the autobiographical subject. Recalling David Hume's proposition that identity is a fiction constructed to counter the ravages of time, De Quincey claims that every individual is subject to a fundamental dispersal of identity over time.[16] In 'Finale to Part I—Savannah-La-Mar', this radical discontinuity is explained in terms of Zeno's Paradox: in an attempt to discover the present, each moment is split into an infinite number of parts, only to find that the present is but 'a mathematical point': he writes, 'by infinite declensions the true and very present, in which only we live and enjoy, will vanish into a mote of a mote, distinguishable only by a heavenly vision' (C, 159). As every part of each moment is different from the last, the past becomes an ever-expanding and contradictory mass of incompatible events. The dilemma of the individual is that he must make sense of the disparate events that constitute his life.

Thus a recurrent theme of *Suspiria* is the disjunction between his life as an adult and as a child. Yet although childhood experience is offered as a key to adult behaviour, there is no necessary continuity between what are presented as two separate modes of life. 'The reader must not forget', he writes, '. . . that, though a child's feelings are spoken of, it is not the child who speaks. *I* decipher what the child only felt in cipher' (C, 113 n.). As the subject is placed in time, the fragmentation it suffers can only be negotiated through an act of interpretation: the adult's former self becomes a text that is only later available for reading. Significantly, the passing of time does not so much textualize the past as allow the consumption of the past's texts. It is the act of interpretation, the deciphering, that draws together the distinct parts of the man's life. The structure is similar to that suggested by the palimpsest discussed in Chapter 3, in which the 'potent

---

[16] David Hume, *Treatise of Human Understanding*, ed. L. A. Selby-Bigge, 2nd edn., rev. P. H. Nidditch (Oxford: Clarendon Press, 1978), 259: 'Sameness of person is nowhere to be found; the identity which we ascribe to the mind of man, is only a fictitious one.'

convulsion of the system' (C, 146) allows one to look back and draw together the various inscriptions of the past.

At the beginning of *Suspiria* he calls on the idea of *sympathy*, a familiar term from the vocabulary of aesthetic response, as a mode of reconciling past and present selves.[17] Sympathy operates by finding correspondence between substantially different objects. Thus,

> An adult sympathizes with himself in childhood because he *is* the same, and because (being the same) yet he is *not* the same. He acknowledges the deep, mysterious identity between himself, as adult and as infant, for the ground of his sympathy; and yet, with this general agreement, and necessity of agreement, he feels the differences between his two selves as the main quickeners of his sympathy. (C, 92)

Time incurs the fragmentation of the subject because it not only disrupts a particular identity, but also undermines the logical contingency for identity, for it allows the simultaneous production of incompatible events: the awkward syntax points to the difficulty of comprehending a situation in which the self '*is* the same, and because (being the same) yet he is *not* the same'. Sympathy heals the divided identity by negotiating the contradictions that confound the rational senses, that are indeed 'the main quickeners of his sympathy'. As before, a mode of aesthetic consumption heals the disjunctions incurred in time.

In *Suspiria* the divided subject is to be healed through the consumption of itself as an aesthetic object; the self is united by being both consumer and consumed. Nevertheless, in the more traumatic moments of the text, this strategy is not sustained and the multiplication of subject positions it requires becomes a source of anxiety. Thus in his childhood nightmare of the expanding book order, when his greedy wish for books is fulfilled in the form of a never-ending delivery of books, he weaves an extremely complex scenario in which his story is in fact an episode from the *Arabian Nights*, but also a retelling or a reproduction of the story that has already been told; moreover he not only realizes that he has

[17] On sympathy in 18th-cent. aesthetics, see James Sambrook, *The Eighteenth Century: The Intellectual and Cultural Context of English Literature, 1700–1789* (London: Longman, 1986), 121–3. For its prominence in Victorian aesthetics, see *Victorian Scrutinies: Review of Poetry 1830–1870*, ed. Isobel Armstrong (London: Athlone Press, 1972), 9.

already read his own story himself, but, worse, he has been read before by another people in another time and place:

> Here now was the case, that had once seemed so impressive to me in a mere fiction from a far-distant age and land, literally reproduced in myself. . . . It appeared, then, that I had been reading a legend concerning myself in the *Arabian Nights*. I had been contemplated in types a thousand years before on the banks of the Tigris. It was horror and grief that prompted that thought. (C, 135)

Both producer and produced, consumer and consumed, De Quincey is reproduced as a story that he has already produced, and consumed as a fiction that he has already consumed himself. Rather than healing his subjectivity, this multiplication of subject positions bespeaks his radical fragmentation.

It is crucial to understand the implications of this passage. *Suspiria* suggests that the consumption of the subject as an aesthetic object is a mode of achieving unity and order. Yet this passage demonstrates that this unity can never be attained since it incurs a multiplication of subject positions that is ultimately disabling. A sublime over-production takes place, and he can find no stable position from which to speak. The problems of individual agency and autonomy continue to haunt the autobiographical text, for it is the very mode of unification that is the text's undoing.

As the boy De Quincey is left floundering between Europe and Arabia, between 1845 and a thousand years before, we see that the aestheticization of the subject has engendered an unsettling abandonment of chronology and cultural hierarchies. It begins to become apparent that the problems of lost agency expressed in the autobiographies are entwined with the distant concerns in the East. The bolstering of the self is required to fend off encroachments and contaminations from abroad: from the Malay who haunts his dreams in *Confessions*, to the Dark Interpreter of *Suspiria*, who knows more than he about himself, De Quincey's autobiographies contain menacing oriental figures against whom he must defend himself.

In the next section I will suggest that the threat that the East constitutes, which is evident in his writings of the late 1830s and 1840s, is associated in De Quincey's mind with troubled Sino-British relations which result in the Opium War. The removal of opium from the centre of his autobiographical project in the 1840s is motivated by an intricate network of concerns that include issues of national sovereignty and the balance of trade, as well as concerns closer to his private life.

Opium

A sign of opium's changing image in British public life between the 1820s and 1840s was the fact that in 1834, the literary establishment was scandalized by De Quincey's exposure of Coleridge as a drug addict and plagiarizer.[18] On both charges De Quincey was hardly innocent himself. Plagiarism and drug addiction are interestingly related vices, for both are disavowals of authenticity and integrity: the plagiarizer commits literary theft and abandons the semblance of originality, while the opium-eater relinquishes his will to a greater agency, as his integrity is usurped by the omnipotent drug.

An opium-eater, like all addicts, risks loss of personality. *Confessions* bears witness to this for, as we have seen, in this work opium became 'the true hero' of his autobiography, leeching on his identity to such an extent that it usurped the subject of his life story. In the later autobiographies, this loss of identity was more troubling, and in the revised *Confessions*, which had previously been published anonymously, he was at pains to assert his identity, appending a long note on the De Quincey genealogy (III: 457–9). In fact the initial anonymity of the work had allowed its authorship to be claimed by another writer, since Thomas Griffiths Wainewright, a man infamous for his crimes of forgery, poisoning, and opium-eating, did profess to have written the

---

[18] 'Samuel Taylor Coleridge', *Tait's*, NS, 1 (Sept., Oct., Nov. 1834), 509–20, 588–96, 685–90, and NS, 2 (Jan. 1835), 3–10. For an account of this episode, see Lindop, *Opium-Eater*, 314–6. On the changing reputation of opium in the 1830s, see Christine Barnes Stevenson, 'The Shade of Homer Exorcises the Ghost of De Quincey: Tennyson's "The Lotus-Eaters"', *Browning Institute Studies*, 10 (1982), 117–41. Stevenson argues that Tennyson's revisions of 'The Lotus-Eaters' reveal a need to re-evaluate his Romantic heritage. Reading the poem as an exploration of addiction, she focuses on the representation of opium as the bearer of the increasingly unsatisfactory values of Romanticism.

Confessions.[19] The Wainewright saga shows that if opium causes one to lose one's own agency, it nevertheless enables one to claim another's.

The consumption of opium tends to undermine notions of authenticity, originality, and individuality, striking a blow at the heart of the bourgeois subject. Moreover it is similarly troublesome in relation to the production of literature, for it negates the values for which literature is conventionally praised. In accounts of Romantic literature, in which drug experiences were not marginalized but rather a feature of much of the best writing, the problem of authenticity—the extent to which writers known to be addicts might nevertheless be held responsible for their literary products—is a recurrent one. Indeed the Romantics often praised opium as the agent of artistic creativity, functioning in the same way as other exterior agents necessary to the Romantic idealist aesthetic in which, following the structures of the sublime, a mountain, a breeze, a solitary woman, or a nightingale's song moved the perceiving subject to write.[20] Nevertheless its disturbing physical effects raised special problems: while the wonders of nature might have excited a man to literary production, they did not, like opium, cause physical and psychological distress and dependency, the shaking hands, pale diminished form, and the torpor which were the characteristics of the nineteenth-century opium-eater.

During the mid-twentieth century when New Critics placed the notions of authenticity and authorial integrity high on the critical agenda, the Romantics' interest in drug-induced states of altered consciousness was resuscitated as a point of critical debate. Various strategies emerged for asserting the poet's authorial power despite its loss incurred by opium. For instance, M. H. Abrams in

---

[19] See Alethea Hayter, *Opium and the Romantic Imagination* (London: Faber & Faber, 1968), 105. On Wainewright, see Oscar Wilde, 'Pen, Pencil and Poison, a Study in Green', in *The Artist as Critic: The Critical Writings of Oscar Wilde*, ed. Richard Ellmann (London: W. H. Allen, 1970), 320–40. For De Quincey's memories of Wainewright, see V: 246–50.

[20] Cf. Clifford Siskin in *The Historicity of Romantic Discourse* (Oxford: OUP, 1988), 179–94, who argues that critical accounts of Romanticism have tended to emphasize the correspondences between the effects of drug experiences—and in particular, the structure of addiction—and Romantic literature itself.

The Milk of Paradise (1934), and Alethea Hayter in *Opium and the Romantic Imagination* (1968) argued that opium had a significant effect on writing, for it gave access to a new experience, or as Abrams put it, a 'new world'.[21] This world was recognizable by its strange oriental landscapes which, like the orient, were ahistorical and unchanging. But as the poet articulated these new and common experiences to the best of his ability, poetic agency appeared to have been reinstated. Indeed, for these critics, the consumption of opium did not challenge the notion of authenticity. Instead it provided a mode of asserting the timelessness of experience and the unchanging nature of the world, a means of a common experience that was individual and never collective, and within which a semblance of agency might be restored.

Similarly, Elisabeth Schneider, writing in 1953, was motivated by the anxiety that drugs threaten to usurp poetic genius.[22] She drew on the evidence of contemporary medical science to prove that not only was opium not bad for the health, but also it had no particular or necessary effect on the writings of a habituated consumer. The consistency of imagery in the writings of opium-eaters was due to a common set of textual references, rather than the shared experience of the drug. Using the responses of a class of schoolchildren who had been presented for the first time with the poem 'Kubla Khan', she demonstrated that the marks of the creative genius of the poet, uncompromised by the effects of opium, persisted in the poem, and were recognizable to innocent and fresh readers who were untainted by the judgements of past critics.

The striking point about these accounts of opium in Romanticism, however, is their range of opinion as to its capacity to affect literature. While Abrams and Hayter attribute opium the power to infiltrate literary production and create an entire 'new world', Schneider regards its effect as negligible. Such differing representations are repeated with uncanny regularity in accounts of opium in the Romantic and Victorian eras in a number of different discourses. In early nineteenth-century medicine, opium was a benign and powerful anodyne, a cure for all ailments, but also a

---

[21] Abrams, *Milk of Paradise*, 48.

[22] E. Schneider, *Coleridge, Opium and 'Kubla Khan'* (Chicago: University of Chicago Press, 1953).

poison, a familiar agent for suicide.[23] As an intoxicant, it was considered on the one hand less harmful than alcohol, and alternatively a dangerous compelling drug, causing guilt in the consumer and pity in his or her contemporaries. While many of the discrepancies in these accounts might be ascribed to ignorance of its powers, it is nevertheless significant that a similar range of opinions persists today in discourses on drugs, despite medical knowledge: recent attitudes have ranged from the sensationalist message of the 1980s anti-heroin campaign in Britain which bandied the notion that one shot meant certain death, or at very least a protracted life of abject misery, to the alternative view that it is the criminalization of drugs that causes physical, psychological, and social problems, and that even an addictive drug such as heroin might be incorporated into 'normal' social behaviour.[24]

These conflicting attitudes towards opium can also be identified in the debate over the 1839–42 Opium War. Sparked off by an incident in the Chinese government's campaign to eliminate the trade in opium, the war was the result of a conflict of interests between the British desire to expand its share of world trade, and the Chinese desire for autonomy. However, discussion of the rights and wrongs of the war tended to be displaced on to the controversial powers of opium, the drug.

Although the Chinese government had banned the import of opium since the late eighteenth century, British merchants had persisted in their lucrative trade in the drug, which was cultivated for the Chinese market in India by the East India Company.[25] The export of opium from India to China greatly increased in 1834 when the East India Company lost its monopoly in China, and trade was thrown open. By 1838 it was estimated that in some provinces nine out of ten people were opium addicts.[26] The opium

---

[23] Berridge and Edwards, *Opium and the People*, 80–1.

[24] On the social construction of representations of drugs, see Marek Kohn, *Narcomania: On Heroin* (London: Faber, 1987).

[25] The economic urgency for Britain to continue the opium trade with China is noted by Hsü, who cites House of Commons' Select Committee reports of 1830 and 1832: 'it does not seem advisable to abandon so important a source of revenue as the East India Company's monopoly of opium in Bengal.' See Hsü, *The Rise of Modern China*, 225.

[26] Ibid. 223. Cf. Fairbank, *History of China*, 178.

trade also caused acute damage to the Chinese economy. Until the escalation in opium imports, around 90 per cent of the shipments to China from the East India Company had been gold to exchange for Chinese goods such as silks and tea; only 10 per cent of imports took the form of commodities. By the mid-1820s, the balance had slipped completely the other way, and by the 1830s, Chinese silver was pouring out of the country, partly because the illicit nature of the trade in opium meant that opium was exchanged for cash, rather than the traditional method of exchange by barter. For the British, opium allowed trade with China to be conducted without incurring a substantial monetary defecit. Thus when in 1838 Lin Tse-hsü, the imperial commissioner attributed with the charge of suppressing the opium trade, organized a stringent campaign to rid China of opium, imprisoning dealers and even executing addicts, arresting British smugglers and confiscating their cargoes, the British prime minister, Lord Melbourne, declared war in defence of the trade, beginning a bloody military campaign. The signing of the Treaty of Nanking in 1842 formally ended hostilities, and provided the basis for a temporary peace. As well as a large payment of 'compensation' for the confiscation of British opium, the Chinese ceded Hong Kong to the British; opened a number of ports to trade and for the residence of British consuls, merchants and their families; and ended the traditional Chinese monopolistic system of trade.[27] The matter did not rest here, however, for new campaigns began in the 1850s and lasted until 1860.

In Britain, the war was supported by Whigs and Radicals, who, as supporters of free trade, saw the world as a market-place in which everyone should have equal rights to trade. In January 1839, Dr William Jardine, the wealthiest trader in Canton, whose company, Jardine, Matheson and Company, handled about a third of the total opium in China, gathered the support of some three hundred Midlands textiles firms in his efforts to persuade

---

[27] On the monopolistic trade, see Fairbank, *History of China*, x. 164–71. One point conceded to the Chinese in the treaty was equality in official correspondence. This was a point of contention throughout the affair as the British merchants refused to approach the Chinese government in the manner considered appropriate in China. Likewise, in 1839 Commissioner Lin sent a letter to Queen Victoria through a British envoy, but this was not recognized as an official document by the British government. The point highlights the problems of cultural difference that provoked the situation.

the government to protect the interests of trade in China.[28] Opposition to the war was led by the Tories, Robert Peel and James Graham, who spoke in the name of the moral conscience of the nation.[29] Capturing this spirit of moral concern, Gladstone, still a Peelite Tory at the time, declared that he did not know of a more 'unjust and iniquitous war.'[30] This vocabulary was echoed by the other main opposition group to the war, radical evangelicals, whose views were expressed in periodicals such as *Eclectic Review* and *Household Words*: the importers of opium were 'demoralizing' the Chinese population; a Christian government had a duty to send missionaries to 'civilize' the Chinese, and not to poison them.[31] Parliamentary opposition, however, was greatly diminished when the war began to be presented as a cause of national honour rather than as an infringement of Christian duty: by impounding British opium and imprisoning its owners, it was held, the Chinese were guilty of an affront to British dignity, and should be taught to respect its citizens and its property. Such nationalist fervour united parliament behind the war, which was transformed into a just and honourable campaign in support of British sovereignty.[32]

---

[28] Fairbank, *History of China*, x. 193–5.

[29] Bernard Semmel, *The Rise of Free Trade Imperialism: Classical Political Economy, the Empire of Free Trade, and Imperialism, 1750–1850* (Cambridge: CUP, 1970), 152.

[30] Cited by Semmel, ibid. 152.

[31] For example, Nathan Allen, in an article taken from his pamphlet, *The Opium Trade Including a Sketch of its History, Extent, Effects, etc, as Carried on in India and China* (Boston, 1850), wrote, 'the English are constantly supplying the Chinese with a deadly poison with which thousands yearly put an end to their existence' ('The Opium Trade', *People's Journal*, 10 (1850), 53). Similarly J. J. Darling commented: 'The war with China has begun, and already several hundred Chinese have been murdered by our cruisers, because the government will not allow us to poison its subjects; in which poisoning it appears, we have obtained a vested right' ('Political Register', in *Tait's*, NS, 7 (March 1840), 201–4). A commentator in the *Eclectic Review* notes that the insidious effects of opium contaminate all who are involved in the trade: 'The health and morals of the people suffer from the production of opium. Wherever opium is growing, it is eaten and the more it is grown the more it is eaten; this is one of the worst features of the opium question. We are demoralizing our own subjects in India; one-half of the crime in the opium districts, murders, rapes and affrays, have their origin in opium-eating.' If the opium industry were eliminated, 'we should in the end be richly rewarded, by having a fine healthy force of men growing up for our plantations, to fell our forests, to clear the land from jungle and wild beasts and to plant and cultivate the luxury of the world [tea].' *Eclectic Review*, NS, 7 (1840), 718–19.

[32] Hsü claims that the opposition between 'the Chinese claim to universal overlordship and the Western idea of national sovereignty' was at the heart of the conflict. Hsü, *The Rise of Modern China*, 246.

De Quincey's essay 'The Opium Question with China in 1840', published in *Blackwood's* in June of that year, expressed jingoistic support for the war. In line with the proponents of the war, he argued that opium was a harmless intoxicant in great demand by the evil and greedy Chinese whose government had banned Indian opium only so that it might fulfil the demand with home-grown supplies.[33] Greed motivated the Chinese both in their consumption of the drug, and in their desire to reap the profits of this valuable commodity. On the other hand, opponents of the war considered opium to be a dangerous poison; the reason to withdraw from the campaign was not an abhorrence of imperialist aggression, but rather the immoral nature of the goods that were imported. Indeed the fears concerning opium that dominated the anti-war rhetoric tended both to deflect and to repeat anxieties about the alien nature of the Chinese: the use of opium was a mark of foreignness signifying a cultural difference that was best eliminated. The difficulties of this position were illustrated by Nathan Allen's call in 1850 for 'a Wilberforce' to free the Chinese from their enslavement to opium. It passed notice that Wilberforce himself had used laudanum for many years.[34]

This discussion exemplifies the general point that the range of popular representations of opium—from the all-transforming, pernicious killer-drug to the harmless and controllable intoxicant—tends to be replicated throughout history and in different contexts. It is perhaps because opium experiences induce changed states of consciousness and are thus in the normal sense unknowable, that they present to the understanding a blank spot that is always ready to be filled with fanciful explanations that bear little relation to opium itself. Mystified and over-determined in its meanings, there is a sense that debates about opium are always in fact about something else, and that opium itself functions in a

---

[33] Cf. T. H. Bullock in 'The Opium Question of India considered in Connexion with Mr. Laing's Last Budget', *Fraser's Magazine*, 66 (Oct. 1862), 403: 'Opium is neither very much better nor very much worse than gin.'

[34] 'As the East India Company is shortly to petition parliament for a renewal of its charter, who will fearlessly come forward like Clarkson and Wilberforce, to examine into this evil, expose its terrible effects and call for their removal?' Allen, *The Opium Trade*, 63. Although the name itself was left blank in the original preface to *Confessions*, in the revised edition, De Quincey listed 'the eloquent and benevolent William Wilberforce' as among the distinguished opium-eaters of the time (III: 212 n.).

covert way as a means of representing the desires and values of those who speak about it.

From among the accounts considered so far, opium is connected with two recurrent but opposed models of representation. The two rest on a sharp distinction between the ideal and the material: in the first, opium invokes an escape into the shadowy world of ideal forms; in the second, an abrupt return to the certainties of material life. The two will be familiar, for they are comparable with the two kinds of writing to be found in De Quincey's work already outlined.

In the idealist form, opium incurs an addiction to writing, and transport to a realm of aesthetic discourse that exists explicitly outside history, as witnessed in the store of oriental imagery that Abrams and Hayter identify as the mark of opium-induced writing. The incomprehensibility of the opium experience renders it sublime, and it provokes discourses in which the referent is curiously displaced and acquired through a logic that is always devious. As the direct relations of reference have been severed, the discourses of opium are unbounded and straggling, so that writing becomes a kind of contagion that spreads through reading. Thus De Quincey's *Confessions* provoked a proliferation of writing that included his own over-burgeoning body of unfinished texts and those of writers fascinated by his style and addiction. Various parodies followed the publication of *Confessions*: for instance, *The Confessions of a Green Tea Drinker*, and Wilson's 'Noctes Ambrosianae'; and Baudelaire's translation and expansion of De Quincey's *Confessions* as *Les Paradis artificiels*. Indeed to a large extent De Quincey set the tone for a still-growing sub-genre of drug literature.[35]

Confessions has inspired not only literary works. More surprisingly, it has also been incorporated into scientific and medical accounts of opium. Robert Macnish's popular philosophical-cum-medical treatises, *Drunkenness* (1827) and *Sleep* (1830) made extensive reference to De Quincey's accounts of intoxication and

---

[35] Anon., 'Confessions of a Green-Tea Drinker', *Monthly Religious Magazine*, 25 (1860), 317–9; John Wilson, 'Noctes Ambrosianae', *Blackwood's*, 14 (Oct. 1824), 484–503; Charles Pierre Baudelaire, *Les Paradis artificiels: opium et haschisch* (Paris, 1860). For subsequent 'drug narratives', see *Hashish Club: Anthology of Drug Literature*, ed. Peter Haining, 2 vols. (London: P. Owen, 1975).

dreams. Schneider, in 1953, went so far as to argue that *Confessions* retained its status as empirical evidence for medical research even into the twentieth century, a strange phenomenon given its idiosyncratic literary style.[36] In defiance of this literariness, it has also been held responsible for the drug experimentations of others. As early as 1836, Walter Cotton published his account of drug experiences which were supposedly incited by his reading of the *Confessions*.[37] Hayter's more recent anxiety, expressed in the introduction to *Opium and the Romantic Imagination*, that her book might induce its readers to experiment with drugs, reiterates the popular belief, that drug literature has the power to cause addiction in others.[38] In this case, it is as though the impossibility of representing the experience of the drug provokes a repetition of that experience: not, as in the former case, an escape into language, but a resort to action in the face of the failure of language. It is a gesture similar to that of nineteenth-century scientific discourse which accepted the *Confessions* as an empirical document, for both suggest that these representations of drug experiences step out of the realm of discourse into a sphere of direct action in the world. This then is the second model of representation, a model in which writing coerces action, which is always a compulsive repetition of the represented action: in the case of drug narratives, the repeated action is the consumption of the drugs and consequent addiction. It is a familiar model, for it corresponds to what I have called the aesthetic of force.

The two models of representation that opium suggests—representation as contagion, and representation as compulsion, or the aesthetic of force—match the two models of writing at work in De

---

[36] 'It would have delighted [De Quincey's] vanity to know that almost alone he dominated the scientific as well as the literary explanations of the effects of opium for nearly a hundred years.' Schneider, *Coleridge, Opium and 'Kubla Khan'*, 28. See also Hayter: '[De Quincey] is not often given credit for the impulse which his book undoubtedly gave to the scientific investigations which have helped and saved other addicts.' *Opium and the Romantic Imagination*, 35.

[37] Walter Cotton, 'Turkish Sketches', *Knickerbocker*, 7 (Apr. 1836), 421–5. Cf. Hayter: 'De Quincey is often blamed, and rightly, for the terrible fascination of his masterpiece in drawing in others to follow his example': see Hayter, *Opium and the Romantic Imagination*, 35.

[38] Hayter, *Opium and the Romantic Imagination*, 11–15. She makes a similar point in her introduction to her edition of the *Confessions* (Harmondsworth: Penguin, 1971).

Quincey's texts. De Quincey's works contain a struggle between these two kinds of writing, one digressive and circuitous, in which his own will is lost in an infinite proliferation of writing, and the other which forcibly inscribes the will of the writer, and demands submission on the part of the reader. Opium enters into this struggle in an ambiguous way; if initially it seems to be an agent which incurs the writer's loss of will, a usurper of a never-to-be-regained authority, it also endorses the second model, becoming itself a tyrannical force of order and conformity. If at first opium consumption marked a deliberate relinquishing of agency, it now suggests a model of representation in which a certain power is reclaimed with force, for the writer may not have control over his own writings, but through his writing he can direct the behaviour of others. The overwhelming power of opium comes to suggest a semblance of agency in the violence and coercion of spectacle.

In the later works, De Quincey was able to find in opium an aid to the reconstitution of social order. This is strange given that, as we shall see, in the political writings De Quincey declared opium addiction among the Chinese to be a sign of decadence within China's social fabric; moreover in his late autobiographies, opium is demoted from its prior status as the structuring agent in his life. Nevertheless in the introduction to *Suspiria*, he claims that opium and intense exercise are the unlikely pair of agents that will restore to men and women the power of dreaming which has been destroyed by the 'mighty revolutions amongst the kingdoms of the earth', caused by 'steam in all its applications, light getting under harness as a slave for man, powers from heaven descending upon education and accelerations of the press, powers from hell (as it might seem, but these also celestial) coming round upon artillery and the forces of destruction' (C, 87). Thus opium figures as the last hope against all the forces of change that he deplores: industry, advances in communications and in education, increased democracy, social change. De Quincey's monotonous diatribe against modern life is met by a surprising solution—opium.

In the political discourse of the time, however, opium marked the weak spot of the British economy, for the opium trade in China was an important source of revenue that sustained the British balance of trade. China's attempt to outlaw the opium trade threatened to cause deflation and poverty in Britain. This

structure of trade resembles that of addiction: Britain's depend-
ence on the Chinese market assigned a dangerous power to the
consumer, the withdrawal of whose custom would have devastating consequences in Britain. This situation partially explains the
difference between the estimation of opium in the early and late
autobiographies, for at this juncture, opium's capacity to usurp a
subject's identity and agency parallels similar concerns in the
economy. While in the 1820s opium's power to usurp agency
might be celebrated and aestheticized as a sublime moment, in the
1840s it has distasteful economic reverberations. In an uncanny
reversal, the structures of addiction always turn back on themselves, for the power of consumption usurps the power of production, just as the pleasures of opium slip into its pains. Imperial
trade becomes an addiction that replicates the patterns of De
Quincey's own drug addiction: if in the 1820s Britain enjoyed the
pleasures of foreign trade, the 1840s brought about its pains. De
Quincey's concerns for lost agency explored in *Suspiria* are intensified by the worry that national sovereignty might be usurped by
the Chinese.

The meanings of opium shift in response to factors external to
it. But De Quincey's experience of addiction persisted, despite his
attempts to free himself from his enslavement.[39] In the final section of this chapter, I will suggest that *Suspiria* marks an attempt
to describe the condition of being addicted, without reference to
opium, the agent of that addiction. *Suspiria* is a traumatic text
because it dares to explore the psychic consequences of addiction,
the unpalatable trajectory of which, in economic terms, is the
potential of the Chinese to ruin the British economy.

Addiction

By the late eighteenth century, the East India Company had
recognized opium's potential as a commodity for the generation of large profits, and had perfected methods of its wide-scale

---

[39] Lindop observes that *Suspiria* 'was begun under the pressure of the sudden
upsurge of dreaming produced by a partial withdrawal from opium': Lindop,
Opium-Eater, 353. Later De Quincey decided that a life without laudanum was
unendurable and 'resigned himself to remaining an opium-eater until his dying
day' (368).

cultivation and production. The processes of preparation and refinement were labour-intensive: entire Indian villages were engaged in its production, from the harvesting of the poppies to the packaging of the drug for transport to the ports of Calcutta and Bombay.[40] But Indian labour was cheap, and at each stage of production the value of the opium increased rapidly, reaping vast profits for the British landlords. Moreover large amounts of revenue were derived from taxes levied on the production of opium and on its passage through the different regions of the Indian subcontinent, as it was transported to entrepôts on the coast. The manufacture and circulation of opium, and the seemingly unlimited wealth it produced, strangely resemble De Quincey's nightmare visions of endless reproduction and accumulation.

At the Indian ports, the opium was auctioned to merchants who carried the drug to China and traded it for Chinese silver. In the anti-opium trade rhetoric in Britain, the nature of this transaction became a focus of attention. An article in *Household Words* of 1857 commented that

the opium is paid for, before delivery, and the payment is in nothing less than Sycee silver, lumps of the purest silver estimated by weight at so much per ounce: no bills, no bonds, no barter: Sycee, and nothing but Sycee, in exchange for the opium. The history of commerce presents nothing more solid or direct than the purchase price of opium.[41]

The solidity of the silver becomes fetishized, for at the end of the line, the opium had transcended the fluctuations of capital to become a physical substitute for a tangible piece of silver. The processes of refinement multiplied alongside the drug's rapidly increasing economic value, generating profits and allowing the distribution of wealth among various parties. However, at the point of exchange, the processes of the accumulation of wealth came to a halt, and the social problems incurred by opium began to take over. The acceleration of social degradation in the

[40] See 'The Opium Trade and War', *Eclectic Review*, NS, 7 (June 1840), 699–725; 'Opium: Chapter the First, India,' *Household Words*, 16 (Aug. 1857), 104–8; W. S. Fry, *Facts and Evidence Relating to the Opium Trade with China* (London, 1840); Allen, *The Opium Trade*; and Robert Alexander, *Rise and Progress of British Opium Smuggling, and its Effects upon India, China, and the Commerce of Great Britain* (London, 1856).

[41] 'Opium,' *Household Words*, 16 (Aug. 1857), 182.

consumers mirrored the accumulation of wealth for the pro-
ducers: as a commodity that caused habituation in its consumers, opium had created a constant market at the same time
as it produced seemingly limitless poverty.

The social effects of opium addiction lay at the centre of arguments against this trade. Nathan Allen encapsulated liberal outrage when he asked, 'How long is it to continue to drain the
country of its specie—embarrass its finances—corrupt its offi-
cers—impoverish and ruin its inhabitants?'[42] The effect of opium
was to infect the social apparatus and cause the complete decay of
its institutions. Part of the problem caused by the drug was the
characteristic torpor it produced in its consumers, for widespread
addiction caused a collapse in the Chinese labour supply.[43] In his
essay of 1840, De Quincey argued against the claim that the
opium trade with China 'palpably affect[s] the public industry'
(XIV: 168), on the grounds that the price of the commodity auto-
matically excluded the lower classes from its consumption. However, later in the same essay he contradicted his claim by pointing
out the direct connection between poverty and the widespread
use of opium. As a means of retribution for Chinese aggression,
De Quincey recommended that the British relinquish its tea trade
with China; this would have widespread effects, causing steep
inflation. He wrote, 'Jails will be filled, suicides will multiply,
taxes will be unpaid, opium-eating will prosper' (XIV: 183).
Opium typically contradicts the logic of good household
economy, for it thrives on poverty, creating uncontrollable desires
that supersede the financial limitations of the consumer.

Continuing his speculations in the 1840 essay, as to the fate of
the Chinese, De Quincey wrote:

Wealth is the surplus arising after consumption is replaced. Now, it is
certain that upon every British family, not being paupers, such a surplus
arises. But upon the vast body of the Chinese, living on rivers, and eating
the garbage rejected by the meanest of the comfortable classes, though
not paupers, yet no surplus at all arises. (XIV: 183)[44]

---

[42] Allen, *The Opium Trade*, 52.
[43] On the damage to the Chinese economy, see Hsü, *Rise of Modern China*, 224,
and Fairbank, *History of China*, x. 178–9.
[44] Cf. Marx on the Irish: 'The Irishman has only one need left—the need to
eat, to eat *potatoes*, and, more precisely, to eat *rotten potatoes*, the worst kind of

The model of wealth as surplus is wielded in an effort to assert the superior strength of the British despite their much smaller population. The British, who consistently produce more than they consume, are wealthy, while the Chinese, who cannot produce enough for their vast population, are impoverished. But this model of wealth as surplus only functions when there is a foreign market to buy the excess goods: without this, there would be a situation of glut and overabundance. The Chinese theoretically provided an ideal market for British goods, but De Quincey's description of them, living on waste, implied that in fact they were able to exist and reproduce themselves outside the economy; their poverty provided the best resistance to British trade.

The argument here should be seen as part of De Quincey's conception of the strategy to impel the Chinese to trade with Britain. De Quincey's recommendation of an embargo on the import of Chinese tea into Britain was based on his understanding of Ricardo's principles of land economy: De Quincey argued that although the trade in tea was slight in comparison with the trade in opium, such a sanction would nevertheless have a devastating effect on the entire Chinese economy. But if the British could ruin the Chinese by withdrawing the purchase of tea, the Chinese, in view of their large consumption of opium and the vast expanses of British poppy plantations in India, had still greater powers over the British.

The point he insisted on in the 1840 essay was China's resistance to trade. It was this that marked China out as an 'inorganic' nation, 'having no commerce worth counting, no vast establishments of maritime industry, no arsenals, no shipbuilding towns, no Portsmouths, Deals, Deptfords, Woolwiches, Sunderlands, Newcastles, Liverpools, Bristols, Glasgows,—in short, no vital parts, no organs, no heart, no lungs' (XIV: 176). '[A]t present [China] is an inorganic mass—something to be kicked, but which cannot kick again' (XIV: 176). But if colonization and trade were

potatoes.' See Karl Marx, 'Economic and Philosophical Manuscripts' in *Early Writings*, trans. Rodney Livingstone and Gregor Benton (Harmondsworth: Penguin, 1974), 360. On sewage and waste, see Peter Stallybrass and Allon White, 'The City: the Sewer, the Gaze and the Contaminating Touch' in *The Politics and Poetics of Transgression* (London: Methuen, 1986), 125–48.

the marks of organic life, it was these that would become Britain's weakness, for the rapid expansion of trade in the East made Britain vulnerable to attack. 'It is a subject of just alarm', he wrote, 'that not only will the occasions for revenge be multiplied, but the chances of provoking revenge by offending those unnatural laws will even outrun our increased scale of intercourse' (XIV: 191). Ultimately the organic growth of the empire made it undefendable and steadily less able to be controlled. In this, De Quincey repeated the familiar Romantic image of the decay that is inherent in all organic growth; Keats' images of overproduction and glut are called to mind, for the aesthetic images of Romanticism articulated the economic problems associated with the expansion of trade in the mid-nineteenth century. If organic growth ironically contained the seeds of its own destruction, so too did foreign trade; for not only were the outposts of the empire difficult to protect, but the refusal of foreign consumers to buy the produce of British emporia produced a glut of unsellable opium, the ultimate consequences of which would be the decline of the British economy, the decay of the over-productive nation. This is the structure of addiction, in which pleasure turns into pain, and pain and pleasure merge into one another. It is pleasure's excess that is always the problem, just as the excess of production caused problems in the British economy. Thus it is significant that one can detect differences between the articulation and theorization of excess in the early and late autobiographical works, particularly in the representation of pleasure.

In the *Confessions*, De Quincey provided an elaborate account of his own first purchase of opium. The point which aroused his constant wonder was the 'humanity' of the 'sublunary druggist', the 'unconscious minister of celestial pleasures' (C, 38), who administered to him the small tincture of the drug. De Quincey focused on various details of the transaction that confirmed the apothecary's human status despite his mystical powers. Of these, the coin returned as change became a sign that it was a usual economic exchange: 'out of my shilling, [he] returned me what seemed to be a real copper halfpence, taken out of a real wooden drawer' (C, 38). That opium had an exchange value, and one moreover that was far beneath its pleasure value, was the cause of De Quincey's overwhelming wonder. The pleasurable excess that opium caused surpassed economic representation, and took off into the realm of the supernatural. The sublime powers of the drug superseded the conditions of natural life, and the druggist unnaturally disappeared. 'I believe him to have evanesced, or evaporated,' De Quincey wrote. 'So unwillingly would I connect any mortal remembrances with that hour, and place, and creature' (C, 38).

In the writings of the post-1840 period, however, De Quincey attempted to ascertain opium's value, but as a drug with specific medical functions. In the revised *Confessions*, he expounded at great length various theses concerning the medicinal powers of opium, particularly as a cure for pulmonary diseases.[45] Moreover he argued that if an insurance broker were to calculate the premium on the life of an opium eater, the consumption of opium would only be a relevant factor in the equation in so far as it indicated that the person possibly suffered from some other complaint, for opium itself would not unnaturally foreshorten life. The hedonist who took opium purely for pleasure would be of no concern to the insurance broker.[46] The argument between De Quincey and Coleridge as to which was the 'worse' addict, revolved around a similar denial of the pleasurable aspects of opium: the claim which both writers laid against the other was that, while the accuser was a victim of the addictive capacities of a drug taken only for relief from physical symptoms, the other took the drug purely for pleasure.[47] The addictive capacity of opium could only be considered as a danger to which the consumer was an unwitting and passive victim: neither De Quincey nor Coleridge could entertain the idea that this addiction might have been entered into wittingly and for pleasure, for addiction suggested a masochism that transcended both comprehensibility and the economy.

Despite this, there is an important sense in which *Suspiria* does attempt to represent pleasure. Recounting an anecdote concerning a tourist in the Lake District searching for the quickest route to Keswick, De Quincey replies: 'Most excellent stranger, as you come to the lakes simply to see their loveliness, might it not be as

[45] Cf. Berridge and Edwards, *Opium and the People*, 67.
[46] Cf. Virginia Berridge, 'Opium-Eating and Life Insurance,' *British Journal of Addiction*, 72 (1977), 371–7.
[47] See, for example, III: 231–2.

well to ask after the most beautiful road, rather than the shortest? For if abstract shortness, if τὸ *brevity* is your object, then the shortest of all possible tours would seem, with submission— never to have left London' (C, 93). What is to be explored in this work is pleasure as it exists for itself, for *Suspiria* contains the representation of pleasure apart from opium. He writes:

The true object in my 'Opium Confessions' is not the naked physiological theme—on the contrary, *that* is the ugly pole, the murderous spear, the halbert—but those wandering musical variations upon the theme—those parasitical thoughts, feelings, digressions, which climb up with bells and blossoms around the arid stock. (C, 94)

Not the agent of addiction, but the addiction itself is the subject of *Suspiria*. Abandoning himself to excess, De Quincey represents in aesthetic discourse what cannot easily be assessed in economic terms: the masochistic pleasures of addiction.

The text thus engages directly with the pleasurable loss of power incurred in addiction. This discourse of pleasure is beset with dangers, for it is always inscribed with the threat of death. '[V]iew me', he writes, 'as one . . . making verdant, and gay with the life of flowers, murderous spears and halberts—things that express death in their origin, . . . things that express ruin in their use' (C, 94). Throughout, his own selfhood is at stake in the structures of excess: in the excesses of opium, in which pleasure turns to pain, in the excesses of writing, and the excesses of production—each turns back on De Quincey, to swamp his own self.

The figure of the Brocken Spectre illustrates this process. This strange phenomenon that occurs under specific atmospheric conditions, is an apparition of a giant image of the perceiving subject. De Quincey describes the appearance of this figure that mirrors all his movements. Testing its powers of representation, he declares, 'You are now satisfied that the apparition is but a reflex of yourself; and, uttering your secret feelings to *him*, you make this phantom the dark symbolic mirror for reflecting to the daylight what else must be hidden for ever' (C, 156). The Brocken's supreme powers of reflection represent aspects of the self that are otherwise hidden, producing a giant and unfamiliar copy. In a process of excess and reversal, it usurps the self.

De Quincey calls this apparition the Dark Interpreter, granting it surprising powers of intellect. It is, however, significant that the

Brocken should be implicated in the process of literary consumption, for it is in the process of consumption that his self is lost; as in the book dream, the consumption of a textualized self, which is offered as a strategy for healing the fractured subject, incurs deeper and more troubling fissures. Here the 'reflex' of the self has associations with alien cultures that are profoundly disturbing: 'He is originally a mere reflex of my inner nature. But as the apparition of the Brocken sometimes is disturbed by storms or by driving showers, so as to dissemble his real origin, in like manner the Interpreter sometimes swerves out of my orbit, and mixes a little with alien natures' (C, 156). The Dark Interpreter's intercourse with 'alien natures' indicates excursions to the East. As in the book dream, De Quincey's own self is consumed and reproduced in the orient.

In *Confessions* the most striking representation of the orient is in the dream of the Malay. In this, his own self is scattered in a terrifying amalgam of all eastern landscapes:

Under the connecting feeling of tropical heat and vertical sun-lights, I brought together all creatures, birds, beasts, reptiles, all trees and plants, usages and appearances, that are found in all tropical regions and assembled them together in China and Indostan. From kindred feelings, I soon brought Egypt and all her gods under the same law. I was stared at, hooted at, grinned at, chattered at, by monkeys, by paroquets, by cockatoos. I ran into pagodas: and was fixed for centuries, at the summit, or in secret rooms; I was the idol; I was the priest; I was worshipped; I was sacrificed. I fled from the wrath of Brama through all the forests of Asia: Vishnu hated me: Seeva laid wait for me. I came suddenly upon the Isis and Osiris: I had done a deed, they said, which the ibis and the crocodile trembled at. I was buried, for a thousand years, in stone coffins, with mummies and sphynxes, in narrow chambers at the heart of eternal pyramids. I was kissed, with cancerous kisses, by crocodiles: and laid, confounded with all unutterable slimy things, amongst reeds and Nilotic mud. (C, 73)

In this over-burgeoning orient, China, India and Egypt come together in an awe-inspiring glut of the exotic. As in the Piranesi dream, his own self is multiplied in a variety of fantastic and compromising positions. However, the passage is punctuated by the insistent interjection of the first person: despite the traumatic multiplication of the self, there is nevertheless a certain confidence in the continuity of his subjectivity that is lacking in later works. In this context, the significant feature of the dreams of the early *Confessions* is the assertion of himself as a producing subject; like the architect, Piranesi, he builds himself in dreams and fantasies. Although there is undoubtedly an anxiety concerning his imminent loss of control incurred through this boundless self-reproduction, which is aestheticized as the sumptuous generation of literary images of the orient, this is crucially different from the total dissolution of self that is implied in the later works.

As I have suggested, the dreams of the late autobiographies are best characterized by the nightmare of the expanding book order in *Suspiria*. In this De Quincey fears that he will be simultaneously swamped by an infinite pile of books, and drowned in the flooding 'river' of his debts. The physicality of the images indicates that his anxieties reverberate around a fear of bodily loss that is different from the sense of infinite self-reproduction in evidence in the early work. In the book dream, his fears culminate in the awareness that his experiences have already been read, hundreds of years before, in the *Arabian Nights*: his identity and agency are lost in a fracturing of his self between his simultaneous and incompatible positions of producer and produced, consumer and consumed. Significantly the topic of the books he has ordered is 'a general history of navigation, supported by a vast body of voyages' (C, 131): it is the exploratory impulse, the desire to cover the vast globe that incurs this loss of self. In its geographical dimensions, this anxiety is reminiscent of his concern for the expanding size of the Empire and the difficulty of protecting British merchants' ships expressed in the 1840 essay, 'The Opium Question with China'. The dream explores the troubling notion of the 1840s, that the European subject is at risk of losing itself in a dangerous and unprotected world, the same issue that is discussed in the political writings on the relations between Britain and China. De Quincey's anxieties concerning his own loss of self through over-consumption of books presents an analogy with his anxieties of loss of self in opium addiction; but they are also analogous with the threat to national power he perceives in the venture into trade with distant and alien societies.

In *Suspiria*, De Quincey describes the masochism of addiction producing his elaborately tortured text. The economic corollary of addiction, the crisis in colonial trade, which repeats the same masochistic structure, cannot be similarly countenanced, for in this case the stakes—national sovereignty—are too high. Instead, he must resort to a different strategy: the brutal campaigns of the Opium War, the uncompromising violence of the imperial representation of power. He writes: 'What we want with Oriental powers like China, incapable of a true civilization, semi-refined in manners and mechanic arts, but incurably savage in the moral sense, is a full explanation of our meaning under an adequate demonstration of our power' (XIV: 193). To supplement the representation of Britain's powers to an enemy lacking the intellectual capacity to interpret them correctly, a demonstration of strength is required, whose meanings cannot be misunderstood by the most ignorant audience: the spectacle that he demands is one of military violence and force. He thus condones the aggressions that were at that time taking place in China. Contemporary accounts of the campaigns tell of demonstrations of military power that were excessive for a war against an enemy much less sophisticated and less able to defend itself: the brutal destruction of entire villages, and massacre of large groups of people.[48] For De Quincey, the Opium War is an assertion of agency that unequivocally interprets the messages of the British; a textual aid for the Chinese that transcends the ambiguities that are an unavoidable aspect of representation.

This instance of state violence and coercion mimics the aesthetic of force, for like the murderer-artist, or the army concealed behind the curtain in the denouement to *Klosterheim*, the British army displays its intentions in its incontrovertible acts of aggression. The display of state power conforms to one of the models of representation suggested by opium, when writing about opium compels the reader to repeat the writer's addiction, even in the face of the lost agency of the writer. This aesthetic model provides the justification for the infliction of physical force and violence on the Chinese at the point at which British control is at risk. Through this aesthetic model, De Quincey condones and naturalizes the brutal campaigns of the British, the uncompromising violence of imperial representations of power.

As the source of his impoverishment, the cause of his ill health, the agent of his lost will, the origin of his dreams, the material of

---

[48] See J. J. Darling, 'Political Register', *Tait's Edinburgh Magazine*, NS, 7 (Mar. 1840); and 'Opium Trade and War' in *Eclectic Review*, NS, 7 (June 1840).

his best work, and the genesis of his identity, opium was surely the single most important factor in De Quincey's life. As we have seen, it is also the pivot between his political and aesthetic writings, underpinning a discursive economy in the same way as the opium trade supported the British economy. For opium connects the two aesthetics that are at work in his writings, endorsing both the aesthetic of lost agency that celebrates his receding selfhood—the aesthetic of the 'impassioned prose' and the impersonal literature of power—and the aesthetic of force, that compels action, protects the family, restores traditional values, and overturns the loss of power suffered through Britain's addiction to Chinese markets. Opium functions as a panacea beyond even De Quincey's imaginings.

Epilogue

I am at the last gasp.

De Quincey to Robert Blackwood, 12 July 1842[1]

Having confidently predicted his own death frequently throughout his life, De Quincey finally died at 9.30 a.m. on 8 December 1859, aged 74, at Mavis Bush Cottage, Lasswade, outside Edinburgh. This was the home procured by his children twenty years before then, but to which De Quincey was, at first, unable to move, 'held hostage' as he then was in his lodging by his landlord to whom he owed money.[2] In his final days he was nursed by his daughters, Emily and Margaret, two of the three remaining children—he had outlived his five sons. This was a quiet and respectable death for one whose life had been lived on the social margins. Moreover it had been a remarkably long life for a long-term drug addict and man of hypochondriacal tendencies. Lindop notes that a rumour circulated after De Quincey's post-mortem, to the effect that none of his organs had been damaged by the effects of opium.[3] The apparent resilience of his body is a final contradiction in De Quincey's extraordinary life and writings.

But if his body resisted the effects of opium, his literary reputation has remained in its shadow, for it is as the Opium-Eater, and author of *Confessions*, that his name endures. This has tended to obscure the fact that De Quincey was a prolific journalist, whose work as a popularizer of a vast range of topics was well known in his own time, and latterly won him a degree of respectability. In subsequent critical studies, however, the bulk of his writings has tended to be neglected. Some of these works have been considered in this study—not from a desire to seek out lost literary jewels, but rather from an interest in the works as disseminations of different kinds of knowledge. An exceptional and eccentric

---

[1] National Library of Scotland, MS 4060 fo. 250.
[2] See Ch. 2, p. 44.
[3] Grevel Lindop, *The Opium-Eater: A Life of Thomas De Quincey* (Oxford: OUP, 1985), 387.

writer, De Quincey's works nevertheless illuminate a small part of the complex structure of Victorian culture and society. It is the very abundance and variety of his work that has made him a useful writer for my purposes, for by tracing the shared concerns and literary tropes between the different areas of knowledge he addresses, it has been possible to understand the work in the broader context of the intellectual, political, and social concerns of his time. Moreover by the same count, De Quincey's works offer a commentary on the formation of knowledge in a particular context, and at a particular time. This book, I hope, makes some modest contribution to the study of disciplinization in the early Victorian period.

I have not covered all De Quincey's writings, but the framework that I have formulated here for reading his works might be extended, for example, to his works on theology and classical history, themes which were high on his list of enthusiasms. These remain the most neglected of all his works, and have yet to receive adequate critical attention.

Despite De Quincey's own intellectual range, his place in history is preserved only in the English literary tradition and as a curio in the history of pharmacology. This is a situation partly of his own making. His terms, the literature of power and the literature of knowledge, set up an opposition between literature and science that still dominates British culture: literature (the literature of power) is the place of transcendent and unchanging truths, while science (the literature of knowledge) produces knowledge of local and material relevance. As Jerome McGann has argued in *Towards a Literature of Knowledge* (1989), this has led to a situation in which knowledge is considered incompatible with the Truth of poetry, and as a consequence, literature tends to be emptied of its content.[4] McGann is among a number of critics working to dismantle this opposition, and to find 'knowledge' in literature.

Although McGann's title draws on De Quincey's terms, he makes only passing reference to De Quincey's work, as a conservative transmitter of Wordsworth's work.[5] The present study has attempted to put De Quincey back into the literary tradition in

---

[4] Jerome McGann, *Towards a Literature of Knowledge* (Oxford: Clarendon Press, 1989).
[5] McGann, *Literature of Knowledge*, 130.

which he is so often represented as a shadowy bit-part player, but one who nevertheless speaks some of the crucial lines. He was one of the key writers who relay a highly influential version of Romantic values to subsequent generations, and as such, it is important to understand the particular interests of his work within its own context. De Quincey is significant as a writer who enunciates the influential power/knowledge dichotomy, and against which much of the current critical work is aimed. To read against that economy is to perceive that his frequently unnoticed legacy in the history of English literature is the deeper inscription of forms of social violence in an ostensibly disinterested aesthetic.

Selected Bibliography

PRIMARY SOURCES

Books

DE QUINCEY, THOMAS, *De Quincey's Writings*, ed. J. T. Fields, 20 vols. (Boston, 1851–56).
—— , *Selections Grave and Gay from Writings Published and Unpublished*, 14 vols. (Edinburgh, 1853–60).
—— , *Collected Writings*, ed. David Masson, 14 vols. (Edinburgh, 1889–90).
—— , *Walladmor: Freely translated into German from the English of Sir Walter Scott and now Freely Translated from the German into English* (London, 1825).
—— , *Klosterheim; or, the Masque* (Edinburgh, 1832).
—— , *The Logic of Political Economy* (Edinburgh, 1844).
—— , *China, by Thomas De Quincey: A Revised Reprint of Articles from 'Titan', with Preface and Additions* (Edinburgh, 1857).
—— , *Uncollected Writings of Thomas De Quincey*, ed. James Hogg, 2 vols. (London, 1890).
—— , *Posthumous Works*, ed. Alexander H. Japp, 2 vols. (London, 1891).
—— , *New Essays by De Quincey: His Contributions to the Edinburgh Saturday Post and the Edinburgh Evening Post, 1827–1828*, ed. Stuart M. Tave (Princeton, NJ, 1966).
—— , *Selected Essays on Rhetoric*, ed. Frederick Burwick (Carbondale, Ill., 1967).
—— , *Recollections of the Lakes and The Lake Poets*, ed. and intro. David Wright (Harmondsworth, 1970).
—— , *Confessions of an English Opium-Eater*, ed. Alethea Hayter (Harmondsworth, 1971).
—— , *Confessions of an English Opium-Eater and Other Writings*, ed. and intro. Grevel Lindop (Oxford, 1985).
—— , *Confessions and Other Writings*, ed. Aileen Ward (New York, 1966).

Articles not Reprinted in Collected Writings

Blackwood's Edinburgh Magazine

'The Duke of Wellington and Mr Peel', 25 (March 1829), 294–302.
'French Revolutions', 28 (September 1830), 542–58.
'France and England', 28 (October 1830), 699–718.
'Political Anticipations', 28 (November 1830), 719–36.

'The Late Cabinet', 28 (December 1830), 960–81.
'The Present Cabinet in Relation to the Times', 29 (February 1831), 143–58.
'On Approaching Revolution in Great Britain and its Proximate Consequences in a Letter to a Friend', 30 (August 1831), 313–29.
'The Prospects of Britain', 31 (April 1832), 569–91.
'Dilemmas on the Corn Law Question', 45 (February 1839), 170–6.
'Foreign Politics', 47 (October 1840), 546–62.
'Conservative Prospects', 49 (March 1841), 406–22.
'Sir Robert Peel's Position on Next Resuming Power', 50 (September 1841), 393–409.
'Canton Expedition and Convention', 50 (November 1841), 677–88.
'Sir Robert Peel's Policy', 51 (April 1842), 537–52.
'Anti-Corn-Law Deputation to Sir Robert Peel', 52 (August 1842), 271–80.
'The Repeal Agitation', 54 (August 1843), 264–74.
'The Game Up with the Repeal Agitation', 54 (November 1842), 679–86.

Manuscripts

All manuscripts are from the National Library of Scotland and are cited by volume and, where relevant, folio number.

972
1670
4027 fos. 79–88.
4029 fos. 147–54.
4032 fos. 179–93.
4035 fos. 174–80.
4038 fos. 208–9.
4046 fos. 140–5.
4047 fos. 219–45.
4051 fos. 108–77.
4055 fos. 138–91.
4060 fos. 225–75.
4065 fos. 168–212.
4070 fos. 194–216.
4074 fos. 178–90.
4789 fos. 1–67.
4937 fos. 39–40.

SECONDARY MATERIAL FIRST PUBLISHED BEFORE 1900

ANONYMOUS, Review of *Confessions of an English Opium-Eater*, *Album*, 2 (November 1822), 177–207.

——, Review of *Confessions of an English Opium-Eater, The British Critic*, NS, 18 (November 1822), 531–34.

——, Review of *Confessions of an English Opium-Eater, New Edinburgh Review*, 4 (January 1823), 253–74.

——, Review of *Confessions of an English Opium-Eater, Eclectic Review*, NS, 19 (April 1823), 366–71.

——, 'West India Slavery', *Eclectic Review*, 26 (February 1826), 97–113.

——, 'Burman Empire', *Westminster Review*, 7 (April 1827), 505–27.

——, 'The Anti-Slavery Society', *Fraser's Magazine for Town and Country*, 1/5 (June 1830), 610–22.

——, 'Anti-Slavery Crisis', *Eclectic Review*, NS, 3 (April 1838), 458–80.

——, 'Present State of the Anti-Slavery Cause', *Eclectic Review*, NS, 3 (January 1838), 54–77.

——, 'How do Poor Men Live?' *Tait's Edinburgh Magazine*, NS, 6 (January 1839), 13–22.

——, 'The Opium Question and the Suspended Trade with China', *Fraser's Magazine*, 21 (March 1840), 365–75.

——, 'The Opium Trade and War', *Eclectic Review*, NS, 7 (June 1840), 699–725.

——, 'The Present State of the Anti-Slavery Cause', *Eclectic Review*, NS, 13 (June 1843), 673–90.

——, 'Thomas De Quincey and His Works', *Hogg's Instructor*, 3 (July 1854), 1–15.

——, 'Opium', *Household Words*, 16 (August 1857), 104–8, 181–5.

——, 'Confessions of a Green-Tea Drinker', *Monthly Religious Magazine*, 25 (1860), 317–9.

——, 'The Opium Revenue of India', *Eclectic Review*, NS, 5 (January 1861), 39–47.

——, Review of *Works of Thomas De Quincey, British Quarterly Review*, 38 (July 1863), 1–29.

——, 'Opium Smokers in East London', *London Society*, 14 (1868), 68–73.

ALEXANDER, ROBERT, *The Rise and Progress of British Opium Smuggling, and its Effects upon India, China, and the Commerce of Great Britain* (London, 1856).

ALLEN, NATHAN, *An Essay on the Opium Trade Including a Sketch of its History, Extent, Effects, etc, as Carried on in India and China* (Boston, 1850).

——, 'The Opium Trade', *People's Journal*, 10 (1850), 24–5, 51–3.

BAUDELAIRE, CHARLES PIERRE, *Les Paradis artificiels: opium et haschisch* (Paris, 1860).

BLUMENBACH, J. F., *A Short System of Comparative Anatomy, With Additional Notes and an Introductory View of the Classification of Animals, by the Translator*, trans. William Lawrence (London, 1807).

BROWNING, ELIZABETH BARRETT, *Aurora Leigh* (1856; London, 1978).

[BULLOCK, T. H.], 'The Opium Revenue of India considered in connexion with Mr Laing's last budget', *Fraser's Magazine*, 66 (October 1862), 399–417.

BURKE, EDMUND, *A Philosophical Enquiry into the Origin of our Ideas of the Sublime and Beautiful*, ed. James T. Boulton (Oxford, 1987).

——, *Reflections on the Revolution in France and on the Proceedings in Certain Societies in London Relative to that Event*, ed. C. C. O'Brien (Harmondsworth, 1969).

CARLYLE, THOMAS, 'On History', in *Critical and Miscellaneous Essays* (London, 1899).

——, *Selected Writings*, ed. Alan Shelston (Harmondsworth, 1971).

——, *Early Letters of Thomas Carlyle*, ed. C. E. Norton, 2 vols. (London, 1886).

COLERIDGE, SAMUEL TAYLOR, *Poetical Works*, ed. Ernest Hartley Coleridge (1912; repr. Oxford, 1980).

——, *Biographia Literaria, or Biographical Sketches of My Literary Life and Opinions*, eds. James Engell and W. Jackson Bate, 2 vols. (London, 1983).

——, *On the Constitution of the Church and State*, ed. J. Colmer (1829; London, 1976), in *Collected Writings*, vol. x.

CORY, WILLIAM, *Extracts from the Letters and Journals of William Cory*, selected and arranged by Francis Warre Cornish (Oxford, 1897).

COTTON, WALTER, 'Turkish Sketches', *Knickerbocker*, 7 (April 1836), 421–5.

CROLY, GEORGE, 'Things of the Day', *Blackwood's Edinburgh Magazine*, 51 (February 1842), 141–52.

CRUMPE, SAMUEL, *An Inquiry into the Natural Properties of Opium; Wherein its component principles, mode of operation, and use or abuse in particular diseases, are experimentally investigated, and the opinions of former authors on these points impartially examined* (London, 1793).

DARLING, J. J., 'Political Register', *Tait's Edinburgh Magazine*, NS, 7 (March 1840), 201–204.

DAY, HORACE B., *The Opium Habit, with Suggestions as to the Remedy* (New York, 1868).

ENGELS, FREDRICK, *The Origin of the Family, Private Property, and the State*, intro. Evelyn Reed (New York, 1972).

FEARON, SAMUEL TURNER, 'The Opium Smoker', *Bentley's Miscellany*, 17 (January 1845), 65–9.

FERRIER, JAMES, 'An Introduction to the Philosophy of Consciousness', *Blackwood's Edinburgh Magazine*, 43 (February 1838), 187–201; (April 1838), 437–52; (June 1838), 784–91; 44 (August 1838), 234–44; (October 1838), 539–52; 45 (February 1839), 201–11.

FRY, WILLIAM STORRS, *Facts and Evidence Relating to the Opium Trade with China* (London, 1840).

FUSELI, HENRY, *Life and Writings of Henry Fuseli*, ed. J. Knowles, 3 vols. (London, 1831).

GILFILLAN, GEORGE, *A Gallery of Literary Portraits* (Edinburgh, 1845).

—— , 'Thomas De Quincey', *Eclectic Review*, 27 (April 1850), 397–408.

GORDON, MARTHA H., *Christopher North: A Memoir of John Wilson*, 2 vols. (Edinburgh, 1862).

GREGG, W. R., 'The Slave Trade and the Sugar Duties', *Westminster Review*, 41 (June 1844), 486–515.

HAINING, PETER (ed.), *Hashish Club: Anthology of Drug Literature* (London, 1975).

HAMILTON, SIR WILLIAM, *Discussions on Philosophy and Literature, Education and University Reform* (London, 1852).

—— , *Lectures on Metaphysics and Logic*, ed. Henry L. Mansel, and Veitch, John, 4 vols. (London, 1877).

HAZLITT, WILLIAM, *Complete Works*, ed. P. P. Howe, 21 vols. (London, 1930–34).

HERDER, JOHANN GOTTFRIED, 'Essay on the Origin of Language', trans. Alexander Gode, in *On the Origin of Language*, intro. Alexander Gode (Chicago, 1966).

HOGG, JAMES, 'Nights and Days with De Quincey', *Harper's New Monthly Magazine*, 80 (February 1890), 446–56.

HUME, DAVID, *Treatise of Human Nature*, ed. L. A. Selby-Bigge, 2nd edn., rev. P. H. Nidditch (Oxford, 1978).

[JACOX, FRANCIS], 'The English Opium-Eater', *People's and Howitt's Journal*, 8 (1849), 217–21.

—— , 'The Humour of Thomas De Quincey', *Colburn's New Monthly Magazine*, 96 (October 1852), 142–7.

—— , 'Thomas De Quincey's Autobiographic Sketches', *Colburn's New Monthly Magazine*, 98 (June 1853), 142–3.

—— , 'The Pathos of Thomas De Quincey', *Colburn's New Monthly Magazine*, 98 (August 1853), 389–99.

KANT, IMMANUEL, *Critique of Judgement*, trans. James Creed Meredith (Oxford, 1928).

KEBBEL, T. E., Review of *Selections Grave and Gay*, *The Quarterly Review*, 110 (1861), 1–35.

LAIRD, MACGREGOR, 'Remedies for the Slave Trade', *Westminster Review*, 34 (June 1840), 125–65.

LAWRENCE, WILLIAM, *Lectures on Physiology, Zoology, and the Natural History of Man* (London, 1819).

LESSING, GOTTHOLD EPHRAIM, *Werke*, ed. Herbert G. Gopfert, 8 vols. (München: 1970–9).

—— , *Laocoön*, trans. Robert Phillimore (London, 1874).

LEWES, G. H., *Problems of Life and Mind*, 5 vols. (London, 1874–9).

MCCULLOCH, J. R., *The Literature of Political Economy. A Classified Catalogue* of Select Publications in the Different Departments of that Science with Historical, Critical, and Biographical Notices (London, 1845).

——, 'Life and Writing of Mr Ricardo' in *The Works of David Ricardo*, ed. J. R. McCulloch (London, 1846).

MacNish, Robert, *The Anatomy of Drunkenness* (Glasgow, 1827).

——, *The Philosophy of Sleep* (Glasgow, 1830).

[Maginn, William], 'The Humbugs of the Age, no. 1–The Opium Eater', *John Bull Magazine and Literary Recorder*, 1 (July 1824), 21–4.

Malthus, T. R., *Definitions in Political Economy Preceded by an Inquiry into the Rules which Ought to Guide Political Economists in the Definition and Use of these Terms, with Remarks on the Derivation from these Rules in these Writings* (London, 1827).

——, *An Essay on the Principle of Population; or A View of its Past and Present Effects on Human Happiness*, 6th edn., 2 vols. (London, 1826).

——, *The Measure of Value, Stated and Illustrated, with an Application of it to the Alterations in the Value of the English Currency since 1790* (London, 1823).

Martineau, Harriet, *Biographical Sketches* (New York, 1869).

Marx, Karl, *Early Writings*, intro. Lucio Colletti., trans. Rodney Livingstone and Gregor Benton (Harmondsworth, 1975; rev. edn. 1981).

——, *Capital: A Critique of Political Economy*, introd. Ernest Mandel, 2 vols., i trans. Ben Fowkes, ii and iii trans. David Fernbach (Harmondsworth, 1976–81).

——, *Grundrisse: Foundations of the Critique of Political Economy (Rough Draft)*, trans. Martin Nicolaus (Harmondsworth, 1973).

——, *Surveys from Exile*, ii, *Political Writings*, ed. and introd. David Fernbach (Harmondsworth, 1973).

——, and Friedrich Engels, *The German Ideology, part one; with selections from parts two and three together with Marx's 'Introduction to a Critique of Political Economy'*, ed. and introd. C. J. Arthur (London, 1970).

Mayhew, Henry, *London Labour and the London Poor: a Cyclopaedia of the Conditions and Earnings of those that will work, those that cannot work, and those that will not work*, 4 vols. (1861–2; repr. London, 1967).

Mill, J. S., Review of *Logic of Political Economy*, Thomas De Quincey, *Westminster Review*, 43 (June 1845), 319–31.

——, *Principles of Political Economy with some of their Applications to Social Philosophy*, 2 vols., 2nd edn. (London, 1849).

——, *Mill on Bentham and Coleridge*, introd. F. R. Leavis (London, 1950).

Minto, Walter, *A Manual of English Prose Literature* (London, 1872).

Morton, Samuel George, *Crania Americana: or, a comparative view of the skulls of various Aboriginal Nations of North and South America: to which is prefixed an essay on the varieties of the Human Species* (Philadelphia, 1839).

——, 'Crania Aegyptiaca; or, Observations of Egyptian Ethnography, derived from Anatomy, History, and the Monuments', in *The Transactions of the American Philosophical Society*, 9 (Philadelphia, 1844).

NISBET, H. B. (ed.), *German Aesthetic and Literary Criticism: Winckelmann, Lessing, Hamann, Herder, Schiller and Goethe* (Cambridge, 1985).

OLIPHANT, MARGARET, *The Literary History of England in the End of the 18th and beginning of the 19th Centuries*, 3 vols. (London, 1882).

——, *Annals of a Publishing House: William Blackwood and his Sons*, 3 vols. (Edinburgh, 1897–8).

POLLITT, CHARLES, *De Quincey's Editorship of the Westmorland Gazette, with selections from his work on that Journal from July 1818 to November 1819* (Kendal, 1890).

RICARDO, DAVID, *The Works and Correspondence of David Ricardo*, ed. Piero Sraffa with collaboration of M. H. Dobb, 10 vols. (Cambridge, 1951–73).

ROUSSEAU, JEAN-JACQUES, *The Confessions of Jean-Jacques Rousseau*, trans. and intro. J. M. Cohen (Harmondsworth, 1953).

——, 'Essay on the Origin of Languages', trans. John H. Moran, in *On the Origin of Language*, introd. Alexander Gode (Chicago, 1966).

RUSKIN, JOHN, *The Works of John Ruskin*, lib. edn., ed. E. T. Cook and Alexander Wedderburn, 39 vols. (London, 1903–12).

RUSSELL, C. W., 'Palimpsest Literature and its Editor, Cardinal Angelo Mai' in *Afternoon Lectures on Literature and Art* (London, 1867).

SIMPSON, DAVID (ed.), *German Aesthetic and Literary Criticism: Kant, Fichte, Schelling, Schopenhauer, Hegel* (Cambridge, 1984).

SMITH, ADAM, *An Inquiry into the Nature and Causes of the Wealth of Nations*, 3 vols., ed. R. H. Campbell and A. S. Skinner, 2 vols. (Oxford, 1976).

SPENCER, HERBERT, *System of Synthetic Philosophy*, 10 vols. (London, 1862–93).

STEPHEN, LESLIE, *Hours in a Library* (London, 1874).

STEWART, DUGALD, *The Collected Works of Dugald Stewart*, ed. William Hamilton, 11 vols. (Edinburgh, 1854–60).

WARREN, SAMUEL, *The Opium Question* (London, 1840).

WILDE, OSCAR, *The Artist as Critic: The Critical Writings of Oscar Wilde*, ed. Richard Ellmann (London, 1970).

WILSON, JOHN, 'Noctes Ambrosiana', *Blackwood's Edinburgh Magazine*, 14 (October 1824), 485–503.

WORDSWORTH, WILLIAM, *The Prelude; or Growth of a Poet's Mind*, ed. Ernest De Selincourt, 2nd edn., rev. Helen Darbishire (Oxford, 1959).

——, *The Prose Works*, ed. W. J. B. Owen and Jane Worthington Smyser, 3 vols. (Oxford, 1974).

SECONDARY SOURCES PUBLISHED AFTER 1900

AARSLEFF, HANS, *From Locke to Saussure: Essays on the Study of Language and Intellectual History* (London, 1982).

—— , *The Study of Language in England, 1780–1860* (London, 1983).

ABRAMS, M. H., *The Milk of Paradise: The Effect of Opium Visions on the Works of De Quincey, Crabbe, Francis Thompson and Coleridge* (1934; repr. New York, 1970).

—— , *The Mirror and the Lamp: Romantic Theory and the Critical Tradition* (New York, 1953).

—— , *Natural Supernaturalism: Tradition and Revolution in Romantic Literature* (London, 1971).

AGULHON, MAURICE, *Marianne into Battle: Republican Imagery and Symbolism in France, 1789–1830*, trans. Janet Lloyd (Cambridge, 1981).

ALTICK, RICHARD D., *The English Common Reader: A Social History of the Mass Reading Public 1800–1900* (Chicago, 1957).

ANDERSON, BENEDICT, *Imagined Communities: Reflections on the Origin and Spread of Nationalism*, 2nd edn. (London, 1991).

ARMSTRONG, ISOBEL (ed.), *Victorian Scrutinies: Reviews of Poetry 1830–1870* (London, 1972).

ARMSTRONG, NANCY, *Desire and Domestic Fiction: A Political History of the Novel* (Oxford and New York, 1987).

ASHTON, ROSEMARY, *The German Idea: Four English Writers and the Reception of German Thought* (Cambridge, 1980).

ATTRIDGE, DEREK et al., *Post-Structuralism and the Question of History* (Cambridge, 1987).

BALDICK, CHRIS, *The Social Mission of English Criticism, 1848–1932* (Oxford, 1984).

—— , *In Frankenstein's Shadow: Myth, Monstrosity and Nineteenth-Century Writing* (Oxford, 1987).

BARKER, FRANCIS, *The Tremulous Private Body: Essays on Subjection* (London, 1984).

BARRELL, JOHN, *The Infection of Thomas De Quincey: A Psychopathology of Imperialism* (New Haven, Conn., 1991).

BAXTER, EDMUND, *De Quincey's Art of Autobiography* (Edinburgh, 1990).

BEER, JOHN, 'The Englishness of De Quincey's Ideas', in *English and German Romanticism: Cross-Currents and Controversies*, ed. James Pipkin (Heidelberg, 1985), 323–47.

BENJAMIN, WALTER, *Charles Baudelaire: A Lyric Poet in the Era of High Capitalism*, trans. Harry Zohn (London, 1983).

—— , *One Way Street and Other Writings*, trans. E. Jephcott and K. Shorter (London, 1979).

BERG, MAXINE, *The Machinery Question and the Making of Political Economy,*

1815–1848 (Cambridge, 1980).

BERRIDGE, VIRGINIA, 'Opium-Eating and Life Insurance', *British Journal of Addiction*, 72 (1977), 371–7.

——, and EDWARDS, GARETH, *Opium and the People: Opiate Use in Nineteenth-Century England* (New Haven, Conn., 1987).

BILSLAND, JOHN W., 'On De Quincey's Theory of Literary Power', *University of Toronto Quarterly*, 26 (1957), 469–80.

——, 'De Quincey's Opium Experiences', *Dalhousie Review*, 55 (1975), 419–30.

BLACK, JOEL, *The Aesthetics of Murder: A Study in Romantic Literature and Contemporary Culture* (Baltimore, Md., 1991).

BLAUG, MAURICE, *Ricardian Economics: A Historical Study* (New Haven, Conn., 1958).

BRISTOW, JOSEPH (ed.), *The Victorian Poet: Poetics and Persona* (London, 1987).

BRUSS, ELIZABETH W., *Autobiographical Acts: The Changing Situation of a Literary Genre* (Baltimore, Md., 1976).

BURWICK, FREDERICK, 'The Dream-Visions of Jean-Paul and Thomas De Quincey', *Comparative Literature*, 20/1 (1968), 1–26.

——, (ed.), *Approaches to Organic Form: Permutations in Science and Culture*, Boston Studies in the Philosophy of Science, CV (Dordecht, 1987).

BURY, J. P. T. (ed.), *The New Cambridge Modern History*, x, *The Zenith of European Power, 1830–70* (Cambridge, 1960).

BUTLER, MARILYN, *Romantics, Rebels, and Reactionaries: English Literature and its Background, 1760–1830* (Oxford, 1981).

CAMERON, DEBORAH, and FRASER, ELIZABETH, *The Lust to Kill: A Feminist Investigation of Sexual Murder* (Oxford, 1987).

CARTER, ANGELA, *Sadeian Woman: An Exercise in Cultural History* (London, 1979).

CASEBY, RICHARD, *The Opium-Eating Editor: Thomas De Quincey and the Westmorland Gazette* (Kendal, 1985).

CASSIRER, ERNST, *The Philosophy of the Enlightenment*, trans. Fritz C. A. Koelln and James P. Pettegrove (Princeton, NJ, 1951).

——, *Kant's Life and Thought*, trans. James Haden (New Haven, Conn., 1981).

CHRISTENSEN, JEROME, *Coleridge's Blessed Machine of Language* (Ithaca, NY, 1981).

CHRISTIE, J., 'Human Sciences: Origins and Histories', *History of the Human Sciences*, 6 (1993), 1–12.

CLARK, ANNA, *Women's Silence, Men's Violence: Sexual Assault in England, 1770–1845* (London, 1987).

CLARK, J. C. D., *English Society 1688–1832: Ideology, Social Structures and Political Practice During the Ancien Régime* (Cambridge, 1985).

COLEMAN, BRUCE, *Conservatism and the Conservative Party in Nineteenth-*

Century Britain (London, 1988).

COLLEY, LINDA, 'Whose Nation? Class and National Consciousness in Britain, 1750–1830', *Past and Present*, 113 (1986), 97–117.

——, *Britons: Forging the Nation, 1707–1837* (New Haven, Conn., 1992).

COLLINS, MAURICE, *Foreign Mud: Being an Account of the Opium Imbroglio at Canton in the 1830s and the Anglo-Chinese War that Followed* (London, 1946).

COOKE, MICHAEL G., 'De Quincey, Coleridge, and the Formal Uses of Intoxication', *Yale French Studies*, 50 (1974), 26–40.

COPLEY, STEPHEN, and WHALE, JOHN, *Beyond Romanticism: New Approaches to Texts and Contexts, 1780–1832* (London, 1992).

COUSINS, MARK, and HUSSAIN, ATHAR, *Michel Foucault* (London, 1984).

CORVINO, WILLIAM, 'Thomas De Quincey in the Revisionist History of Rhetoric', *Pre/Text*, 4/2 (1983), 121–36.

CRAWFORD, DONALD W., *Kant's Aesthetic Theory* (Madison, Wis., 1974).

CRITCHLEY, T. A., and JAMES, P. D., *The Maul and the Pear Tree: The Ratcliffe Highway Murders 1811* (London, 1971).

CROWLEY, TONY, 'A History of "The History of the Language"', *Language and Communication*, 6/4 (1986), 293–303.

——, *The Politics of Discourse: The Standard Language Question in British Cultural Debate* (Basingstoke, 1989).

CUNNINGHAM, HUGH, 'The Language of Patriotism, 1750–1914', *History Workshop Journal*, 12 (1981), 8–33.

CURRAN, STUART, *Poetic Form and British Romanticism* (Oxford, 1986).

DARBISHIRE, HELEN (ed.), *De Quincey's Literary Criticism* (London, 1909).

DAVIES, HUGH SYKES, *Thomas De Quincey* (London, 1964).

DE BOLLA, PETER, *The Discourse of the Sublime: Readings in History, Aesthetics and The Subject* (Oxford, 1989).

DELEUZE, GILLES, *Kant's Critical Philosophy: The Doctrine of the Faculties*, trans. Hugh Tomlinson and Barbara Habberjam (London, 1984).

DE LUCA, V. A., *Thomas De Quincey: The Prose of Vision* (Toronto, 1980).

DE MAN, PAUL, *Allegories of Reading: Figural Language in Rousseau, Nietzsche, Rilke, and Proust* (New Haven, Conn., 1979).

——, *Blindness and Insight: Essays in the Rhetoric of Contemporary Criticism*, 2nd edn. (London, 1983).

——, *The Rhetoric of Romanticism* (New York, 1984).

DENDURENT, H. O., *Thomas De Quincey: A Reference Guide* (Boston, Mass., 1978).

DERRIDA, JACQUES, *Of Grammatology*, trans. Gayatri Chakravorty Spivak (Baltimore, Md., 1976).

——, *Writing and Difference*, trans. Alan Bass (London, 1978).

——, 'Living On: Borderlines', in Harold Bloom *et al.*, *Deconstruction and Criticism* (London, 1979), 75–176.

——, 'Scribble (Writing-Power)', trans. Cary Plotkin, *Yale French Studies*,

58 (1979), 117–147.

——, 'La Loi du Genre/The Law of Genre', *Glyph*, 7 (1980), 176–232.

——, 'Economimesis', trans. R. Klein, *Diacritics*, 11/2 (1981), 3–25.

DEVLIN, D. D., *De Quincey, Wordsworth, and the Art of Prose* (London, 1963).

DOWNING, RICHARD, 'De Quincey and the Westmorland Gazette', *Charles Lamb Bulletin*, 23 (1978), 145–56.

DYOS, H. J., and WOLFF, MICHAEL, (eds.), *The Victorian City: Images and Realities*, 4 vols. (London, 1976–78).

EATON, HORACE AINSWORTH, *Thomas De Quincey: A Biography* (New York, 1972).

EAGLETON, TERRY, *The Ideology of the Aesthetic* (Oxford, 1990).

EVANS, ERIC, *Britain Before the Reform Act: Politics and Society, 1815–1832*, (London, 1989).

FAIRBANK, JOHN K. (ed.), *The Cambridge History of China*, x, *Late Ch'ing 1800–1911, pt 1* (Cambridge, 1978).

FERGUSON, FRANCES, *Wordsworth: Language as Counter-Spirit* (New Haven, Conn., 1977).

——, 'The Sublime of Edmund Burke, or the Bathos of Experience', *Glyph*, 8 (1981), 62–78.

——, 'Legislating the Sublime', in *Studies in 18th-Century British Art and Aesthetics*, ed. Ralph Cohen (Berkeley, Calif., 1985).

FETTER, FRANK W., 'The Economic Articles in *Blackwood's Edinburgh Magazine*, and their Authors, 1817–1853', *Scottish Journal of Political Economy*, 7 (1960), 85–107, 213–231.

——, 'The Rise and Decline of Ricardian Economics', *History of Political Economy*, 1 (1969), 67–84.

——, *The Economists in Parliament 1780–1868* (Chapel Hill, NC, 1980).

FLEISHMAN, AVROM, *Figures of Autobiography: The Language of Self-Writing in Victorian and Modern England* (Berkeley, Calif., 1983).

FONTANA, BIANCAMARIA, *Rethinking the Politics of Commerical Society: The Edinburgh Review, 1802–1832* (Cambridge, 1985).

FOUCAULT, MICHEL, *The Order of Things: An Archaeology of the Human Sciences* (London, 1970).

——, *The History of Sexuality*, i, trans. Robert Hurley (Harmondsworth, 1981).

——, *Power/Knowledge: Selected Writings, 1972–1977*, ed. and trans. Colin Gordon (Brighton, 1980).

FOWLER, J. H., *De Quincey as Literary Critic* (London, 1922).

FREUD, SIGMUND, *The Standard Edition of the Complete Psychological Works*, 24 vols., trans. James Strachey (London, 1953–74).

GALLAGHER, CATHERINE, *The Industrial Reformation of English Fiction: Social Discourse and Narrative Form, 1832–1867* (Chicago, 1985).

GASH, NORMAN, *Sir Robert Peel: The Life of Sir Robert Peel after 1830*

(London, 1972).

GENETTE, GERARD, *Figures of Literary Discourse*, trans. Alan Sheridan (Oxford, 1982).

Genre, 4/1–2 (1973).

GILBERT, SANDRA, and GUBAR, SUSAN, *The Madwoman in the Attic: The Woman Writer and the Nineteenth-Century Imagination* (New Haven, Conn., 1979).

GOLDMAN, ALBERT, *The Mine and the Mint: Sources for the Writings of Thomas De Quincey* (Carbondale, Ill., 1965).

GOOTZEIT, MICHAEL J., *David Ricardo* (New York, 1975).

GORDON, BARRY, *Political Economy in Parliament 1819–1823* (London, 1976).

—— , *Economic Doctrine and Tory Liberalism 1824–1830* (London, 1979).

GOULD, STEPHEN JAY, *The Mismeasure of Man* (New York, 1981).

GROVES, DAVID, 'Thomas De Quincey, the *Edinburgh Literary Gazette*, and the *Affinity of Languages*', *English Language Notes*, 26/3 (1989), 55–69.

HALÉVY, ELIE, *The Growth of Philosophic Radicalism*, trans. Mary Morris (London, 1928).

HAMILTON, PAUL, *Coleridge's Poetics* (Oxford, 1983).

HARRISON, J. F. S., *The Early Victorians: 1832–1851* (London, 1971).

HAVENS, MICHAEL KENT, 'Coleridge on the Evolution of Language', *Studies in Romanticism*, 20 (1981), 163–183.

HAYDEN, JOHN O., 'De Quincey's *Confessions* and the Reviewers', *Wordsworth Circle*, 6 (1975), 273–279.

HAYTER, ALETHEA, *Opium and the Romantic Imagination* (London, 1968).

HEINZELMAN, KURT, *The Economics of the Imagination* (Amherst, Mass., 1980).

HELSINGER, ELIZABETH, SHEETS, ROBIN, and VEEDER, WILLIAM, *The Woman Question: Society and Literature in Britain and America, 1837–1883*, 3 vols. (Manchester, 1983).

HERTZ, NEIL, *The End of the Line: Essays on Psychoanalysis and the Sublime* (New York, 1985).

HEYCK, T. W., *The Transformation of Intellectual Life in Victorian England* (London, 1982).

HILTON, BOYD, *Corn, Cash, Commerce: The Economic Policies of the Tory Governments, 1815–1830* (Oxford, 1977).

HIRSCHMAN, ALBERT O., *The Passions and the Interests: Political Arguments for Capitalism Before its Triumph* (Princeton, NJ, 1977).

HOBSBAWM, ERIC, and RUDÉ, GEORGE, *Captain Swing* (London, 1969).

—— , and Ranger, Terence (eds.), *The Invention of Tradition* (Cambridge, 1983).

HOLLANDER, SAMUEL, *The Economics of David Ricardo* (London, 1979).

HOLLIS, PATRICIA, *The Pauper Press: A Study of Working-Class Radicalism in the 1830s* (Oxford, 1970).

HOUGHTON, WALTER E., *The Victorian Frame of Mind 1830–1870* (London, 1957).

HSÜ, IMMANUEL C. Y., *The Rise of Modern China*, 2nd edn. (New York, 1975).

INGLIS, BRIAN, *The Opium War* (Sevenoaks, 1976).

JACK, IAN, 'De Quincey Revises his "Confessions"', *PMLA* 72 (1957), 122–46.

JACOBUS, MARY, *Romanticism, Writing and Sexual Difference: Essays on The Prelude* (Oxford, 1989).

JANOWITZ, ANNE, *England's Ruins: Poetic Purpose and the National Landscape* (Oxford, 1990).

JESPERSEN, OTTO, *Language, its Nature, Development, and Origin* (London, 1922).

JONES, GARETH STEDMAN, *Languages of Class: Studies in English Working-Class History, 1832–1982* (Cambridge, 1983).

JORDAN, JOHN E., *Thomas De Quincey, Literary Critic: His Method and Achievement* (Berkeley, Calif., 1952).

——, *De Quincey to Wordsworth: A Biography of a Relationship with Letters of Thomas De Quincey to the Wordsworth Family* (Berkeley, Calif., 1963).

——, (ed.), *De Quincey as Critic* (London, 1973).

KELLEY, THERESA, *Wordsworth's Revisionary Aesthetics* (Cambridge, 1988).

KENWOOD, SYDNEY H., 'Lessing in England', *The Modern Language Review*, 9 (1914), 197–212, 344–358.

KLANCHER, JON P., *The Making of English Reading Audiences, 1790–1832* (Madison, Wis., 1987).

KNIGHTS, BEN, *The Idea of the Clerisy in the Nineteenth Century* (Cambridge, 1978).

KOHN, MAREK, *Narcomania: On Heroin* (London, 1987).

LACOUE-LABARTHE, PHILIPPE, and NANCY, JEAN-LUC, *The Literary Absolute: The Theory of Literature in German Romanticism*, trans. Philip Barnard and Cheryl Lester (Albany, NY, 1988).

LEASK, NIGEL, *British Romantic Writing and the East: Anxieties of Empire* (Cambridge, 1992).

LEJEUNE, PHILIPPE, *On Autobiography*, ed. Paul John Eakin, trans. Katherine Leary (Minneapolis, 1989).

LENTRICCHIA, FRANK, *After the New Criticism* (London, 1980).

LEVINSON, MARJORIE, *The Romantic Fragment Poem: A Critique of a Form* (Chapel Hill, NC, 1987).

——, (ed.), *Rethinking Historicism: Critical Readings in Romantic History* (Oxford, 1989).

LINDOP, GREVEL, *The Opium-Eater: A Life of Thomas De Quincey* (Oxford, 1985).

LOGAN, JOHN FREDERICK, 'The Age of Intoxication', *Yale French Studies*, 50 (1974), 81–94.

LYONS, JUDSON S., *Thomas De Quincey* (New York, 1969).

McDONAGH, JOSEPHINE, 'Writings on the Mind: Thomas De Quincey and the Importance of the Palimpsest in Nineteenth-Century Writing', *Prose Studies*, 10/2 (1987), 207–224.

—— , 'Do or Die: Problems of Agency and Gender in the Aesthetics of Murder', *Genders*, 5 (1989), 120–134.

—— , 'Opium and the Imperial Imagination', in *Reviewing Romanticism*, ed. Philip W. Martin and Robin Jarvis (Basingstoke, 1992).

McFARLAND, THOMAS, *Romanticism and the Forms of Ruin: Wordsworth, Coleridge, and the Modalities of Fragmentation* (Princeton, NJ, 1981).

McGANN, JEROME, *The Romantic Ideology: A Critical Investigation* (Chicago, 1983).

—— , *The Beauty of Inflections* (Oxford, 1985).

—— , *Towards a Literature of Knowledge* (Oxford, 1989).

MANDLER, PETER, *Aristocratic Government in the Age of Reform: Whigs and Liberals 1830–1852* (Oxford, 1990).

MANIQUIS, ROBERT M., 'Lonely Empires: Personal and Public Visions of Thomas De Quincey', in *Literary Monographs*, 8, ed. Eric Rothstein and Anthony Wittreich jun. (Madison, Wis., 1976).

MEEK, RONALD L., *Economics and Ideology and Other Essays* (London, 1967).

MEHLMAN, JEFFREY, *Revolution and Repetition: Marx/Hugo/Balzac* (Berkeley, Calif., 1977).

MERQUIOR, J. Q., *Foucault* (London, 1985).

MERRIMAN, JOHN M. (ed.), *1830 in France* (New York, 1975).

METCALF, JOHN CALVIN, *De Quincey: A Portrait* (New York, 1963).

MIERS, SUZANNE, *Britain and the Ending of the Slave Trade* (London, 1975).

MILLER, J. HILLIS, *The Disappearance of God: Five Nineteenth-Century Writers* (Cambridge, Mass., 1975).

MONK, SAMUEL H., *The Sublime: A Study of Critical Theories in 18th-Century England* (1935; repr. Ann Arbor, Mich., 1960).

Modern Language Notes, Autobiography and the Problem of the Subject, 93/4 (1978).

MOORE, DAVID CRESAP, *The Politics of Deference: A Study of the Mid-Nineteenth-Century English Political System* (Hassocks, 1976).

MORETTI, FRANCO, *Signs Taken for Wonders* (London, 1983).

MOREUX, FRANCOISE, *Thomas De Quincey: La Vie—l'homme—l'ouevre* (Paris, 1964).

NISBET, H. B., 'Laocoön in Germany: The Reception of the Group since Winckelmann', *Oxford German Studies*, 10 (1979), 22–63.

OLNEY, JAMES, *Metaphors of Self: The Meaning of Autobiography* (Princeton, NJ, 1972).

—— , *Autobiography: Essays Theoretical and Critical* (Princeton, NJ, 1980).

OWEN, W. J. B., *Wordsworth as Critic* (London, 1969).

——, 'De Quincey and Shoplifting', *Wordsworth Circle*, 21/2 (1990), 72–76.

PARRINDER, PATRICK, *Authors and Authority: a Study of English Literary Criticism and its Relation to Culture 1750–1900* (London, 1977).

PARSSINEN, TERRY M., *Secret Passions, Secret Remedies: Drugs and British Society, 1820–1930* (Manchester, 1983).

PAULSON, RONALD, 'Burke's Sublime and the Representation of Revolution', in *Culture and Politics from Puritanism to the Enlightenment*, ed. Perez Zagorin, (Berkeley, Calif., 1980), 241–269.

——, *Representations of Revolutions (1789–1820)* (New Haven, Conn., 1983).

PEDERSEN, H., *Linguistic Science in the Nineteenth Century: Methods and Results*, trans. J. W. Spargo, (Cambridge, 1931).

PHILLIPS, RODERICK, *Putting Asunder: A History of Divorce in Western Society* (Cambridge, 1988).

PINKNEY, DAVID H., *The French Revolution of 1830* (Princeton, NJ, 1972).

PLATZNER, ROBERT L., 'De Quincey and the Dilemma of Romantic Autobiography', *Dalhousie Review*, 61/4 (1981–2), 605–17.

PLOTZ, JUDITH, 'On Guilt considered as One of the Fine Arts: De Quincey's Criminal Investigations', *Wordsworth Circle*, 19/2 (1988), 83–88.

POULET, GEORGES, 'Timelessness and Romanticism', *Journal of the History of Ideas*, 15 (1954), 3–22.

PRAZ, MARIO, *The Romantic Agony*, trans. Angus Davidson (1933; London, 1960).

——, *The Hero in Eclipse in Victorian Fiction*, trans. Angus Davidson (Oxford, 1956).

PROCTOR, SIGMUND K., *Thomas De Quincey's Theory of Literature*, University of Michigan Publications, Language and Literature 19, (Ann Arbor, Mich., 1943).

RAJAN, TILOTTAMA, *Dark Interpreters: The Discourse of Romanticism* (Ithaca, NY, 1980).

REED, ARDEN, 'Abysmal Influence: Baudelaire, Coleridge, De Quincey, Piranesi, Wordsworth', *Glyph*, 4 (1978), 188–206.

—— (ed.), *Romanticism and Language* (London, 1984).

REISNER, THOMAS A., 'De Quincey's Palimpsest Reconsidered', *Modern Language Studies*, 12/2 (1982), 93–95.

RICE, C. DUNCAN, 'Controversies over Slavery in Eighteenth- and Nineteenth-Century Scotland', in *Anti-Slavery Reconsidered: New Perspectives on the Abolitionists*, ed. Lewis Perry and Michael Fellman (Baton Rouge, La., 1979).

——, *The Scots Abolitionists, 1833–1861* (Baton Rouge, La., 1981).

ROE, NICHOLAS, *Wordsworth and Coleridge: The Radical Years* (Oxford, 1988).

RUSSETT, MARGARET, 'De Quincey's Gothic Interpreter: De Quincey Personifies "We Are Seven"', *Studies in Romanticism*, 30 (1991), 345–65.

RZEPKA, CHARLES J., 'The Literature of Power and the Imperial Will: De Quincey's Opium War Essays', *South Central Review*, 8/1 (1991), 37–45.

SACKVILLE-WEST, EDWARD, *A Flame in Sunlight*, ed. John Jordan (1936; repr. London, 1974).

SAID, EDWARD, *Orientalism* (1979; repr. Harmondsworth, 1985).

SAINTSBURY, GEORGE, *A History of English Criticism, being the English Chapters of a History of Criticism and Literary Taste in Europe, Revised, Adapted and Supplemented* (Edinburgh, 1911).

SAMBROOK, JAMES, *The Eighteenth Century: The Intellectual and Cultural Context of English Literature 1700–1789* (London, 1986).

SCHNEIDER, ELISABETH, *Coleridge, Opium, and 'Kubla Khan'* (Chicago, 1953).

SCHUMPETER, JOSEPH A., *History of Economic Analysis*, ed. Elizabeth Boody Schumpeter (London, 1953).

SCHWAB, RAYMOND, *The Oriental Renaissance: Europe's Rediscovery of India and the East, 1680–1880*, trans. Gene Patterson and Victor Reinking (New York, 1984).

SEDGWICK, EVE KOSOFSKY, *The Coherence of Gothic Conventions* (1976; repr. London, 1986).

SEMMEL, BERNARD, *The Rise of Free Trade Imperialism: Classical Political Economy, the Empire of Free Trade, and Imperialism, 1750–1850* (Cambridge, 1970).

SHAFFER, E. S., *'Kubla Khan' and 'The Fall of Jerusalem': The Mythological School in Biblical Criticism and Secular Literature 1770–1880* (Cambridge, 1975).

SHAPIRO, FRED R., 'Words for the OED from De Quincey', *American Notes and Queries*, 22/3–4 (1983), 49–50.

SHATTOCK, JOANNE, and WOLFF, MICHAEL (eds.), *The Victorian Periodical Press: Samplings and Soundings* (Leicester, 1982).

SHAW, W. DAVID, *The Lucid Veil: Poetic Truth in the Victorian Age* (London, 1987).

SHELL, MARC, *The Economy of Literature* (Baltimore, Md., 1978).

——, *Money, Language, and Thought: Literary and Philosophical Economics from the Medieval to the Modern Era* (Berkeley, Calif., 1982).

SHOWALTER, ELAINE, *A Literature of Their Own: British Women Novelists from Brontë to Lessing* (Princeton, NJ, 1982).

——, *The Female Malady: Women, Madness, and English Culture 1830–1980* (London, 1987).

SIMPSON, DAVID, *Irony and Authority in Romantic Poetry* (London, 1979).

SISKIN, CLIFFORD, *The Historicity of Romantic Discourse* (Oxford, 1988).

SMITH, OLIVIA, *The Politics of Language, 1791–1819* (Oxford, 1984).

SNYDER, ROBERT LANCE (ed.), *Thomas De Quincey: Bicentenary Studies* (Norman, Okla., 1985).

——, 'De Quincey's Literature of Power: A Mythic Paradigm', *Studies in*

English Literature, 26/4 (1986), 691–711.

SPECTOR, STEPHEN J., 'Thomas De Quincey: Self-Effacing Autobiographer', *Studies in Romanticism*, 18 (1979), 501–20.

SPENGEMANN, WILLIAM C., *The Forms of Autobiography: Episodes in the History of a Literary Genre* (New Haven, Conn., 1980).

STALLYBRASS, PETER and WHITE, ALLON, *The Politics and Poetics of Transgression* (London, 1986).

STEVENSON, CATHERINE BARNES, 'The Shade of Homer Exorcises The Ghost of De Quincey: Tennyson's "The Lotus-Eaters"', *Browning Institute Studies*, 10 (1982), 117–41.

SULLIVAN, ALVIN (ed.), *British Literary Magazines: The Romantic Age, 1789–1836* (Westport, Conn., 1983).

THOMPSON, E. P., *The Making of the English Working Class* (Harmondsworth, 1980).

THOMPSON, F. M. L., *English Landed Society in the Nineteenth Century* (London, 1963).

TRIBE, KEITH, *Land, Labour, and Economic Discourse* (London, 1978).

—— , 'Ricardian Histories', *Economy and Society*, 104 (1981), 451–66.

TYSON, BRYAN, ' "The Frightful Co-Existence of the *To Be* and the *Not To Be*': Antinomy and Irony in De Quincey's "Sir William Hamilton"', in *Philosophical Approaches to Literature: New Essays on 19th- and 20th-Century Texts*, ed. William E. Cain (London, 1984), 73–90.

VISWANATHAN, GUJARI, 'The Beginnings of English Literary Study in British India', *Oxford Literary Review*, 9/1–2 (1987), 2–26.

WALEY, ARTHUR D., *The Opium War Through Chinese Eyes* (London, 1958).

WALVIN, JAMES (ed.), *Slavery and British Society, 1776–1846* (London, 1982).

—— , *England, Slaves, and Freedom* (Basingstoke, 1986).

WARREN, ALBA H., JUN., *English Poetic Theory, 1825–1865* (Princeton, NJ, 1950).

WEBB, R. K., *The British Working-Class Reader 1790–1848: Literacy and Social Tension* (London, 1955).

WEISKEL, THOMAS, *The Romantic Sublime: Studies in the Structure and Psychology of Transcendence* (1976; Baltimore, Md. and London, 1986).

WELLBERG, DAVID, *Lessing's 'Laocoön': Semiotics and Aesthetics in the Age of Reason* (Cambridge, 1984).

WELLEK, RENÉ, *Immanuel Kant in England, 1793–1838* (Princeton, NJ, 1931).

—— , *Confrontations: Studies in the Intellectual and Literary Relations between Germany, England, and the United States during the Nineteenth-Century* (Princeton, NJ, 1965).

—— , *A History of Modern Criticism, 1750–1950*, 5 vols. (London, 1966).

WHALE, JOHN C., *Thomas De Quincey's Reluctant Autobiography* (London, 1984).

WILLIAMS, RAYMOND, *Culture and Society, 1780–1950* (1958; repr. Harmondsworth, 1982).

——, *The Country and the City* (London, 1973).

——, *Keywords: A Vocabulary of Culture and Society* (London, 1983).

WILNER, JOSHUA, 'Autobiography and Addiction: The Case of De Quincey', *Genre*, 14/4 (1981), 493–503.

WINCH, DONALD, *Classical Political Economy and Colonies* (London, 1965).

WOOF, ROBERT, *Thomas De Quincey: An English Opium-Eater 1785–1859*, Catalogue to an exhibition at the Grasmere and Wordsworth Museum, 24 June–31 October 1985, and the National Library of Scotland, 16 November–31 June 1986. Cumbria: Trustees of Dove Cottage, 1985.

YEAZELL, RUTH BERNARD (ed.), *Sex, Politics and Science in the Nineteenth-Century Novel* (Baltimore, Md., 1986).

YOUNG, ROBERT, 'For Thou Wert There', in *Glyph Textual Studies*, i, *Demarcating the Disciplines: Philosophy, Literature, Art*, ed. Samuel Weber, (Minneapolis, 1986), 103–128.

——, *White Mythologies: Writing, History, and the West* (London, 1990).

Index